Magic Mike Likey:
A Man for All Seasons

Dr. Michael H. Likey

DEDICATION

I dedicate this book to my parents Louis and Rachel, whom I know are watching and are proud.

CONTENTS

Acknowledgments

ACKNOWLEDGMENTS

My deep appreciation and gratitude goes to everyone in my beloved Winnipeg, Manitoba that I personally knew, know, and met, for their continued inspiration and encouragement; Montreal, next to New York, the greatest city on earth, for being my place of origin, shaping the person I am today; Toronto, and the people I met and personally knew when I was living there, for opening my mind; finally, Vancouver, for opening up my heart about spirituality, and just opening up my eyes in general; my parents, whose unconditional love and support have been unparalleled; finally, to my wife Susan, for her unconditional love, support, and patience.

My further gratitude and appreciation goes to all of you, the real Magic Mike Likey fans, who after thirty-four years, still remember and support me.

Nothing's forgotten. Nothing is ever forgotten.

1 FORWARD

It's June 2018 and as I sit and contemplate my life on this typically rainy west-coast Canadian day, I feel an eagerness and anticipation towards the future. This is a different kind of anticipation, for it is filled with a slight sense of loss about my father-in-law who passed from this earthly realm last October, leaving my wife and myself now completely "parentless", so-to-speak. It is as if the rug was pulled out from beneath us, taking from us the last semblance of the past, and perhaps even a "safety net", if-you-will. But what of the future? What about all that there is to look forward to that is ahead of us, as opposed to what no longer remains behind us?

As long as we have our memories, the past (with all of its joys and sorrows) still exists, unless you have "selective memory", which I suppose I have, rendering me with mostly good past memories, joyful even! As for the future, what of it?

Shall we sit here, wringing our hands in fearful anticipation of something that does not yet (nor may ever) exist? I think not!

Somebody once said that we build (and we learn) from our past, and I most heartily agree. The past (technically) does not exist, so why dwell there mournfully or even regretfully, except to perhaps transform it (magically or miraculously) into something that one may expand on for a practical and even a greater good, or at the very least, as a sort of a positive inheritance for future generations?

This is the way that I've recently began to think, or philosophize: what am I handing down for future generations? My step-kids (now approaching their forties) have more-or-less cut out a relatively clear future for themselves, so all that remains, really, is for myself to ponder what I am handing down to future generations, other than for my own kids.

Apparently (and not withstanding) I have contributed much (according to my wife Susan) to the well-beingness (on an emotional and on a spiritual

1

level) of my patients and clients as my career as Dr. Michael Likey, Clinical Hypnotherapist and Doctor of Theocentric Psychology. Most of this career has been executed on Canada's west coast from 1994-2018; sure, life-altering for my clients and patients, and certainly gratifying for myself.

Twenty-five years earlier on the Manitoba prairies of central Canada, (and decades separating me from the west coast) as well as in my native Montreal and Toronto, my main careers were graphic design/illustrating for big-city ad agencies, magazines and newspapers, as well as editorial cartooning, and my greatest joy and passion: magic! How does a humble Jewish boy from Montreal transform himself from graphic designer, to magician, to therapist, all the while enjoying the landscapes across Canada spanning some forty-one years?

This is the subject of this book.

When I first landed in Winnipeg from Toronto, and after a while, I checked out the local magic club, I remember meeting a magician whose business card read "A Man for All Seasons, Magic for All Reasons"; this is where the title of this book was inspired from!

I've also changed the names and identities of most of the people here, as well as some of their careers/jobs, and the names of some places, and organizations for the sake of privacy/anonymity. Any resemblance to any person living or dead is purely coincidental.

This is the story of my life of positively affecting my public in printed media, the medium of television, and finally the therapist's couch and in social media. Some have called me a "Renaissance Man", I choose to refer to myself as "A Man for All Seasons".

Decide for yourself.

Enjoy!

Rev. Dr. Michael H. Likey

Coquitlam, Canada.

June 2018

2 MONTREAL: BEGINNINGS
1956-1979

For you to fully understand this process, this series of transformations (or adaptations) if-you-will, that I've endured, I will now provide for you the text from one of my book, *Magic Still Happens.*

The earliest remembrances I have as a child in Montreal are truly magical, as were most of my memories growing up in that ancient and sophisticated metropolis. I remember laying on my back while I was resting in something, (I later found out it was a pram) and looking to my left at a nearby table filled with small toys: a metal train, a rubber multi-colored ball, and some beads. The colors, sights, sounds and smells around me filled me with both comfort and excitement. I could hear my mother and father (now both of them gone) always chatting in the kitchen, located down the hall from my room. Their voices soothed and comforted me with warmth, joy, and optimism, even at that distance. Little did I know that my mum, a homemaker, was fraught with anxiety over when and where my father, a gifted musician, (a show drummer) would work again: I learned of this in my late teen years. It seems that my father was out of work maybe a handful of times while I was growing up; Montreal was (and still is) a cultural Mecca; a leader in the arts, culture and science, so time between "gigs" was short, and his skills were always in demand for the thousands of live-music outlets there. Nearby Toronto, I was told as a child, paled in comparison, in fact, I would always hear the jokes and comments about Toronto, even in the media: "I hear Toronto just got electricity and roads put in", quipped the local weatherman on the 6:00 o'clock news when I was around eight years old. These friendly jabs may have been a result of a sort

3

of envy towards Toronto, I'm not sure to this day. When I visited Toronto in 1971, the city, generally, struck me as very clean and "sanitized" compared to Montreal. Nonetheless, it did seem to lack the quicker pace and sophistication of Montreal. Toronto was also called "Toronto The Good" by many Montrealers, again, I suspect for its very "straight-and-narrow" conservative perspective and feel. To me, the differences didn't mean one city was better than the other, only different from each other, and this thrilled me; I enjoyed (even to this day) comparing cultural differences, manner of speech and attitude of people all over the world; that always held a fascination for me, those differences. Perhaps it's a way to gauge my growth? I don't know.

High-Jinx

Around that same time, I recall while laying in my crib, (I have very vivid memories of jail-like bars preventing me from exiting this juvenile Alcatraz) the desire to surprise my late parents who were sitting and chatting in the kitchen as usual.

This would entail sticking my foot out from between the bars, and pushing against the wall, which the crib rested against. I don't know how I knew to do this, I just knew that this was a necessary component of my great surprise.

So I began to do this, and sure enough, the crib (which rested on wheels) began to move!

I continued pressing my foot against the wall, and with each press, the crib moved more and more along the wall and out the door of my room. I continued this action to my amusement, after all, who would have expected that I would have invented at this point in my infancy a method of propulsion that could potentially move millions of other infants? Nonetheless, I continued to do this, as the crib, in turn, moved along the long corridor between my bedroom and the kitchen's entrance. As I did this, I could hear my parents' voices getting louder and louder as I made my way closer and closer. I remember feeling a growing excitement within me at the prospect of eventually surprising my parents, and in retrospect, I believe that I still carry to this day the ethic of working hard until I accomplish something positive for others. I continued focusing, almost fixating, on my foot and the wall, and the repetitive movements necessary for propelling me down the hall. I could feel and see the progress, though slow, towards my goal, which I knew would eventually happen. At this point I was wearing a sort of one-piece, yellow-fleece body suit, with my feet resting in the foot-bottoms, which slipped occasionally from against the wall, adding to the challenge. I remember wearing this sort of one-piece jump-suit a lot, and how comforting and familiar it felt. I still have black-

and-white photos of myself in this outfit, (complete with bonnet!) and I can't be more than one or two years of age! My mum and dad always reminded me of this, and other incidences (or "high-jinx", as they called them) around this time, insisting I was only two, but I never believed them until I saw the photographs.

Finally, the entrance to the kitchen was just upon me, I merely needed to maneuver the crib somehow, pivoting it so that it would enter through the narrow doorway; I utilized, one last time, my dependable foot, with which I gave one last great push against the wall, and voila...the crib made its appearance just inside the kitchen's entrance! I'll never forget my parents expression, which I carry with me to this day: it was a combination of surprise, delight, and pride, framed with huge smiles and eyes wide-opened!

I remember laughs and hugs, combined with feelings of amusement and amazement on my parents' part, that "Baby Mikey" could accomplish this (pardon the pun) feat/feet! They would continue to share this story for many years with myself, friends and other family members. I remember my chest filled with pride and a feeling of accomplishment, as well as pleasure because I made my parents react in such a manner.

More High-Jinx

Following are a few more stories from "Baby Mikey's" life.
One of the other strong emotions or feelings I recall as an infant besides the aforementioned ones, plus wonderment, and joy, was unfortunately a "need" or desire to escape! It's a wonder I never became an escape-artist, or a magician who specialized in Houdini-like illusions. If there was ever a potential or even a hint for restraint or imprisonment, I would immediately rebel. I don't know where these feelings originated from, other than perhaps it was "in my blood" from my father's dad who abandoned him and his family early in life; I may have inherited this feeling, which, far from being non-committal, was more like a desire to continue to "breathe" and be free.

Although I remember this vividly, this incident is another story that my parents would enthusiastically share throughout my childhood, with an air of amazement.

One day around the time of the crib incident, I was playing in our living room, sitting on my rear and playing with colorful children's blocks. It was a typical Montreal summer's day, with the sun shining brightly with no clouds in the sky, and a trace of a warm breeze winding its way through our apartment. I could hear the chirping of birds in the distance, and my ever-present yellow-flannel jump-suit hugging me. I felt contentment, joy and in-the-moment enthusiasm and gratitude for my toys. Suddenly, I looked up at the screen-door, secured with hooked-hasps, which when opened, led to the metal fire-escape stairs which winded down to our back-yard. How I enjoyed numerous times with my mum in that back-yard consisting of a slide, swings, sand-box, and lots of parents and friends my age. I was filled with the excitement, desire, and almost obsessive feeling at the prospect of exiting the living room, going down the fire-escape, (which also fascinated me) with its black-shiny paint and interesting patterns in the stairs. The bonus reward that awaited at the bottom of the stairs was far too much for me to endure: I knew at that point I had to make my escape!

I noticed a wooden broom resting against the wall beside the screen-door, which also, by-the-way, fascinated me, what with its tactile screen, which I occasionally caressed, as it felt nice against my small palms. It gave me many chances to observe the flies which came to rest on the outside of the screen as well; some of the flies, I observed, had green, semi-transparent bodies, while others had black-only bodies; I often pondered why that was. Nonetheless, the time was nigh, my escape down the fire-escape was imminent!

I took the broom close to the bottom of its handle, and enjoyed a feeling of smooth white wood and some red lettering painted on it, which was slightly raised or embossed; I could smell the paint as well, which was not completely unpleasant. These sensations reminded me of my red-metal-and-wood wagon, which I so loved. Then, I proceeded to lift the broom handle up towards the top-most hook, managing to raise the hook up and out, thus liberating the hook (and soon myself) from it's resting-place. I did this two more times, as there were actually three hooks securing the door.

My heart pounded as I lay the broom aside; there was the door, now slightly ajar; somehow I felt this was wrong, but yet the desire to be out in the fresh air and playing in the sand-box below out-weighed everything else; all logic was now gone! I had to liberate myself! Quietly, I made my way out of our apartment; the warmth of the sunshine beating down on me, easing slightly, my trepidation. I began to go down each step while sitting on my bum. Suddenly I heard laughter, a familiar laughter, and I looked back and up. Standing there on the top step was my mum. In retrospect, she probably saw the whole thing, saying nothing and observing just how far I'd go. Now she knew. I would be from here on in to her, a potential escapee from our home, a veritable convict from Sing-Sing prison. There was no fooling the "warden", and she knew it, and I knew it.

Scooping me up into her arms, she was still laughing, and I never forgot the feeling of her amazement, warmth, and how impressed she seemed to be of her little "Houdini". She seemed to think these acts were brilliant and unusual for my age, continuing to share this, and the crib incident, for the rest of her life. Myself, I don't know if the way I acted and thought was unusual or not for my age, (one or two years of age) so I never shared all of this until now. One more incident occurred, which left me somewhat shaken, and yet relieved.

The Bridge

I remember an incident that occurred when my mum picked me up in her arms on another occasion.

I remember sitting on a hard, dark-wood, polished table which was resting against a wall, with a decoratively-framed picture on the wall just above this. I remember seeing several interesting objects casually laying on the table beside me; a decoratively-painted small metal box, pearl beads, rings, baubles and bracelets, all, obviously belonging to my mother. Suddenly, as I was admiring these trinkets, my mum surprised me and picked me up, startling me. My first instincts were to extend my arms up and outward in a sideways movement, opening them.

Apparently I must have inadvertently hit my mum in the mouth with the back of one of my hands, as I heard a loud scream, and looking down at the table from her arms, I could see what looked like her teeth falling and hitting the table, bouncing and landing with a kind of a jangling sound; I noticed a thin, odd-looking black wire that accompanied this display. I'd never seen anything like that before; it came from my mum, and it scared me, because instinctively I felt that these things should still be inside my mother! Had I inadvertently extracted her beautiful teeth? Would she die? Would she be angry or hurt in some way? This new experience really shook me up, as previously her and my father were always pleased, and/or amused with me and my actions.

She quickly and gently set me back down on the table beside my handiwork, moaning with a worried (not painful) groan; "How will we pay for this?" was what she said over and over, and I felt frozen with fear; I didn't know what "pay" meant, but I felt responsible, and regardless, that to "pay" for this was like a punishment and/or out of our reach/realm of possibilities. Scooping me up again in her arms, and looking deeply into my eyes, she said, "It'll be okay, it's not your fault". I felt a great relief, and emotion filled my head and heart, with my eyesight seeming foggy; I was probably crying at that point. I don't remember this experience of crying too much in my early childhood, which is probably a good thing. I remember reaching out and lightly touching my mum's mouth at this point, as if to fix, heal, or make things better for her, and/or even to make up for what just happened. I still to this day look at a couple of black-and-white pictures from that time, of my mum holding me up, next to that decorative picture hanging just above that same table. I'm around one or two, wearing a white bonnet, and my infamous jump-suit with the feet. This is how I know the time-frame of this and those two other incidents, which even to this day, so many years later, are as vivid as if they happened just yesterday.

My mother, by-the-way, mentioned this incident in a non-blameful way, as if it were a minor emergency, for many years to come.

Television: More "Magic"

From the moment television in Montreal signed on the air as the second English-speaking television station in Montreal, pure magic manifested for me, watching that channel!

Up until that point in January of 1962, I had endured relatively "dry" arts-and-culturally-based programming on the only English-language Montreal station at the time. Now there were game-shows such as "A Kin To Win" with host the sophisticated (and late) Jimmy Tapp, which I loved watching so much, that my father bought me the "home-game" version of that show for us to play with each other! There were the kids' programming, such as Ted Zeigler's show, "Johnny Jellybean" and Magic Tom Auburn's "Surprise Party"; (all of them deceased as well) everything and everybody on that station seemed more bright, alive, and interesting! I credit those early years' programming for influencing me personally and professionally. More television-related memories and products marketed include the "Nestle Quick" puppet mascots, one red and the other blue, which my parents ordered for me by saving the labels from the Quick box; a "Johnny Jellybean" beanie, along with a life-size foam-replica of Ted Zeigler's head, which you could place your hand into and make the mouth move! A "Bat Man" kite, masks and cape, "The Monkees" hand-puppet which consisted of a glove-like affair, with four "Monkees" heads on each finger, and which, with the help of a battery-driven devise built into it, could say "Monkees" sayings; imagine each band-member "talking" to you! I adored this toy and still have it stored away, along with a larger, stuffed "Bat Man" doll. This was the magic of television and marketing, which I never forgot about.

My Parents-Their Influence

Here's some quick info on my now-deceased parents, which might shed more light on them, their likes, dislikes, behavior, etc. and how they influenced my development.

My parents-to-be got together when my mother was forty and my father, thirty-five; they were introduced to each other through mutual friends. Both of them had previously been engaged to be married to other partners.

Within the first few years of their formal union, my mum became pregnant twice, but twice the babies perished before they were born. My mother always blamed the second death on a late family member, who allegedly pushed her down a flight of stairs, allegedly jealous of her own inability to become pregnant.. Tension remained between my mother and this family member for the duration of their lives, I assume due to the aforementioned unfounded or founded allegations. I also assume that my mum's over-protectiveness of me was as a result of her finally successfully giving birth to me, and her subsequent fear of losing me, as she did with the other two. Regardless of my mum's early childhood tragedies, and early traumas/fears of losing her father to consumption (Tuberculosis) while growing up in post-war Europe, she seemed to always be singing throughout my childhood; everything from "Mona Lisa" to "Oh My Man, I Love Him So", and many more! She would sing with great passion and conviction, never too shy to "belt out" a good one! I'm sure her musical attitude influenced me later in years to not be shy, and regardless of my technical abilities, to drop self-consciousness and to just sing from my heart Later on, I would add drumming, (my father's influence) and finally guitar (Cat Stevens' influence) to my vocals! As a teen, I found myself singing along, with great passion, joy, and satisfaction, to songs on the radio, records, and television! In fact, I would passionately sing along to many of the famous pop stars of the day. I wanted so much to sing and play, that I constructed out of cardboard an "electric" guitar, so that I could sing and "play" along to the 1960's musicians who appeared on various television programs. Come to think of it, I suspect that I used my drawing abilities to make my desires a "reality": I constructed a huge, six-foot-wide, full-color "weather map" of Canada, because I liked the one on the local news; later on, I constructed a miniature model of "The Monkees" set, complete with a small, winding metal staircase that I adored; finally, "The Odd Couple" set, complete with "walls" separating the living room from the kitchen and a "metal gate" separating the living-room from the hallway! I even constructed a huge paper weather-map of Canada, as I was also mesmerized by the animated suns and clouds on those television weather-maps! Keep in mind most of this occurred between ages nine to fourteen! My sense of wonder was always aroused in anticipation of the appearance of a little puppet-mouse, "Topo Gigio" on the "Ed Sullivan Show" when I was around age seven; I never forgot how watching this little puppet made me feel: wonder, love, joy, curiosity, and a sense of familiarity, because of "Topo's" regular appearances. Perhaps this is why, likely because of my early Disney-characters' influences in "Little Golden" story-books, that my cartoon drawings and characters resembled those same almost innocent, wide-eyed characters: there was a "magic" to them that is hard to define. Later, in my early '20's, I even received formal "Disney-style" cartoon training...but more on that later! I like to think that my newer cartoon-characters to this day still project a kind of innocent magic and wonder of life. The same applied to my magic, in regards to "just doing it": practice,

practice, practice, then drop self-conscious awareness of proficiency, and just do it: just entertain and move people, either to laughter, to tears, or to amazement.; maybe to all! I never cared how proficient my draws, singing, magic, or guitar proficiencies were, I just wanted to do it, hopefully also succeeding in the process of projecting a kind of passion, magic, and wonder. This energy is all that ever really mattered (or still matters) to me. Love something, then just share it! In reality, after having come full-circle with my spiritual journey, this is also "the answer": Find what you love, do what you love, love what you do, and then share it as best you can. If I had to give a metaphysical lecture today, I would summarize it all in that way. That's not to say that my parents weren't guilty of pressuring me to be "number 1", or even a "nice Jewish doctor!"

I remember my mother, herself a European immigrant, spouting anti-immigrant verbiage, calling them "green-ah's", or "greenies" in English. How ironic, and how soon people can forget their humble beginnings and opportunities and compassion offered to them in order to get their start in a new land; what ever happened to gratitude? Oh. well. What pushed my buttons even more, was her bias against non-Jews, or "goyem" as she called them, equating non-Jews with having illegitimate children or "mumsers"; ("bastard-children") "goyem" apparently were less intelligent than Jews because they ate pork, according to my mother; thank goodness, as a child, I intuitively knew that didn't "feel right", so I largely ignored her rants. Her dislike for blacks, or "call-ear-tah's", ("colored") or "shvartzah's", or "blacks" was unfortunate, considering how many black-people there were in Montreal, particularly in our area; how uncomfortable she must have felt!

This prejudice also angered me.

"Bribing Me"

My mother would often "bribe" me into eating my dinner, or finishing it completely, by offering me a ride on her broom if I listened to her. As a three-year-old, I actually believed that she could actually do this, as she held up her broom, miming riding on it. I asked her, "where will we go?" She answered "To outer-space!" Needless to say, I always finished my dinner, with the hope that I would "fly" with her on her broom to far-away places, which of course, never became reality. I think I felt somewhat cheated back then!

Far Away Places And Novelties

Because television shows such as "Jet Jackson, The Flying Commando" and "Fireball XL5" were largely science-fiction shows, my imagination was constantly stimulated, and also ran rampant. Some of the novelties my father brought home were made in "exotic" lands such as India and Japan. One of the Indian-made novelties included a small piece of charcoal, which when lit on fire, created a huge cloud of smoke; when the smoke would clear, the charcoal had transformed into a black, elongated object, that moved, writhed, and "danced around" like a real snake! This both amazed and puzzled me, and to this day, I have no explanation for this. The other Indian-made toy was a small, ivory elephant, which, when you placed the supplied mini-cigarette in it's mouth and then lit it, would "blow" smoke-rings! Yes, small rings of smoke would emanate from the tip of the cigarette! Again, I have no scientific explanation for this, nor do I want my "bubble burst"! Yet another Indian-made toy were two small, rectangular cardboard pieces, covered with a pale-green Indian-influenced, exotic pattern, approximately two inches by four inches, and one-eighth of an inch thick. Connecting these two pieces were two criss-crossing strips of cardboard, creating a hinged "wallet" of sorts. When I would place the supplied toy paper-money in the wallet, closed it, then turned it over and opened it again, the money would be gone! this principle I'm familiar with today, and is even used in the world of magic, employing genuine-looking, leather wallets. A way to "switch" and "transform" objects placed in the wallet. All of these things contributed to a most magical childhood!

At the same time, I remember certain "challenges" such as choking on food, having some small object fall into my eye creating discomfort for several days until it was finally identified and removed, throwing up after drinking Nestle Quick "Banana Flavor", and the "cigar incident": while flailing my arms about, I accidentally made contact with my dad's lit cigar which he was holding in one hand; that really hurt! So did the dart I used in a bow-and-arrow set, accidentally jabbing the webbing between my thumb and forefinger, creating a minor hemorrhage, which my mum quickly bandaged up! No darts were henceforth allowed in my immediate vicinity from age three until age ten!

I remember, roughly from the age of four until I was around eight, whenever my parents and I were at a social function, or had family or friends over to our home, my mum would say to our guests, "Tell them what you want to be when you grow up, Michael..." To which I would give the previously-coached answer, "A Pediatrician!" The look in the peoples' eyes, and their facial expressions are still with me to this day: it was a similar surprise and delight that my parents expressed when I wheeled my crib into the kitchen! They would even buy me toy doctor kits, which I did adore; I loved the stethoscope, the toy plastic "injection needle", ever-present regardless of the brand of doctor's kit. My favorite one was the one that came with multi-colored candy "pills" in a clear plastic, capped-bottle; I believe this was the "Ben Casey Doctor's Kit", which consisted of a white-plastic carrying-case, whose plastic or rubber odor I remember to this day!

To me, this smell wasn't unpleasant, only distinctive; it was my beloved white-rubber/plastic cat, "Tinkerbelle", with her adorable chin, (I still love real kitty's chins to this day!) that had this same odor. My father had given me this toy when I was in the hospital having my tonsils and adenoids removed, around age six. My mother encouraged my father to bring me something soft, that I could cuddle with; initially he brought me a wooden bobble-head replica of a character from a local television and print-ad commercial; then, followed a beautiful clear acrylic cube containing the image of one of Montreal's brand-new skyscrapers at the time; I suppose my father just didn't understand the concept of "cuddly", though to be fair to him, he did previously buy me a couple of large, black-and-white teddy-bears, one of which I named "Gracie", (for the actress/comedienne Gracie Allen) and with which I impersonated her husband, comedian George Burns of "Burns and Allen" television fame. I would wear plastic "George Burns Glasses" and smoke a plastic cigar, just like him, while speaking like him to my teddy bear. I carried on this vaudeville show for the sick kids in the same hospital I was staying in, and also drew them a cartoon of Fred Flintstone on the large blackboard in the common room where they politely watched all of this. Nevertheless, eventually my father brought me "Tinkerbelle", which I loved for years to come; in fact, I loved, cherished, and appreciated everything my parents ever gave me. Occasional jokes and sarcasm would emanate from me, even at a young age, especially by eight years of age, when I voraciously was reading my "monster" magazines: one day, after my mum asked me to tell a friend of hers what I wanted to grow up to be, I uttered the words, "An Undertaker!" Imagine my mothers' surprise and discomfort; the friend looked puzzled as my mother quickly apologized for me and said, "He wants to be a Pediatrician". I knew that this would now be my "stock-answer" for any further questions of this type from my mother, after all, it got a "reaction", and a different one at that: one that amused me more than the other reactions of surprise and delight! This was to also be somewhat of the groundwork of my adult personality!

I never did share my somewhat "metaphysical" experience I had experienced during my tonsillectomy with anyone, until now. As the ether was being administered and they had me counting down from "ten" down to "one", besides the familiar rubber-like scent which I was experiencing, I could see very clearly (even though I was aware of my being "under") floating farther and farther from the earth; from my perspective, it was as if the earth was going farther and farther away from me, appearing smaller and smaller, stopping, moving around in space somewhat, then coming back to me, closer and closer until it "engulfed" me. The public at that time (and science) had no clear, measurable color pictures of planet earth from outer space, so my images were not influenced by that, I'm certain; I forgot the experience until the Apollo Eleven moon-landing and subsequent walk in 1969, specifically, at 4:00 p.m. Eastern Time on July 20th, the date of my birth, by-the-way. The full-color pictures of earth taken from outer space were identical to the images I had experienced while "under" during my operation! The photos clearly brought back that previous experience, and I thought it ironic, anyway, because my astrological sign is "Cancer", or "Moon-Child", ruled by the moon, and that the moon-walk took place on my thirteenth birthday.

Another "incident" involving the moon, was the summer I was turning six, I believe. My mom and dad bought me a "Beany" doll, from my favorite television cartoon, "Beany and Cecil"; I had begged and begged for this expensive toy, and finally received it, although it was the less expensive, "non-talking" model. I nonetheless cherished it, and clutched it firmly while my parents and I were seated on our couch during the total solar eclipse tat summer. For whatever reason, my mother feared some catastrophe would occur during the eclipse. My hearted pounded and pounded, and was the first time in my life that I felt real fear; finally, the eclipse was over, and we could all breathe a sigh of relief. I looked at "Beany" in an even more appreciative way.

The "Croup"

Along with the aforementioned "challenges" was possibly the one that was the longest-lasting, from age six to fourteen.

Early one morning, I awakened unable to breathe! With a sort of "braying" like a struggling donkey, I attempted to inhale, but instead, found myself making loud sounds, and even attempting to cough, again with difficulty and some pain. Naturally, this would be startling for a six-year-old, let alone an adult, and visibly panicking and shaking, I continued to struggle to breathe, managing to hoarsely bray out a "Mom! Help me!"

Running in from the other room, my mother began to visibly panic, as she kept asking me, rather pleading with me to breathe! I was jumping up and down now, in fear, on my bed: I was never previously unable to breathe...what could I do? Unable to catch my breath, I sat back down on my bed, crying now and making it all worse. "I'll call your father at the club!" shouted my mother, as I begged her to call the doctor instead. My pediatrician in those days was a kind and elderly gentleman. Besides his fascinating doctor's bag, rimless eye-glasses, and distinct chemical-smell he emitted, (was it alcohol in retrospect?) this man of medicine had previously made countless house calls when I had tonsillitis, high fevers, flu, etc., but never this; would he even be able to make it to our home in time at this hour? Instead, my mum opted to quickly heat up some milk, and then adding a raw egg and sugar to this strange European concoction called a "Guggle Muggle", insisted that I swallow it all at once, and quickly; I figured at that point that if my brain didn't perish from oxygen deprivation, I would likely choke to death! Somehow, I managed to get it all down; (and keep it down!) I tried to cough again, and miracle of miracles, the hardened phlegm in my bronchial tubes and throat were slightly softening, allowing me to cough, albeit painfully! I continued to cough and cough, all the while feeling this potentially deadly obstruction beginning to break up enough for me to cough it up. I remember that in-between the coughing, my inhaling sounds were sounding like a sort of screeching sound; again, a brand-new and frightening experience. I wasn't at that point in my life able to objectively and curiously observe this condition as I've learned to, many years later.

Nonetheless, up came small, green, glue-like hardened substances, about the size of dimes, onto the newspaper which was laid before me on the floor by my mum. By then my head was pounding, due to the labored and continuous coughing. I could breathe more easily now; I happened to glance at the nearby clock: it was 5:00 a.m., and I could hear my father put his key into the lock, and turning and opening it, entered our apartment. Usually my dad, who didn't drive, used public transit in Montreal which ran all night. He likely missed his bus.

Feeling more calm, I sat on my bed, my mother by my side, with my dad asking what happened? My mum's conclusion was that I had had an allergic reaction to the glue I used to make one of my plastic model kits with, the previous day. We all accepted her diagnosis, and I substituted an odorless, white glue from that point on, to make my models. I never went back to the cement, nor did I use paint on my models, as they emitted a rather pungent odor. It was at age fourteen, when I had outgrown these "croupy" attacks, (as predicted by the doctor) that I began to paint my models again, but chose to never again use the cement. At age seven, my parents took me to an allergy specialist who, after making eight or nine needle scratches on my back and then on my arm, determined that I was allergic to dust and feathers. My mother was already an immaculate house-keeper, and my budgie had just recently passed, so it was a waiting and observing game now. My almost monthly (certainly quarterly) colds always culminated with the croup; the headaches and sore-throats that always preceded these colds made me feel depressed and anxious, in anticipation of a whole night of coughing and subsequent headaches; would I be able to bring up the phlegm this time, or would I choke to death? This was always on my mind near the end of each cold, until age fourteen. Apparently, later in life, my mother shared with me that her father had suffered from the same syndrome, but before she discovered her "miracle remedy" of the mysterious "Guggle Muggle", she would call out from the window of her parents' home in Europe, desperately calling out to the neighbors for help for her father. I never learned how her siblings reacted to any of this.

The Magic of Photography

During the time of the croup, my parents "introduced me" to the wonder and marvels of photography, which I still experience to this day. I can still smell the wonderful plastic of the Instamatic camera, the whine of the "Magic Cube" disposable flash, and the excitement and anticipation of my father returning from the local pharmacy, developed prints in his hand! What would those black-and-white remnants, nay, reflections of my life and its joys look like from a different perspective? Would the beauty and love I felt at that time for my budgie, "Pretty Boy" be reflected in the photos I took of him? And what about my parents? Could simple, flat pictures mirror the love and laughs we all shared for and with each other? Miraculously, they did!

Each photo was a treasured reminder, a literal snapshot of the near-past, which to this day, is the now-distant past! As I still occasionally gaze upon these times long-gone, they become almost as vivid, almost as fresh as the moment I captured these memories, these events, these loved ones and places that I called my life. Though long dead, they remain immortalized in these photos: my mother with her arm around my father, both lovingly smiling at me through the camera; my beloved and trusting "Pretty Boy" perched upon my finger; the outside facade of our apartment building on Goyer street; my last day of grade two, three, and then, in color, the last day of grade four! I could see an evolution of sorts of myself, my ever-changing glasses, hairstyles, and clothing, which also further fascinated me, since my parents continued to consistently appear to be unchanged in those photos.

Even the color, Polaroid pictures of the 1960's, portrayed my unchanging parents as very down-to-earth and loving; this is the image and feeling I carry with me today, even though I look at these long-gone images. How I loved my hard-plastic "Expos" helmet, and furthermore, how it looked on my head in the photos; even the cloth "Expos" cap looked great on me, with it's red, white, and blue insignia of that newly-formed team. I loved my hat; I loved my parents; I loved my school; I loved my life, and my Polaroid camera which helped me to remember and hang onto these memories.

To this day, I still enjoy capturing memories with my digital camera, and viewing those images on my laptop, in many instances, sharing them on social media. My, how miraculously technology has evolved!

Superstition or Fact?

I grew up with my mother speaking mostly Yiddish to relatives and to some of her friends. To others, she chose to speak perfect English. "Yiddish" is a dialect of Eastern European Jews, a derivative of German and Jewish.

Depending on your country of origin, the dialect varied a bit, and Jewish people (I was told by my mum, and this was suggested in Mordecai Richler's "The Apprenticeship Of Duddy Kravitz") sometimes teased at each others' pronunciation of certain words.

She also seemed to relate more to our elderly friends and family members, for some reason, as opposed-to her peers. Who knows why? Perhaps she was an "old soul"?

One of her idiosyncrasies included her talking to her dead mother, and her father! I remember many a summer night, as she gazed out the window towards our clear, starry nights, she was crying and pleading for peace and love for them, speaking some Yiddish words I wasn't familiar with, but the gist being her expressing her loneliness for them, as well. The experience of them communicating with each other seemed real to her, filled with emotion, so I never gave it all a second thought: I assumed that European Jews had some special "gift", abilities, depth, or "wisdom"; at the very least, it would be some sort of "intuition", and I seemed to always have it!

I could always "see" accurately, seconds before I received a graded paper in school, exactly the mark I had received. In time, I began to trust these flashes of information, or "hunches" as I called them; my "heart" (as my mother called it) was rarely wrong. "Follow your heart", she said, "And you'll never go wrong"; that and "If you don't have faith in yourself, how can others have faith in you?"

Superstition or not, my mum's ways which I had adopted, always worked out fine for me.

I experienced around age ten or eleven, something I have yet to explain to myself, let alone to others. I was laying on my stomach on my bed, peering down at the wooden hardwood floor in my room; suddenly, I became "lost" in the wooden patterns! It was as if I had no body, but my mind and consciousness had blended in with the wooden floor; like I had become "one" with it! This is the only way that I can explain this experience, which some may refer to as Higher Consciousness, or a Cosmic experience. While experiencing this, I felt the most "free" than I had ever felt before this. Little did I realize that I had "stumbled" into a meditative/altered state of consciousness, merely by relaxing completely, focusing on the wood, then merely letting go! To be honest, after a few seconds, I began to feel anxious, this new experience still somewhat unfamiliar to me, so I "snapped back" to this apparent reality. I experimented more and more frequently with this, until I felt more and more comfortable with it, and could "go there" wherever and whenever I wanted! It became an escape, or coping mechanism when I felt sad, or if my parents were arguing for whatever reason; I simply "tuned it all out"! I began to automatically do this whenever I was bored, or felt uncomfortable around visitors to our home; I merely stood there amongst everyone, grin on my face, but in reality somewhere else! I used this too, when my mum lost her temper with me, pulling my hair or whipping me with hangers: I immediately went to this "quiet place", feeling no pain or discomfort until I knew her tirade was over. In retrospect, and as a Clinical Hypnotherapist, I somehow stumbled onto the clinical methodologies for entering into an altered-state, basically the same thing as that which I learned from hypnotherapy college, which was focus on a spot, follow your breathing to relax completely, and then let go! I've simplified things somewhat here for illustrative purposes, but those are the basic meditation/self-hypnosis techniques, except with meditation, you close your eyes and look up into your brow or third-eye area, or stare into a candle-flame, and with self-hypnosis, you stare at a spot on the ceiling, and listen either to the repetitive droning on of someone's voice, music, or your breathing, or a metronome. This, and my out-of-body experience while under ether in the operating-room, were my first metaphysical experiences, along with my mum's mediumistic ramblings.

To summarize my mum and her influence, she gave me a strength of determination, never "settling" for the mediocre, a passion for music and for performing in general, and a hopeful attitude in the face of adversity; she gave me a cynical, sarcastically-mocking view of others; the ability to somehow "make something from nothing", in other words, to always find a way to accomplish whatever you wanted.

My father had his technical musical training as an apprentice/student of some top-notch local Montreal musicians, who took him under their wings. My father began working at the age of twelve as a professional "Show-Drummer", supposedly smoking cigars and hanging out at brothels, my father himself proudly declared! "Show-Drummers" played for vaudeville and burlesque acts, including strippers and variety performers such as magicians and jugglers. My father shared a story which he occasionally repeated about one of the many magicians he played for having lost his eye during a failed attempt at the "bullet catch" trick: rather than catching a bullet fired from a gun or rifle between his teeth, the performer miscalculated resulting in his "taking out an eye". This proved to me (as a professional magician myself) that the entertainer didn't know the actual methodology which was completely safe and fool-proof, or he attempted suicide during a performance. Nonetheless, this incident obviously left quite the impression on my father. I remember when I was around twelve years old, my father humming and playing "air drums" to television's Tony Orlando and Dawn's "Tie a Yellow Ribbon", informing me that he and his trio of musicians played "Knock Three Times" in the night-club they worked in; this was another Tony Orlando tune, and he proceeded to demonstrate the tapping sounds he made at the appropriate point in the song, with his drum-sticks. I found this to be a bit "square", what with rock and roll, "go-go girls", and electric guitars being the current trend. My dad often tutored me on his drums, sitting me down at his drum-kit when I was four, showing me the proper way to hold the sticks, when and how to use the brushes and cow-bell! He then, lowering the stool I was sitting on, put each of my feet on the respective pedals of the drum and the "High-Hat" cymbal, demonstrating the "when's" and the "how's"; I loved it and learned quickly, later in life playing the drums in a sound-a-like "Beatles" group; I merely sat down and played! I was, at that point, playing guitar for ten years, granted, but never a whole drum-kit since age four: I could just "do it" successfully, we all learned, and I went on to playing some Jewish community events, at which some of the women jokingly through their undergarments on stage!

I have vivid memories of my father's health issues throughout my childhood. The first earliest memory I have of this, is my dad stepping out to pick up his usual "New York Daily News" when I was around six, but never returning! Frantically, my mother called all the local hospitals until finally tracking him down at "The Royal Victoria" hospital. Turns out he didn't want to worry us about the blood in his urine that morning; my dad had ongoing issues with kidney-stones, and this time was the first time that I heard about it. The doctors managed to have him pass the stone, and offered him advise about drinking water daily, and avoiding certain over-the-counter cough syrups; they also suggested avoiding mineral water, which evidently encourages a build-up of sediment which eventually formed kidney-stones. I never forgot this, and followed that advice for the rest of my life. My father continued to have several more kidney-stone incidents over the years.

When I was in second-year college, around December or so, I remember my father telling us, after exiting the washroom, that he was going to the emergency ward again; my mum and I assumed it was kidney-stones, but as it turned out, he had developed prostate issues, which resulted in doctors immediately removing it, all relatively routine. Because of the swiftness of the procedure, I suspected that the prostate was cancerous, which was never voiced to us.

One more operation was the removal of my dad's gall-bladder, his nausea and vomiting having necessitated that.

My father always reminded me, when I was impatient with, or intolerant of slow-walking seniors on the street, that I'll "Be old too, one day!" Even to this day, if I find myself in a hurry, and slowed down by others in traffic, or walking slowly in front of me blocking my way, especially if they're seniors, I stop and take a proverbial breath, remembering my dad's words, "Someday, you'll be old like that too."

All I really knew of my family were my parents, until age five or so, when my mum's relative came to visit us. Initially she struck me as a strong, kind, stylish, hip, and funny. Her sarcasm was unparalleled; I seemed to understand sardonic humor even at such a young age, and I suppose it stuck with me into adulthood. My mum's now-late relative's smile warmed me, and I greatly admired her persistence, which she displayed while helping me fix my "View Master". A little of her marital struggles were revealed when I was eleven: her new beau helped her escape from an abusive first marriage; she eventually married this compassionate and intelligent person, who provided for her a prosperous and loving life. I have fond memories of these two visiting us when I was eleven; he would always take the time to sit down with me and take an interest in my toys. I'll never forget them. My mum's female family member passed the morning after my father did, around Father's Day of 1995; her husband passed the following year. Other than them and some family members on my father's side, (they visited us when I was five and later at age fourteen) I knew no other family than my parents. I remember accidentally walking in on my dad's female family member in her underwear as she was changing during one of her visits, and an introduction to average female anatomy this was not! I quickly and embarrassingly turned my head and ran from the room, trying to erase the memory of her in her bra and girdle forever from my mind.

My late mother was the eldest of three children, the other two being my aunt, (the youngest) and my maternal uncle. They and their parents (my maternal grandparents) emigrated from war-time Austria to escape the Nazi's. If I haven't already mentioned, we're Jewish. According to my mum, there are many violin-virtuosos in our family, that creative and artistic genius filtered down to me somehow I suspect, with my love for great art, music, drawing, and yes, instrument-playing.

I have fond memories of my late maternal grandfather, (or "Zeyda" in Yiddish) "the richest barber in Montreal", my mum insisted I mention this when I speak of him to others. He would visit us every Sunday until I was four. My father informed us then, that he had passed of lung cancer after spending some time in a sanatorium in the country; after his passing, I stared at his barber tools and bag that contained them, in fascination for years, as I could still picture his hands holding the electric buzzer, scissors, and comb while working on me. My mum, of course, was heartbroken at his passing; my parents eventually replaced him as my barber with a younger man who made house-calls; to this day I can remember his Halitosis ravaging my nostrils and my senses overall; a nice enough man, it was because of him that I first saw someone wearing leather sandals with wool socks; later in life, I was to see a great many other people (mainly men) wearing socks with sandals in Vancouver, Canada.

Years later, when my parents and I visited Toronto, I was spoiled by the "hip" and "with it" Toronto hairstylist who cut my hair: using a blow-dryer, curling-iron, and a circular brush, he applied the finishing touch of hair spray to my coif! How could I possibly duplicate this upon returning to Montreal? More importantly, who could duplicate all of this for me? The answer would be in an equally hip stylist located at a large, Greco-Roman-style building on Sherbrooke Street in downtown Montreal; he would be the one who would also later perm my hair, resulting in my "trademark" afro. (or "'fro"!)

I digressed; here are more memories of my Zeyda when I was somewhere between ages two and four: I remember vividly his quiet and dignified style and manner. He would sit on the couch, while I would proudly show him my toys, one-at-a-time, taking them from, and returning them to my room. He would respond in an impressed manner. He wore the kind of Ray Ban glasses that are popular today and worn by "Hipsters" and Floyd the barber on the old Andy Griffith television show: plastic tortoise-shell, half-rimmed frames with metal bottom-halves. I believe that style of glasses is referred-to today as "Ray Ban Club" glasses. His moustache was not dissimilar to Hitler's. One day he brought us a beautiful gold cage with a mechanical plastic bird which chirped and flapped its wings when the device was wound up with a key. The cage also seemed to "sweat" some kind of glistening oil on the bars, creating a magical effect overall. This was my first exposure to some thing that seemed truly magical, the mechanics of which I did not understand yet nonetheless fascinated me. I stared and stared all day at this mechanical Austrian marvel. My Zeyda was Austrian, and his wife, my grandmother, (who passed before I could meet her) was of Russian lineage.

"Aunt Zelda"

Around age fourteen, I was introduced to my mum's great aunt, "Aunt Zelda".

Aunt Zelda, from what I gathered, was the real rebel in my mum's family. My mum referred to Zelda (amongst other nicknames in Yiddish) as "The Old Witch". The "old witch" moniker was born out of pure superstition: Zelda had a penchant for reading Tarot cards, or "shpieling-da-cartes", "playing with the cards", again, translated from Yiddish. My mum would say this with an air of secrecy and almost in a guilty, hushed manner. Whether this was true or not, I loved Zelda, who, at the end of her nine-hour smoky visits with us, (the eighty-year-old Zelda would consistently fill our two-bedroom apartment with cigarette smoke!) would look up at me through her metal-rimmed, cat's-eye glasses, and then, pulling me towards her and hugging me, managed to somehow slip a "fin" (or five-dollar bill) into my closed fist; who was the real magician, then? How this five dollars managed to manifest within my clenched palm, I still to this day don't know! Perhaps her "misdirection" were her uncomfortable, amble, and rather pointed breasts which I could feel pressed against me through her clothes during each hug, until I was age fourteen!

She struck me as a very independent woman, frequenting local restaurants and deli's, perched on a stool at the counter. Whenever I visited Montreal from Toronto or Winnipeg, I could almost always count on her sitting in one or the other of these numerous Montreal deli's. She seemed to always delight in my sneaking up on her, surprising her with a hug; "Michal-lah", she would always say, looking into my soul through her glasses. One day, upon my visiting Montreal, I no longer found her sitting at the counter: my mum informed me that she had passed of, surprisingly, natural causes (as opposed to lung cancer!) at age ninety-something.

Other than some American family-members on my father's side, I never met any other paternal family members. They apparently all lived in New York, spread over Brooklyn and Queens; I remember my mother always asking me to tell people that I was from New York; to this day I don't know why; it might have been a status thing. Nonetheless, the only other info I have of my paternal family is this: my father was one of four other siblings. Their father had deserted them, leaving them to support my grandmother, who also passed shortly after my birth. Eventually my aunts and uncles fled to New York from Montreal, leaving my dad in charge of his mother, (who remained in Montreal) whom he supported until he met and married my mother. Noble, I thought. I loved my blue blanket as a baby which apparently, my paternal grandmother had given me. Most of my life, my father proudly spoke of one of his male family members, the American "war-hero" who was so strong, he could "be with several women at the same time"! As a child, I wasn't quite sure what that meant, but I had some idea. My father also proudly displayed his own war ribbons, tags, etc., boasting that his family member had many more plus a "special one". Recently, before another one of my paternal family member's death, he shared with me the story behind this medal. It was apparently the "Congressional Medal of Honor" bestowed upon my father's family member by the U.S. government for his role in the war. The circumstances were somewhat suspect. This was the person my father boasted once or twice to me about, but whom, overall, he dreaded speaking about because of his apparent "connections". According to my mum and dad as I was growing up, that family member "lived somewhere in California", a secret new identity of some kind, the impression was that he was in hiding. My dad was very nervous about this family member. Another paternal family member once shared with me a few years ago, that as a result of some activities in New York a long time ago by my dad's family member, the U.S. government gave him the "option": come work for us and go to war, or face legal consequences. Seemed like a fair offer. I suppose after the war, the government must have given him a new identity. The only other knowledge I have of my paternal family is a female who was born with Down syndrome, a family-member who was the head of a major toy company in New York, and another who was the head of a major denim corporation, their offices having been in the Empire State building. I know that this is all true because when a female paternal member visited us from New York in 1971, she gave me some famous American brand-name jeans, shirts and jackets, (some of which I still have!) and after finishing college as a Graphic Designer/Commercial Artist in 1977 Montreal, I approached my New York "toy corporation" family member for a job interview in Montreal, which he arranged. That was all I ever knew of my family other than my mum and dad; no large family dinners or gatherings. Just myself, my mum and dad as I was growing up in Montreal.

My late mum was interesting. In my late teens, when I moved out, I visited her psychiatrist with many questions about her. He told me that she was "Manic", and that she did not adjust well to my new independence, hence she popped prescribed "uppers" in the morning and "downers" in the evening so that she could sleep. In those days, Montreal was the leader in most fields in North America, so you can well imagine the state of affairs that psychiatry was in, in general! I'm not sure if my mum's "antics" were a "show" for my benefit, or if she was seriously ill; growing up, I never took her actions seriously, so I was never traumatized by them. Generally, my mum was hyper and would over-react. She, like her other family members, was the consummate "entertainer" and would do impressions of friends and family in a mocking manner; to get things "going", she would say outrageous "observational" things to get a laugh. One of my mum's family members would get attention through her turn of a phrase and story-telling skills; my mum's other family member would do much the same. My dad, the balance, was stoic and quiet. Ironically his astrological sign was "Libra", the balance or scales. If you've ever watched the television show "Seinfeld", my parents were somewhat like George's parents. My best and oldest friend pointed that out to me once, but at the time, I didn't see it. I got my "show-biz" antics and creativity from my mum's side, and my introverted nature and musical skills from my father.

My mum would scream to try to scare and control me. It didn't work, but I respected her wishes, nonetheless. One of my dad's belts hung from a door-knob in our home; all that he or my mum had to do to discipline me, was to merely approach the belt...this was threat enough for me! I could go on and even make a separate book in the "Mommy Dearest" vein about my mum pulling my hair once, or whipping me once with a coat-hanger, but truly, I chalk that up to stress, her feeling alone, a low coping threshold with her fear of us running out of money, which we never did. She simply "snapped" once or twice during the course of my childhood. In my early thirties, I approached her about these actions, to which she apologized sincerely, and to my satisfaction, providing me with closure about these matters. To be honest, I believe those violent actions during my childhood contributed to me never wanting my own children (which I never did have) for fear that I myself might be abusive.

I never felt as if we were "poor", even though I grew up in a lower-middle-class neighborhood in Montreal. I never felt I was lacking anything: I had my imagination, my drawing-skills, and top marks in school. I felt truly full and rich!

I loved my father, Lou Likey. I give him a lot of credit for hanging in so long with my mum. I suppose he didn't want to desert us like his dad did. I asked him one day, "Dad, why did you stay with mum for so long?" He responded, "I love her." That was enough for me. My father's inner strength, hopefulness, patience, perseverance, as well as his musical talent truly inspired and influenced me! He played in bands in all the best (and worst) venues in Montreal, and I was blessed enough to watch him when I grew old enough to enter these establishments.

When all is said and done, I'm a combination of my talented and manic mother, with her cynically-optimistic attitude, and my stoic, gifted, and hopeful father.

"Connections"

At least once a year, my traumatized father would tell us that "something happened" at whichever particular club he was playing in.

That usually meant a "hit". Truth of the matter is, I grew numb to watching on television the daily (or weekly) murder count in my beloved city; if you owned a retail establishment of any kind, including fancy upbeat clubs, discos, restaurants, etc. in Montreal, you were usually "protected"; I don't think there was a choice. I remember many times in my late teens, taking a date to an upscale downtown hotel club, and the tall, solid, tuxedo-wearing gentleman were always present. On one occasion, my date was being harassed by a drunk; instinctively, I made eye-contact with one of these gentlemen, who proceeded to "gently" escort the drunk out, leaving us to enjoy the rest of our evening. I'm not sure I knew how I knew to do this, but I did. This was par for the course in a typical evening out: tip the doorman well, (sometimes cutting the line to do this, with a large enough tip, they'd let you in, avoiding the two-hour line-up! This was not an accepted practice in western Canada, I discovered eventually) and you're protected for the night. This seemed to exist in Toronto too. There was an undercurrent of this "feeling" in Winnipeg when I lived there, although I had no direct obvious exposure to it as I did in Montreal. Don't kid yourselves, it's very real, organized and "classy" by eastern standards, not sloppy, young, street-level, and dangerous to the public like in western

Canada. One of my maternal family members might have had some "connections"; he only hinted at it. He spoke of delivering packages between Montreal and Toronto, but having no knowledge of their contents. He might have been what's known as a "runner", but again, I have no actual proof of this. Even a friend of mine from Montreal, the cousin of a major television and movie actor, had an "experience" while driving an upscale vehicle across Canada as a favor for someone. Stopped on the highway just outside of Winnipeg by the police, they claimed that the car was stolen. My friend had no idea of this of course, and asked the police to call the phone-number his friend had given him. Moments later, the officers let my friend proceed on to his destination. One of my maternal family members once spoke of his business partner being incarcerated, (but never himself) for their "aluminum siding" business which they brought to western Canada; I should have suspected something wasn't quite as it appeared when, before they came to Winnipeg, I received a phone-call of inquiry from him, asking about the gullibility of the locals. I merely mentioned how friendly and sincere Winnipeggers seemed. This seemed to clinch their plans to live for awhile in Manitoba. I have a theory about all of this, and the mentality surrounding it all, which you can judge for yourself, by reading Mordecai Richler's "The Apprenticeship of Duddy Kravitz": many European Jews who emigrated to New York, and/or to Montreal during World War 2 got their "break" via connections. Arriving penniless to our shores, they found themselves opening store-fronts and other businesses in short fashion; where did the funds come from? Others took jobs in factories, (especially the women) while the men drove taxi-cabs. My maternal grandparents were of this same demographic. The immigrant European Jews who settled in western Canada appeared to mainly become farmers and peddlers, according to my personal observations. Where did my grandfather get the money to start his barber-shop in Montreal? Did he and his family arrive with funds already? To this day I still don't know. All I know is that my mum spoke glowingly about her parents and their fine taste in furniture and objects d'art. Typical for the east. Another question arose for me, when in my late-teens, one of my friend's father was shot down and killed while in a neighborhood Montreal Laundromat. They were recent Russian-Jewish immigrants to Montreal; did his parents owe anything to anybody?

Oddly enough, as a Montrealer, I was so used to feeling "protected" by the tuxedo-wearing doormen, that I lost perspective, after relocating to points west in Canada, as to whom our real protectors are: the army, the police and R.C.M.P., whom I have a great admiration and respect for. I remember my current wife (who was born and raised in Vancouver, Canada) reminding me of this fact, when I used to tend to ramble on about too much about the "tuxedoes".

The War-Measures Act

Speaking about "protection", thank goodness for the army tanks that rolled in to protect us in 1970 Montreal!

Ordered by our then Prime Minister, he invoked the "War Measures Act", to protect us from the bomb-wielding radical separatists. Regularly, a bomb placed in one or two Montreal mail-boxes would explode; another act of terrorism was the kidnapping (and later release) of a British diploma; from what I understand, the kidnapping was to show the public that those separatists meant "business"; they eventually took it too far, after kidnapping and murdering a local politician! The catalyst for these terrorists' actions, was when, shortly after a diplomat from France visited Montreal in the late 1960's, uttered the now-infamous words to the great crowds that gathered, "Vive Le Quebec Libre"; (long-live a free/separate Quebec) this seemed to be all that the persecuted French majority needed to wage their war against the English inhabitants of Quebec, the goal being to liberate themselves from the rest of Canada and establishing a "sovereign", free-standing and independent province or "state" of Quebec! Eventually the local separatist party leader was elected, with the understanding that he would rally for the cause, which never actually happened, after a failed plebiscite. Unfortunately, the election of a separatist leadership resulted in a mass panic and exodus from Montreal (and Quebec in general) in 1975; most of the major corporations and English-speaking businessmen and university graduates fled to nearby Toronto, which is how that city began its growth-spurt; it eventually grew into the largest city in Canada, surpassing my Montreal size-wise and economically, but certainly not culturally. The other down-side was the alienation of the remaining Quebec "Anglophones" (English-speaking people, as opposed to the "Francophone's") shortly after the separatists being elected: All businesses had to display French-only signs, which the English resented; this law was later modified by the newly-elected provincial Liberal party to include both official languages, with the French-part first and more dominant. Even the Quebec license-plates had in the upper (or was it lower?) margin the words "Je me souviens", or, "We/I remember"; (the harsh treatment of the English over the French) according to my dad who grew up in an early Montreal, the "French were treated as poorly as black people are treated in the south!" (U.S.) No wonder the majority Francophone over-reacted to the French diplomat's original words, but unfortunately rather than insuring justice, they chose violence and revenge, not equality, which everyone deserves.

I'm proud to say that I lived through and witnessed all of this history-in-the-making as a teenager.

The Comic-Books

My father used to bring me home something almost daily, upon his return from work in the "wee-small-hours". Excitedly, I would rush out of bed in the morning, to claim my beloved "prize" of a comic-book (sometimes more than one!) or a "gadget", (a novelty-item of some kind, like a miniature plastic-skull or wind-up character) placed carefully on our couch. This contributed to my childhood being "magical": the anticipation, then the reward, and finally the joy in the actual gift. I appreciated everything my father or mother ever gave me, never taking anything for granted. This is also why I never felt "poor": the emotions of anticipation, joy and gratitude more than filled my heart and spirit.

One day when I was less than four but older than two, I found some old, burnt comic-books that my father had placed out for me to discover. The edges were burned, and the comics had a "smoky" scent to them. He brought them home from "the club" where he played. It was as if the doors to my imagination were opened like never before! Sure, I had experienced the full-color wonders of Disney artwork in the past, but this was different! The characters herein depicted were human-like; later in childhood, I learned that I was in possession of war-time, pre-Marvel comics portraying the adventure of the Sub-Mariner, the Human Torch, and Captain America. I quickly devoured the delicious artwork of (again, later learning) Jack Kirby, who went on to co-author in the early 1960's with Stan Lee a post-war Captain America, Fantastic Four, Silver Surfer, and most of the Marvel comics titles! The heroic images were forever engrained in my mind, and although I couldn't read yet, I followed the story along through the illustrations. This was my original introduction to the world of comics. Seeing my joy and fascination with comics, my dad brought me home one daily from that moment on. I retained the color and action in my head, which eventually I could no longer repress, attempting to draw, at age four, the Bat Man!

The Bat Man: A Revelation

I had a green chalk-board resting on top of our couch, against the wall, which my parents had given me that I adored. There was something magical about the green color, and the white chalk, although I can't remember specifically what made it all so magical at the tender age of three or so. I remember that specific moment in time, as I was trying to copy the image of an early 1960's Bat Man-like superhero onto the board, when suddenly I could. One moment I looked at the circle with the horizontal line I drew three-quarters of the way down through the circle, along with the triangles for ears, when it all clicked: I looked at the comic-book image, which was more squared, sharp, and angular, compared to the circle I had drawn, and it all came together! I quickly erased the circle in an "ah-hah" moment, then I feverishly drew two parallel vertical lines two inches apart, the ears, and nose-part of the mask; two upside-down crescents for the eye-holes, a square chin, and voila! I nailed it! One moment I couldn't see, the next moment I could see, in a clear, unbiased and objective manner; this new vision spurred me on in an almost uncontrollable desire to repeat the drawing act, over and over again, from a famous stone-age character, to the leprechaun on the breakfast cereal box! Nothing could stop me now, I was on a roll! Apparently my parents witnessed all of this, easing me from chalk-board to pen and paper awhile later. I soon discovered "Onion" (tracing) paper, which helped me to first trace Superman over and over straight from the comic-book page, to my drawing him without tracing! Colored pencils were my next passion, again, a gift from my parents as they nurtured my drawing skills; imagine, going from drawing black-and-white action figures to full-color marvels straight out of the comics! All this time, I maintained the original color images in my mind from those old, burned comics my dad gave me a few years before. I was creating magic and amusement for others, (my parents) while at the same time creating magic and amusement for myself! Imagine when I later discovered stage magicians, and the "magic" that would bring me!

Magic: Early Influences

I remember listening to the American television program about magic when I was approximately two or three years of age. It was hosted by a professional magician and his assistant/wife. They also featured a clown character who later performed for years at a major Florida amusement centre. I could only imagine in my mind's eye what was going on visually; this resulted in me becoming more and more curious about this mysterious thing called "magic", and the performers of this art! I had no choice but to listen, because our cable wasn't connected properly, so the picture was "snowy" but the sound was perfect! Ironic, since magic is such a visual thing! My curiosity was later satisfied when, at age four, a local professional magician's TV-show made its debut on the fledgling Montreal channel. Ironically there was also a corresponding radio station of the same name, which simulcast their television programs; this reminded me of the old American magician's TV-show days when I could only hear and not see the magic. Nevertheless, the late Montreal magician's show aired (in various incarnations) on local television for more than twenty years, beginning in the early 1960's, and going well into the 1980's. Everyone in Montreal (of my age range and older) is familiar with this magician, since they either saw him performing live in local venues, and/or grew up watching his television program in English six days-a-week, and in French as well! I was no exception!

Daily, I marveled at this affable man, who produced "magic candy" from attractive (and supposedly empty) containers, cutting and restoring rope, and vanishing and producing big sponge balls, silk scarves, and much more; the children who were guests on his show seemed to enjoy this all too. His Saturday variety program exposed many young variety performers to potential agents and audiences, but for me, the main attraction was waiting for him to do his thing. Even at this young age I hoped to someday do what this legend and the American magician could do!

Later, as a teenager, my father took me to one of the local magic-shops; (back then, Montreal had many "novelty stores" which invariably had a small magic-counter, containing the small "marvels" which I craved.) These shops always had novelties, puzzles, gags, and clown supplies which all also spurned on my imagination. Sometimes they also had comic-books and plastic models to build!

I would beg my parents (almost daily) to take me to another local shop down the street so that they'd "buy me a comic or a model"; oh, how I loved to read my comics and build plastic model kits of Universal's monsters! When a certain 1960's campy superhero television series became popular, as well as other monster and superhero-themed shows, my father would also buy me records containing their theme-songs and other music. Of course, I'll never forget my first "novelty" records, "They're Coming To Take Me Away", (which had the same song on the "B"-side, played in reverse) and "The Mouse" , which I believe in some ways influenced me subconsciously when I wrote, produced, and (still sing) my song "The Bat"! After all, isn't a bat just a "flying mouse"? My passion for monsters, comics, super-heroes, and magic kept growing and was perpetuated by these environmental influences, after all, they were hard to avoid!

The Magic Shop

This is the local magic-shop I alluded to earlier, which my father took me to at age fourteen; my mother tagged along.

It was glorious! I'd never visited such a large variety/novelty store before! The other ones were small and crowded, little "holes in the wall" store-fronts peppered throughout Montreal, but this one was different: spacious and well-stocked.

My heart pounding in eager anticipation, my father and I walked towards the back of the shop, where the magic-counter was. There, behind the counter, was a tall, slender, balding man, sporting a moustache and glasses. I watched his hands and fingers moving deftly and gracefully as he demonstrated some tricks. The crowd dispersed, but my father, mother and myself remained. "This is my son", my father said, introducing me to the magician/proprietor. If I had known how famous this local magician was, (the only difference in reputation between himself and the local television magician, was the television program) I would have been more nervous. I smiled as this "master" magician asked me how old I was. "Fourteen", was my response, upon which time he looked up at my parents declaring, "He'll be in magic for the rest of his life." Little did I realize at that point how true that statement would become. After all, I was completely devoted to high school, my studies, and obsessed with continuing to be within the top ten (and hopefully, top five) so that I might earn scholarship like I did in elementary school. How could I possibly spread myself so thin, allowing myself enough time as well, to becoming adept at this skill, this art called "magic"? After the prestidigitator repeatedly changed the color, from black to white and back again, of a pen-knife, and then visibly and visually transformed a blue silk-scarf to red with merely the passing of his hand through it, I knew I wanted to devote my time to develop the skills to do this; the clincher was, when, after having me select a card and him shuffling it into the deck and supposedly hopelessly losing it, it rose up and out of the pack of cards! Feeling myself almost bursting out of my body, I had to learn the secrets of at least these three tricks; I would devote any amount of time necessary to practice and perfect these minor miracles! I had caught "the magic bug"! "We'll take them", my father said to him, the illusionist beginning to place them into a plain brown wrapper, as if to protect these precious secrets from the public, the idly curious. "You should get these two books too", he said to me; this felt sincere and almost paternal, not like a skilled salesman pushing his wares. I looked over the two soft-cover books. They smelled slightly musty and somewhat old. One was titled "Annemann's Miracles of Card-Magic", the other, "Basics of Card-Magic", I believe. My father purchased these as well for me. The proprietor then proceeded to hand my mother what looked like lip-stick saying to her, "Here, try this." Taking off the cover, she then rotated the bottom-edge of the lip-stick case, revealing a small, flesh-colored penis slowly rising up from its sleeve. Everyone laughed. My mother, not missing a beat, said, "So?" Everyone laughed again. In time, I grew accustomed to this "liberal" Montreal attitude/perspective. In my later teen years, while travelling by bus into downtown Montreal on numerous occasions, I could see in a storefront window which the bus passed, several large dildoes and plastic penises with religious images on them. I assumed that these were some sort of satirical "statements" or novelties, and that they were "okay" by Montreal's Catholic, yet cosmopolitan, standards. Strip-joints abounded in the 1970's along Montreal's main drag, along with silhouettes of females in various states of undress in their second-storey windows for the locals, as well as for tourists to enjoy. Again, nobody commented or complained, so I grew up with this sexually-liberal attitude around me. As I relocated farther and farther west in Canada as time went on, I discovered completely different mores (and morals) existed, but those are other stories I'll share later with you.

Back to magical influences.

Upon returning home, I could barely contain my desire to learn and perfect the secrets to the miracles I witness in the magic/novelty shop. Imagine my disappointment when, upon opening the envelope containing the first illusion, I discovered two small pen-knives: one white on both sides, the other one with a black side, and on the reverse, a white side. How could Mr. Gordon have accomplished what he showed me with these two things? He seemed to accomplish the illusion so smoothly and gracefully, almost effortlessly; then in dawned on me: magic wasn't really magic! It only felt and looked like that to me. At age fourteen I hardly believed in Santa (we were Jewish anyways) or the "tooth-fairy"; I knew stage and close-up magic was merely illusion, but I refused to drop my "Pollyanna", "Peter Pan" attitude in order to learn, practice, and perfect the miracles I witnessed earlier; I made a promise to myself to not become cynical or jaded in the process of learning my new craft. The smiles and wonder I felt, I wished to create in others as well! I would manage to maintain a wonderment, almost a belief in the impossible becoming real for the rest of my life, despite the attitude of others, my environment, or the situations. I became, in time, "Magic Mike" Likey (honoring the television magician), but to this day, I AM "Magic" Mike Likey! I wish others had this same faith/belief in themselves, which is the secret to being "spiritual": faith/belief in yourself results in faith/belief in others, which is equivalent to faith/oneness with the creator/source/higher intelligence/"God"! Funny that I always knew this, yet my journey brought me to earning a Masters, then three Doctorates in metaphysical/university institutions in order to share this knowing in a more palatable and different way to others.

But I digress again.

The summer that I visited that magic shop, I practiced over and over those illusions I initially saw the famous proprietor perform, plus many card-sleights and fancy card manipulations from one book, in order to perform the tricks from the other book. My father, at my request, bought me two trick decks of cards advertised at the time on television, one of them appropriately named "TV Magic-Cards"; I practiced and perfected, that summer, as well, the card miracles contained in the included instructions. I was thrilled that I could perform at that point many card-tricks using either an ordinary deck of cards which I could (and did) borrow in social situation, or the two trick decks, which I easily carried with me in my pockets. These newly-acquired skills not only increased my popularity in school, (I was now the best artist and magician in my high school!) but this also helped me build my self-esteem up, which, due to me being overweight back then, was low. I discovered that I had a sense-of-humor (which I used a lot in my magical presentations) but more importantly, people seemed to like (or tolerate) my pun-filled humor. Because the late Ted Annemann's (the 1940's author of one of the books) specialized in a branch of magic called "Mentalism", (fake mind-reading) I also got hooked on this branch of magic, which was also, coincidentally, being made more popular by a famous American Mentalist and his new television show, syndicated throughout the world at the time, which I watched religiously, in order to figure out his tricks. I had enough magical knowledge to do this, and this gave me a lot of pleasure and a feeling of accomplishment. I recorded the tricks and their secrets in comic-book form, which I was also drawing up and constructing for myself in my spare time. Previously I was drawing super-hero comics for myself.

Card-tricks and "Mentalism" are still my favorite, as opposed to coin-magic. Many magicians are apparently either "card-men" or "coin-men"; I do a few coin tricks in my close-up magic-show, as well as other tricks employing other small props such as rope and sponge-balls just for the variety of the spectators. I also specialize in larger and more colorful kids' magic/magic-shows for children. Little did I realize at the time that I would one day make quite the living from cartooning and as a professional magician, with my own television show! Little did I realize at the time, as well, that in the smaller western Canadian towns (and one of the larger western ones) that stage magic was in their eyes "real magic" and "against God"; many also believe that the famous American television Mentalis does real mind-reading! These facts were real eye-openers for me, and would also eventually conflict with me, my careers, and lifestyle; more on that later.

Regardless, magic gave me (and still does to this day) pleasure from the audiences' responses and a feeling of accomplishment as I perfect, or (now) invent magic illusions; a real "fullness". To me, magic and life are the same thing. I now more personally understand famed Canadian magician, the late Doug Henning's attitude about the craft, which always left his audience, as well as himself, with a sense of wonder.

Movie Monsters and Superhero Serials

I discovered the classic Universal monster movies when I was six or seven. I remember reading in one of my many superhero comics which my father would bring home daily, an ad about a famous 1930's movie vampire with a Transylvanian accent. There was something familiar about him; he had the same sort of "widow's peak" hairline as my dad; he wore my dad's favorite color, black; there was some sort of mystique around the character of this aristocratic vampire, so I shelled out my last two-dollars of my allowance for my first monster "fan-zine", or full-color monster magazine, and boy, I was thrilled when it came in the mail!

This particular issue featured the original 1930's colossus movie-monkey, but also had scores of trivia, information, black-and-white photos from silent as well as "talking" and classic monster movies, but most importantly, herein were contained scores of pictures of my vampire in his numerous movie roles! He not only portrayed the legendary vampire character, apparently, but he also acted in numerous other movies portraying mad scientists, hunchback assistants, generally eerie characters, but to my surprise, he had once portrayed the famous man-made monster in one movie! I realized at that point that the original man-made monster actor was not the only actor to portray that monster! In fact, the famous actor (the son of the silent movie actor, called "The Man of a Thousand Faces") and another (the bartender from a famous 1960's American cowboy television program) had also played the monster. Even my other favorite vampire-actor, an equally aristocratic but far more terrorizing actor, had played him in one of those British 1950's studios movies. Of course, this British vampire actor also portrayed the "undead" count in most of those "Hammer" vampire movies As time went on, and as my father located a local newspaper and magazine depot, I was able to regularly purchase on a monthly basis by beloved monster magazines, thus adding to my movie-monster trivia knowledge! There were also many photos of superhero movies, trivia, and information about the actors who portrayed them. Information and pictures came fast and furiously, and I loved it all! Satisfied that I was completely obsessed with those magazines, my father brought me home comic-book versions of horror tales and original macabre stories in magazine form, the covers lavishly illustrated by legendary artists. All contained "O Henry" (surprise) endings, which I further enjoyed. These magazines gave me a lot of fun and added to my magical childhood. They, along with comic-books, also shaped my interest and obsession with trivia, movie monsters and superheroes; most importantly, they inspired me to obsessively draw superhero comics!

Television Evangelists And Religion

I fondly recall, at age twelve, watching someone on television, and his show, which seemed to be educational about the world tomorrow. Since my parents were Jewish, and naturally did not watch "church" on Sunday mornings, nor did they allow me to watch it, (they reacted in a manner that the fictitious vampire might react to a crucifix!) the only exposure I had to anything vaguely resembling something metaphysical or spiritual, was this show.

I remember this television preacher's manner being soft, yet authoritative. He appeared to be very knowledgeable on current events, and matters of the day in general, including science, space exploration, and the recent social unrest of the day. His salt-and-pepper hair made me feel like he was experienced in life, yet he wasn't intimidating to me as a twelve-year-old youngster. His show felt familiar and cozy to me, as I looked forward to it each week, watching it while my parents were out "making an order": a Montreal term for buying groceries. This television personality seemed to explain with ease the reasons behind current events, and it all made sense to me; I never for one minute connected these facts as being completely religious in nature, as was explained to me later in life; to this day, I'll always have fond memories of him and his show; I suspect that his easygoing presentations heavily influenced the presentations of my own metaphysical lectures.

School

I allowed school, my relationship with and to it, and my academic standing in school to define who I was, from age six until approximately age twenty or twenty-one. This was partly due to the fact that my life in general was limited to home, school, and home again. I had very little, if any, social activities away from home and school; this was due in no small part to my mother's over-protective and controlling manner and personality. She would have me driven to and from school by taxi so that nothing "bad" would happen to me; those "bad" things lived mainly in her imagination, such as my getting kidnapped, or being smothered in a snow storm, or getting fatally ill because of the cold winters we endured. Did I mention that my parents insured that we managed to live in an apartment across the street from my elementary school, and then later my high school? I justify my mother's trepidations being as a result of her losing her unborn children twice, and then finally succeeding in carrying me to full-term, and her great gratitude for succeeding, and then not wanting to lose me after this great "battle". That was how she explained it all to me, any how.

My mum did allow me to bring home friends after school, while I attended elementary school, so that we may play "school", but again, only at our residence. Friends were allowed to come over to our apartment on Goyer Street, again, for us to play in the apartment only, no unsupervised "walks" or trips to the store or playground. I was allowed to go for walks to a nearby playground with my neighbor/school-friend, but again, our mothers chaperoned us. This became "normal" to me, and I looked forward to these get-togethers and walks, as well as my mum, dad, and myself regularly walking to a neighborhood stationary-store, where my parents would buy me a comic, or plastic model-kit of monsters or super-heroes to assemble, or buy me a record album. This combined my love of the comic-books with animation on television and music! To this day, I believe these "limited-animation" shows influenced my current works such as my animated feature-shorts and comic-books. A dream was fulfilled when I was hired in my early twenties to draw a nationally-syndicated comic-strip as well as participate in an "assembly-line" of animators for television commercials; but more on that later.

My oldest friend, was more or less my intellectual friend, with whom I discussed philosophy, television-shows, and yes, love. He was in my grade one class at elementary school, the first time around; the second time around, room 13, (I was held back and had to take grade one again!) there he was again, my classmate and friend, who ended up being ever-present throughout my scholastic "career", in that he seemed to be in many of the classes I took, including college in the 1970's. It was he who, in one particularly long telephone conversation, described in great detail to me the biological methodologies of sex. It was very basic, but it was more than anything my parents had shared with me; I was eight years old, then. I remember one sunny, hot day in Montreal as our mums were walking us back to our respective next-door domiciles from "Kent Park", he stopped, resting himself down for a moment on a concrete-block in front of one of our apartment buildings. Stopping beside him, I asked, "What's up?" His response was, "Just stopping to do some girl-watching." I too, then, took up some real estate beside him, believing this was the right thing to do as well, with my sweater draped around my shoulders and my Montreal "Expos" cap slightly back on my head, we must have been quite the sight for the "debutants" passing by us! He himself was wearing a cotton, striped-patterned white-and-blue golf-shirt with grey dress-pants and shoes, no competition for my casual shorts and sneakers! We nodded and smiled, the sun shining off of my huge, plastic horn-rimmed glasses, my small but over-weight frame beginning to perspire under the thickness of my yellow-polyester golf-shirt; I would, at age fourteen, discover the pleasures (and advantages) to sporting a brand-new anti-perspirant whose scent was like a spring morning!. He remained ever-confident and optimistic that some young lady might give us a second glance, especially with our mother's standing nearby, wringing their hands and mumbling inaudibly between the two of them.

Because my parents entered me into school at age six, I was required to go immediately into grade one, as opposed to kindergarten first; this resulted in me being somewhat traumatized, as I had to adjust to first being separated from my parents for the first time in my life, and then to also try to catch up somehow to the academic/scholastic information being presented, such as arithmetic, spelling, and printing/writing! My classmates were already introduced to all of this already, in kindergarten, and I found myself academically lost, my self-esteem and confidence squashed and nowhere to be found! This resulted in the school diagnosing me as "slow" and with a learning disability! I was required to take "extra gym": exercises for my mind and body which entailed drawing circles over and over again on a blackboard, as well as jumping up and down on a trampoline for fifteen minutes a day; my oldest friend was also a part of this little group. Because I was quite overweight and already had self-esteem issues, this only added to my horrible self-image. Today this syndrome might be diagnosed as autism, (at one lower end of the spectrum) but I suspect that with modern psychological and physiological knowledge and advancements, my inability to achieve might be diagnosed as merely low self-esteem, rather than faulty brain function.

As it turned out, the reason for my "slow learning" and inability to digest the academics as quickly as the other children actually was low self-esteem! During the summer between grade one in room 16 and grade one in room 13, my mother feverishly tutored me, bringing me up to "snuff" with workbooks and flashcards, so much so, that by the time I entered into grade one for the second time, I was actually ahead of my classmates, knowledgeable in fractions, multiplication and long-division! Spelling and writing was no longer an issue too! I'll never forget early in that school year when the teacher reluctantly responded to my hand being up during a quiz, and my answer was correct! Her smile was broad and heartwarming as she scooped me up in her arms in delight and relief at my correct response to her question. Later that same year, she introduced me to more advanced reading, allowing me to take home books that were more creative, colorful, and challenging! I had a confidence in myself and as a student that I'd never experienced before, and this faith in myself and my talents has stayed with me to this day. My mum continued to tutor me until college, when I was able to "run with the ball", so-to-speak, over-achieving for the rest of my academic careers.

Another Friend

My second-oldest friend, Barry, was also friends with him. Barry and I first met in grade 2, when we were both eight years old. I admired Barry's imagination and his love for the same television programs that I enjoyed as well. Barry was the first classmate I knew whose parents separated and subsequently divorced. As Barry and my friendship continues to this day, even though he and his wife reside in eastern Canada, and my wife and I reside on the west coast of Canada, we continue to remain in contact through social-media and phone-calls. My oldest friend and I also maintain our respect for each other and friendship through social-media, specifically, Facebook.

It's comforting to know that friendships that are more than fifty years old can endure.

In broad strokes, so-to-speak, I'd like to summarize my experiences, now, in elementary school. Grade one, twice, I've already shared with you. Grade two and three both seemed similar, including the two different teachers' appearance. (dark hair) What does stand out in grade two, was that the teacher was good-natured, and allowed us to express ourselves, in my case, with practical jokes! How she laughed with surprise at the rubber-spider left on her chair, and the "joy-buzzer" vibrating when we shook hands on April Fool's Day! One of my friends (whose name I've long forgotten) was a spy-movie enthusiast, as were many of us at that time, what with the spy movies and television programs. His passion for spies pushed me to beg my dad for an attaché-case toy "spy kit", marketed on TV. It consisted of a built-in "spy-camera", and a gun that assembled, among other things. Marketed, too, was a "spy" "Sixth-Finger": a flesh-colored index-finger replica that fired toy bullets and miniature darts. How I loved that period!

During grade two and three, I played "Cowboys and Indians", being an only child, I played both roles, dressing up with a feathered head-dress and bow-and-arrows, I pretended to fire at someone else, quickly changing into a cowboy-hat and six-shooters, assuming the other role, and again, firing at myself with my cap-guns! If my mum was watching me from somewhere nearby, she must have had great joy and a great laugh! I would pretend to be hit, falling to the floor in a heap. I recall earlier, in my pre-school days, taking on the roles of both an animated cowboy horse his burro sidekick, interacting with each other with the relevant voices! So much fun! Scholastically, I was a number one student in all grades, except for grade four.

Grade Four

During grade four, I enjoyed a particular popularity as "the artist" with my friend Mathilda. "The Monkees" were very popular that year, as was "Star Trek", and Mathilda continually requested black and white portraits of The Monkees, to which I graciously and willingly obliged. Mathilda, and another female classmate, Arlene, would toss erasers so that they would land just beside and behind a male classmate of ours, Arthur, in an effort to glimpse down his pants, which, as he leaned over at his desk while writing, was revealed to the world due to his pants naturally pulled down and back somewhat; he did not go on to become a plumber, but rather a Toronto University literature professor!

Our teacher, Miss Bartholomew, herself slightly overweight, gave me the occasional "jab" at my own weight, such as "You seem well-fed!" How inappropriate that was, as well as hurtful! I took solace, years later, while my parents and I were walking through the lobby of a fancy Montreal hotel, that I saw this now-former teacher working as a clerk behind the front-desk of that hotel! I wondered if she also mocked the hotel guests. Nonetheless, she was the only elementary school teacher I had who repeatedly gave me average marks, while I was always graded above-average by the others; to this day I don't know why, but I recognize she had some sort of issue with me, and I wish her well. Grade five and six were both academically challenging for me, with the addition of the "Geography" and "History" courses; what I did enjoy of these two courses were the maps we were sometimes called on to make, which I excelled at. Grade seven eventually came along, with the anticipation of earning scholarship and moving onto a new school. A High School! I did earn enough high marks to achieve this, and I still have the scholarship pin and book/documentation. Grade seven did start off sort of uneasily, when, on the first day of school, our teacher Miss Sara suddenly grabbed an annoying student by his face, digging her fingers into both sides of the hollows of his cheeks, lifting him off the ground, pulling him into our classroom, and lifting his small body off the floor, dangling him over a desk, after he kept peering into our classroom while making faces. We stared, shocked! She dropped him to the ground, as he scampered away. All she then said to us was, "I'm not here to win a popularity contest!" We sat in silence, our hearts pounding with fear, and for the first time, fear of a teacher as opposed to the principal, who, throughout elementary school, would strap certain "bad" kids. Imagine this barbaric and ineffective form of punishment being carried out today! But this was Montreal in the late 1960's, where we had to study the songs of Bob Dylan, Simon and Garfunkel, and Leonard Cohen as poetry and works of art. I still love my Montreal! Regardless, I, and a fellow student sitting at her desk beside me both had a lesson in female anatomy when one day, Miss Sara bent over, inadvertently revealing her lack of underwear to the two of us; I can still see Mary Beth's mouth hang open as we looked at each other! This same teacher frequently sat at her desk, legs crossed and feet up on her desk. I'm told by friends in western Canada that this was unheard of; I trust that to be true!

This was the same teacher, who one day, decided to introduce us to a popular comedian and his famous record, consisting of a routine of words you can't say on television; we all knew those words at this point, but never did we expect to hear them by way of our teacher! For whatever reason she shared this material with us. Perhaps she was attempting to expose us to "the real world"? I don't know! Nonetheless, during the playing of that particular segment, into the classroom walked our feared principal! I don't know if this was all planned, or if he was walking by anyway, and upon hearing the language, decided to put an end to it; regardless, storming in and pausing, he merely said, "You playing this stuff to them?" Shaking his head, he exited. She continued playing this epic work of art to us. This was to all lay the ground-work for my impending entrance into puberty in high school; more on that later.

Nevertheless, we all made it through elementary school, relatively unscathed.

The "Bar-Mitzvah"

When a Jewish boy reaches the age of thirteen, he is declared "a man" through the ritual of "The Bar-Mitzvah". For girls, the ritual is called "The Bat- (sometimes "Baz") Mitzvah". It consists of the boy or girl, standing up in "shul", or synagogue, before his/her family and God, reading from the "Torah" (gentiles' version is the "Old Testament", though Jews' "Old Testament" or "Torah" consists of forty-five original mystically-oriented books, sometimes referred-to as "The Kabala"; this has been all been whittled-down to only five books of "The Torah", or the gentiles' "Old Testament") A Jewish boy, from the age of five or six, must attend "Hebrew School" in addition to regular school. There, the Jewish scholar must learn the Hebrew language, each letter a symbol, and a sound, with many, almost infinite interpretations; the combination of these symbols form more sounds, and words, again, with infinite meanings and subtleties; this explains why Jewish scholars, whose aim is to join the clergy and become "Rabbi's" must "argue" (or discuss) with each other and their teacher, the meanings of the biblical texts. It is apparently that way, that one may eventually be "enlightened" or begin to vaguely understand God's Word. By the way, as a Jew, I'm not supposed to say the word "God", but use this expression: "G_d", as in our faith, God is the indefinable, and cannot be reduced to a single word.

My Jewish peers, potential candidates for the ultimate goal of the Bar-Mitzvah, would only have to learn a cursory understanding, reading and writing of Hebrew, along with a history of our people, in preparation for the Bar (or Bat) Mitzvah at age thirteen. In the smaller western cities of Canada, there is this popular misconception that the Bar-Mitzvah is the circumcision ritual, but it is not; the circumcision is performed by a specially-trained Rabbi, called a "Moyle", when the child is seven days old wherein the foreskin is surgically removed. My father took great pride, when I was growing up in Montreal, to share how I "Cried and cried," when the procedure was performed. He had an almost guilty tone in his voice.

Either because, in actuality, my parents did not have enough money to put me through Hebrew, or "Jewish School", and then the inevitable Bar-Mitzvah, (costing upwards of tens of thousands of dollars) they "chose" to not have me "endure" this all; they told me, that they "Wanted me to concentrate on school, and my studies."

Inevitably, I never had a Bar-Mitzvah, nor did one of my maternal cousins. His brother did; we in fact went to Toronto by train from Montreal in 1971 to witness this joyous occasion. I was excited about the trip, as I'd never been outside of Montreal before! Someone pick-pocketed me on the journey there, stealing my wallet and the fifty-dollar contents! I must have looked like a wide-eyed target to the perpetrator of this evil deed. Nonetheless, we all had a great time, staying with my aunt and her new husband. I entertained all with my brand-new passion, magic, and continued to entertain at future family gatherings with my amusing and amazing card-tricks. I even won over the heart of a young lady once or twice while performing my "magic".

Rather than a formal Bar-Mitzvah, in order to acknowledge and celebrate my thirteenth birthday during the summer of 1969, specifically on July 20th, my parents bought me several gifts; although novelties, I kept them and treasured them for years to come. One was a blue, plastic transistor radio with a small white ear-phone, which I used to listen to the music they know that I loved so; I remember singing along to a famous pop-tune by a group of Winnipeg rockers, among many other tunes of the day. Another present was the original "Laughing Bag", consisting of a colorful small cotton draw-string bag containing a small, flesh-colored, plastic devise in which resided a miniature record-player, and a record. It was upon this small record that an audio-sound of continuous laughter originated from, and was activated by a small button which protruded from the devise. When the bag was squeezed, this would activate the devise, and thus, laughter would emanate from the bag! This amused me a great deal, not for the final effect, but because of the clever engineering behind it all; this same admiration and curiosity spurs me on, even to this day, to invent and market new magic tricks and illusions. thus, early exposure to magic-tricks and novelties influenced (and still does influence) my passion for novel, different, magical things. It's like a light turns on within me when I enter a magic, or a novelty-shop. "Dollar" stores, as well as thrift-stores hold this same magical anticipation when I even think of them let alone enter them; I think, "I wonder what unknown treasures reside here, waiting for me to discover them, buy them, and then enjoy them forever?" Obsessive? Maybe, but I don't care! It makes me happy and brings a sense of wonder to my life!

The third and final novelty-gift for my thirteenth birthday was a small, plastic, realistic-looking coffin; small and perfect in every detail. This alone intrigued me, and peaked my curiosity; slowly, I opened the lid of the coffin, and to my amusement and delight, up sat a small, plastic skeleton, spraying water from it's groin-area in the process! I laughed and laughed! What a great twist on the standard water-spraying flower! I loved the simple and clever engineering behind the methodology of this "Urinating Skeleton"! For whatever reason, whenever I share this delightful and amusing story with my current wife, she doesn't crack a smile; she sees no humor in this at all. She is after all, from Vancouver. More on Vancouverites later.

A neighbor and her daughter visited us on my very special day, to present me with a brand-new wallet, to hold the money that they also included with the wallet. I hugged and thanked them, and asked them all about this strange land, California, from which they moved to Montreal in order for the daughter to be schooled. Did Montreal hold some great advantage over California, academically? Did our neighbors hold some secret over Montreal that I was not aware of? Later in life, I vacationed regularly and annually to the south eastern U.S. (as opposed to the south west, where California is) to Miami, "the land of my people", but more on that later.

What a special summer the summer of 1969 was.

High School

The summer of 1969 was indeed an exciting one: besides my thirteenth birthday, "Woodstock" was being televised, and a lot of changes were in the wind. Recently, there was much civil unrest in the U.S., with a black reverend having been assassinated, as well as the brother of a former president. This, of course, impacted the world, but also our family.

We had a framed picture of former U.S. President Kennedy on our wall when I was growing up, and I remember small U.S. flags around the house. My father said that President Kennedy was a great man, and the U.S. was the greatest country in the world. New York City was my dad's home for twenty years before my parents met, with his brothers and sisters still resided there, so I suspect that's where my dad's positive attitude about the U.S. came from. My dad always wanted to move back there, but said that my mother didn't want to do this. I suspect that I inherited this "I'd rather be somewhere else" attitude from him, and carry this melancholic feeling to this day.

The summer of 1969 was also the summer we relocated from Goyer Street to Bouchette Avenue near Legare. The motivation was two-fold: living across the street from my high school, and new beginnings. My parents decided to "cash in" most of my comic-books, leaving me, at my request, only with a few select titles. With dozens of paper grocery-bags in tow, my parents made numerous trips to the corner store with my beloved comics: there went "The Munsters", "I Dream of Jeannie", not to mention all of the "Charlton"-brand comics, "Gold Key" Star Trek titles, "Action", "Superman", "Detective", and "Batman" titles to name just a few. Did I say my goodbyes to "Casper", "Archie" and more titles than I can remember? You bet I did! Still, the prospect of a "new life" and high school superseded any sadness and mourning!

I remember my excitement at the smell of our brand-new leather living-room furniture, and my new desk, lamp, and bed. It truly felt like new beginnings, as I was to start attending high school that fall. Even the television shows were all brand-new it seemed: many were being locally produced. I was truly and eagerly anticipating taking these brand-new classes as well, including something called "Advanced French": I excelled in speaking and writing that language, and so I was placed into an advanced class, as well as having to attend the standard one. I was encouraged to take advanced English and literature classes, where I excelled as well; quite a difference from the traumatized "grade-oner" with a then-diagnosed "learning disability" who subsequently failed grade one, having to repeat it the following year!

Nonetheless, it was the autumn of 1969, and I was attending an amazing, brand-new school!

I loved the fact that all of my classes were not in one classroom; I loved the fact that few knew me, nor did they have any real expectations of me. I looked forward to surprising everyone with my academic "expertise" and artistic ability. This all became a realty in time, as I took "Art" all four years, as well as "Mechanical Drawing", a combination of design, engineering and architecture; again, this was Montreal! I was preparing myself for college, or "C.E.G.E.P." "Cegep" as it is called now, is a publically-funded, pre-university general and vocational college in Quebec. They are post-secondary educational collegiate institutions exclusive to Quebec. One could take a "pre-university" two-year program leading into university, or a complete-in-itself three-year course; I opted for the three-year "Graphic Design" program, but more on that later. All that I knew was that the tuition per semester was only twenty-five dollars, plus expenses for drafting and art supplies, a mere pittance, compared to the hundreds of thousands of dollars to attend some expensive university.

Of course, there were "compulsory" classes I had to attend in high school, some of which I did not enjoy, like "Geometry", despite the expertise of the teacher. Oh, well; this was a means to an end for me, in this case, college and the work-force as a commercial artist/graphic designer. Unlike some of my peers who opted to become doctors, lawyers, scientists, engineers, etc., I knew my first true passion was art, and to make a living from it, I had to be a commercial artist, my ultimate goal being to work as a professional cartoonist, which I also achieved; again, more on that later. I suppose there's something to be said for the fact that my peers and I knew what vocation we wanted to be in; as I lived farther and farther west in Canada over time, I realized that this isn't necessarily the norm, nor is college even an option for most! To this day I realize how fortunate I was. Of course, as usual, I remembered relating to segments and phases of my life through whichever popular songs or television programs were on, and high school was no exception! This television-show about life in a California high School debuted in September, giving me a glimpse (albeit overly optimistic) of what I was in store for: surely many of my teachers and principal would be like these actors; of course, this was not to be, but with the almost etheric theme-song winding its way through a flute and into my heart, I initially "floated" through these "shiny, brand-new" hallways! My ensemble, of course, would also have to be influenced by another brand new show about three mod teenagers recruited by the police to work undercover, after all, the characters seemed so "with it" and "hip" in their bright, multi-colored shirts and trousers! I was eager and ready for whatever high school had in store for me; or so I thought!

Puberty

Puberty hit me with a vengeance, some time in grade eight. I determined this by the fact that I would awaken in the middle of the night, having just experienced a "nocturnal emission". Embarrassed by this, I chose to hide my underwear under my bed, hoping that my mother would not suspect (or discover) that I was now enduring this new "bodily function". Somehow these pairs of undergarments would vanish mysteriously from beneath my bed, reappearing days later freshly washed and dried! To this day I still can't explain these strange occurrences, worthy of a science fiction movie!

Miraculously, an elderly maternal family-member's pornographic novels appeared one day on the seat of one of our couches in the middle of our living room; tawdry tales of sexual acts between poorly-written paragraphs of fiction, and implausible plots and situations! These "works of art" were in the form of several paperback novels, which, without consulting my parents or asking their permission, I voraciously studied; surely people didn't really carry on like the characters in these books; or did they? The answer came that year as well to me, when one night I peered out of my bedroom window, casting a glance at the neighbor's window directly across from my own. 'Lo and behold, our sixteen-year-old, well-"endowed" female neighbor was enjoying herself with her boyfriend, with her mother doing the dishes in front of the kitchen-window, just next door to the girl's bedroom. This was certainly the year for my sex-education! To further add to all of this, on one occasion, while I was throwing out the garbage, I discovered in the incinerator-room, a large, brown paper-bag full of discarded famous pornographic magazines! If I wasn't quite sure of the female-form, I would soon be fully-educated in that "unexplored territory"! To further add to "the year of sexual maturity", my father jokingly offered his solution to my newly-acquired acne: taking me to a "house"! I full well knew what he meant by that. It was the custom in my father's youth, for a young man's father to take him to a brothel, introducing him to a prostitute for his subsequent "de-flowering!" Being relatively self-conscious at this tender age of thirteen, I responded to my father's suggestion with an uncertain and nervous laugh, my mother looking at my dad with disdain. As time went on, and with my previous exposure to teachers without undergarments and neighbors frequently indulging in "coitus", (or as my grade six-educated father called it, "inter-coursing") I accepted the "natural and wide-spread movement" of sex. I began looking at women, and my teachers differently. One of my female grade nine teachers requested, one day, of us that we write a piece of fiction that involved all of our senses. Quite innocently, I described in the terms and manner that I was educated-to by my maternal family-member's books, and my beloved, secret pornography collection, the act of enjoying and eating an orange. At fourteen, I described the tongue "exploring the navel" of the orange, ultimately culminating in the juices of the orange "flowing and flowing"! I received an "A" from this teacher; I didn't understand why she blushed as she returned my paper to me, barely making eye-contact with me. I remember in this class as well, a new immigrant to Montreal, one of my male classmates, asking her to excuse him because he needed to "satisfy" himself. Perhaps it was because of his newly-acquired English language, or perhaps it was something else, I still don't know to this day why he expressed himself in this manner, his face seemingly earnest, as he made this request of her, to be excused. This all contributed to my view of Montreal as a "swinging", hip, and "open" city, despite it's conservative Catholic population-base; perhaps it was because of this conservative base, that the population, generally, needed an outlet; I don't know.

I managed to excel in high school, with my reputation for being a good artist, but by grade ten, I gained the reputation of also being a "Houdini"! My passion for magic grew to the extent that crowds would gather around me at lunch hour, while I did card-tricks and/or won in poker games or "twenty-one". There was another young magician in my high school; together, we successfully participated in the variety show. For the record, one of the tricks I performed was a "Mentalism" effect, in which someone from the audience throws a dart at a board containing all fifty-two cards laid out in random fashion; the card which the dart hit proved to be the same and only card prediction previously turned over in a pack of cards which remained in full sight during the effect. To this day I'm still passionate about Mentalism. Among the other young magician's effects, he performed a "floating ball" kind of effect, which eerily rose up from its pedestal, floating up, in, around, and behind a cloth which he held between his hands, to great applause. I wore a white "Lee" jean-jacket, white "Lee" jeans, pink "Wrangler" shirt from my paternal family-member, and construction boots, like my television hero "Lincoln Hayes" from "Mod Squad". It was this particular performance that always stayed with me, supplying me with confidence and the desire to continue on with magic as a hobby and eventual career!

By grade 10 I wore my hair longer, with prescription aviation sunglasses, sporting denim jackets and jeans, unlike my peers. I didn't believe that I had to dress a certain way just because I was in the top ten academically; I dressed the way I felt most comfortable, even wearing at some point a "sash" the way my hero did, in the "Kung Fu" TV-show. Little did I realize that the Taoist and Buddhist philosophies of the TV-show would profoundly effect my own spiritual beliefs and outlook both personally as well as professionally! That, and the music of Cat Stevens, whose music I also discovered when I was in grade ten, affected me personally as well as professionally. Late one Saturday night in the autumn of 1972 or '73, on a television-show, was featured a certain pop star, whose melodic songs and mystical image, as well as his animated works influenced and captivated me, even still to this day! His solitary singer-songwriter style, combined with his somewhat spiritual songs about nature had a profound effect on me both personally and professionally; his music was like a mirror for me. His songs about peace are still sung to this day, finding a new audience each decade. I even recorded the concert that night of '73 by placing my tape-recorder's microphone near the television; I still have this original recording to this day! There was something etheric and special about his music for me; I could relate to the words, the melodies were infectious, and I played the rhythms with the drum-sticks that my dad had given me; I was making my thighs black-and-blue in the process, but feeling no pain, only bliss. With a couple of classmates, I attended a concert he gave in the 1970's at the Montreal "Forum" which seated more than twenty-thousand people, filled to capacity; what a thrill that was for the eight-dollar ticket-fee! I had the honor of witnessing him breaking a guitar string, and then changing it on stage; in retrospect, wouldn't he have someone change it for him, or just have an extra guitar handy? Nonetheless, the concert named "The Bamboozle Tour" for his newly developed interest in matters spiritual, including Buddhism, was not only a success for the audience, but for the jaded newspaper critics as well. This was not to be the only coincidence that I shared with him, including us both being cartoonists/graphic artists and writing children's books and producing animation! Even later in life, we both have the same eye-glasses and guitars. If this weren't enough, we have a similar birth-date: his July 21st, myself, July 20th. I also share the same coincidences with a metaphysical minister I admire: we are both "Rev. Dr. Michael", and we share the same birth-date! For me, that '70's pop star's music makes me feel more like "myself", and is uplifting for me. I still sing and play his songs on my guitar; his music inspired me to study and play guitar in my spare time, while juggling my love for magic. At age eighteen, feeling overwhelmed, I dropped magic for a few years.

Feeling empowered with the music of that certain pop star and the philosophies of "Kung Fu" in my head, and not belonging to any particular "clique", I walked up and down the hallways of my high school, with nods of mutual respect from everyone but from my peers. It was one particular member of another group who repeatedly called out to me "Hey, Houdini"! which I liked and appreciated.

I remember a handful of students smoking pot in the hallways of my high school, with the smell filling the halls, the principal and two vice-principals being relatively ineffectual in stopping or hindering this. Sex also ran rampant for the same reason. I discovered neither until later in life, but more on that later! My high school also had a reputation for being "tough", regularly being in the local newspapers because a teacher had been accosted, or because of yet another bomb-threat. Nonetheless, my high school and another suburban one both had the dubious distinctions of being tough. I remember visiting in my teens this particular suburb north of Montreal, and it's fast-food restaurant next to a bowling alley; it had an obvious and intimidating presence of security guards! Imagine that! Security guards in a local fast-food restaurant of an affluent suburb! I remember this same fast-food restaurant in my neighborhood having framed pictures of horses on the walls; were they trying to tell the customers something, like the origin of the meat? We thought this to be hysterically funny, until one night someone pointed out that this fast-food establishment was next door to a raceway, where horse-racing occurred! The joke was on us! Across the street we had a huge round, orange building visible for miles! Girls on skates would come up to one's parked car, serving burgers, fries, and frothy orange drinks. Rumor had it that upstairs, within the building was actually a house of ill-repute, and if one ordered a "hot dog with the works", we could also, for a price, be sexually serviced. We never found out., even though, after all, it was Montreal.

One day the local pizza-parlor burned down, to everyone's dismay. I had never partaken of these particular pies, which had an almost legendary reputation, at least in this particular suburb; nothing was as good as the food from this particular pizza-parlor! I couldn't wait for it to be rebuilt, so that I too, could partake of the pie. When I did, I wasn't disappointed! It had a completely unique flavor and appearance; the topping were numerous and more finely chopped than other pizzas.

I experienced the legendary "Montreal Smoked Meat" in my later teens, and discovered why this original, spicy version of a pastrami sandwich was so popular: lots of spicy meat (if requested, "lean") stacked up at least three inches high, between two pieces of rye bread, garnished with mustard! On the side were fries and a "dill" pickle. When one walked into any one of the famous Montreal delis/establishments, the servers automatically knew what you wanted; this and a strawberry cheesecake and a cherry Coke to wash it all down. This was Montreal to me, as well: mile-high meat sandwiches, cheesecake, and the ambiance of a dirty, smoky delicatessen! Walking down rue St.-Catherine in Montreal one could smell these delightful tasty treats wafting through the city's core, thousands of tourists and locals alike being tempted towards a coronary disaster. I love my Montreal.

By grade ten, we were encouraged by the school counselor to prepare ourselves scholastically for college, or "CEGEP", by taking and passing certain classes that we needed in order to "matriculate" or graduate from grade eleven, and thus high school. Without passing our grade eleven matriculation exams and thus securing our "Secondary Five" certificate, we could not apply for, nor enter into college, or Cegep. In Montreal, high school consisted of grades eight through eleven. While writing one of these exams ("History" I believe) with a hundred-and-four temperature and pounding headache, I still managed to get a good mark, despite my fevered state. That was the "summer of measles", as the headache and fever was the precursor to the childhood disease which I had caught, thanks to the epidemic at the time. Needless to say, the summer of 1973 was not a pleasant one thanks to Rubella. Nonetheless, I succeeded in passing, with top-ten marks, all the necessary classes necessary to move onto college!

The Portfolio

One of the requirements for applying for entrance into the three-year "Commercial Art" program at an east-end Montreal college, was a portfolio of my works.

My art teacher, Mr. Intaglio, was extremely kind and helpful towards this goal. I remember, while in grade eight in his art class, one of the taller, physically mature female students approaching him as he sat at his desk. She was wearing a mini-skirt with no undergarment, which she regularly verbally proudly declared to us outside of class, and so she subsequently chose to stand next to him at his desk, one foot perched on top of a small box next to him, giving him an eye full! I can still remember his embarrassment and discomfort as he attempted to avert his glance towards her. One of my high school "English" teachers was driven to nervous exhaustion by several students who repeatedly confounded and harassed him during class; they would run around the classroom, overturning desks, and even once jumped out the first-floor window! This particular teacher could not take control of the situation, and so, after one semester of this, he failed to return, replaced by a tough, mini-skirted and be-spectacled female teacher.

But I digressed.

Mr. Intaglio declared, quietly to me one day, that I would never have respect as an "artist" if I continued to draw cartoons; that cartooning was low on the scale of "high art". Cartooning was my heart and soul, and furthermore, I was quite good at it! I was asked to draw cartoons for our grade eleven school annual! I excelled at portraiture as well, but preferred cartooning! The plan was to get my "Commercial Art" certification to "legitimize" myself and thus eventually become a professional cartoonist. I would not hear of this "nay-saying" teacher, who eventually turned out to be wrong anyway, as I did become a nationally-syndicated cartoonist and political cartoonist; but more on that later! I managed to cobble together the required number of matted samples for my portfolio. Some of the samples were large, full-color, graphic/flat images of my television heroes, such as the protagonist from the "Kung Fu" television series, and "Captain America", a comic-book super-hero. I even constructed a mock music record album for my portfolio, complete with an actual record inside the sleeve, replete with labels! I realized that if I followed my passion, I would do an exceptional job, putting in that extra "something" into the work.

The Interview

The day came, in June of 1974, for my interview for entrance into the Commercial Art program of this particular college. I felt ready, armed with a portfolio that I had put my heart and soul into, as well as following the technical requirements. I trusted that my passion for cartooning would be seen, felt, and respected by the committee, which consisted of a handful of last-year students, plus one or two department heads. I felt more excited than nervous; less judged and more on "display" than anything else, as the friendly committee ushered me into the windowless room. I wondered if the room was also airless?

The interview went smoothly, as they flipped through each piece of my portfolio, smiling, nodding to each other, and then finally, the offer: they asked me if I'd like to be enrolled in the "Graphic Design" program, rather than "Commercial Art". I asked what the difference was, and they said preparing artwork for print was the emphasis, as opposed to focusing on artwork for more three-dimensional uses, such as theatrical set-design, package-design, and so forth. I agreed to the Graphic Design course, not even beginning to realize what a grueling two years I was to endure!

I naively believed, knowing that the top-paying Editorial Cartoonist positions paid in excess of $200,000. annually, (at least in big cities like Montreal) that by age thirty, I might own a "mansion" and drive a Rolls Royce, (like a certain television secret agent) earned through gainful employment as a cartoonist. Marriage and children were never part of my dream, despite my mother's continuous pleas for me to marry, and make her a grandmother. I seemed that the more my mum placed these demands on me, the further I chose to drift from those goals. I was just too excited about working in my chosen fields of Graphic Design and Cartooning at that point in my life.

Graphic Design/Commercial Art

My initial impression on "day one" of the course was how intense this was going to be! First, there were eleven courses per semester, plus the compulsory selection of an "English" and an "Humanities" course, each of which would be at a different campus from the Graphics program. There was a "Magic Bus" which transported students from campus to campus at appointed and scheduled times, allowing students to take courses at any one of several campuses. I opted to take a "Canadian Myths and Literature" course for the English option, but I can't recall the title of the Humanities one. All that I remember was for the "Myths" one that we had to create our own mythical story to explain a natural phenomena, as did the Celts and Indigenous people of every country. For the Humanities course, the professor required of us that we write about anything he wanted, or felt that we were qualified to write about, plus to do a presentation related to the subject of the essay.

I selected "Magic", my then-favorite hobby/passion for this task! I easily wrote a history of magic, consisting of hundreds of pages, in a weekend! The words just flowed, in the same manner that they did for what was to be my future self-help metaphysical books, and yes, even this tome! I did a quasi-mindreading/"Mentalist" show/presentation, wherein a previously-predicted playing card was seen to be spontaneously chosen in class, during the course of my presentation, by the professor! Another "experiment" involved more playing cards: a sealed deck of cards contained another prediction in the form of a reversed (turned face-up amongst faces-down cards) card, the pack held by a fellow classmate. Another student then completely randomly selected a card from a different pack; both were seen to match! I could have easily made the subject-matter of my paper and presentation be on extrasensory perception, but I couldn't, in good conscience do this, for it was trickery after all; deceptions, clever magic-tricks from the branch of magic called "Mentalism", which I felt most comfortable with. I earned a very high mark for this course.

Unfortunately, these two would be the only non-Graphic Design-related courses I would take in my three years at Dawson College; travelling between campuses, plus managing the very difficult and challenging projects/course assignments proved too much for me, as it did with the majority of the other Graphics students. Ninety-percent of my classmates never bothered taking the required two extra courses per semester in order to earn our college certificate; we were after all warned that of the fifty out of two-hundred students selected for the Graphic Design and Commercial Art programs, only ten to fifteen students would see it all through to the end! I didn't believe it when I was told this in the original interview, but this turned out to be true! Even if one managed to be within the final fifteen or so students to make it to the end of the three years, one could not get their certificate without successful completion of the six English and six Humanities courses. Hence, although I made it to the second-to-last month of the three years, I never received my formal diploma; also, at the end of my second year, the administration, in a meeting with me, encouraged me to switch to, for my third year, the Commercial Art program, which they, after all was said and done, felt I was more right for! I ended up getting the best of all worlds: an education for two years on the "bread-and-butter" skills of preparing artwork for print-media, ad layout and designs, as well as learning illustration styles and techniques, photography (in all three years) plus preparing artwork for three-dimensional packaging in third year Commercial Art; what initially seemed as "failure" on my part turned out to give me a more well-rounded Graphics/Commercial Art education! I might add at this point, that most of our Graphic Design and Commercial Art teachers were working professionals, either in the past, or at the time.

One of our "Illustration" teachers was the Editorial Cartoonist of the Montreal Star, it being one of the major English-language papers of the day. A forty-something, slightly over-weight, dark-haired man with a pleasant air about him, he taught us about color portraiture and shading. One day he invited our class to walk a short block to his home, which was bright and airy; a marijuana plant protruded from its pot; it rested on a nearby window-ledge. This plant seemed out of character for him; I guess one never knows. Another teacher was the designer of the logo for a major local bus company; to this day, I marvel at the simplicity of the blue and green design, symbolizing sky and ground! What a fortune he must have made with his creative genius! What great advice he shared with us about the corporate world! I'll never forget the assortment of turtle-neck sweaters he wore under his sport jacket, most notably the yellow sweater, which for some reason reminded me of one of the "Muppets" characters, even though he was tall in stature; perhaps it was the way he stood, neck stretched up and out from his sweater, his head repeatedly turning in quick, jerky motions from side to side as he spoke; perhaps it was his semi-balding head and neat even teeth which protruded over his lower lip, giving him a "cartoony" look; perhaps a "ventriloquist's doll" would be a more apt description of him. Another teacher was the color illustrator of the 1960's magazine ads for a major cheese manufacturer, among many other things. He was thin and nervous-feeling, even though he spoke with a soothing and calm voice. Always dressed in freshly-pressed pants and sports jacket and tie, he also taught us his extraordinary illustrative style, as did another teacher, who taught us her fashion design illustrative style: using just a fine brush and ink, we learned how to draw beautiful three-dimensional-looking things utilizing the same "contour-line" technique I use to this day. I remember her neatly-styled blonde hair which framed her middle-aged face; always sporting contemporary and tasteful garb, she was quick-moving and very clear in what she demanded of us. Yet another female instructor was currently having her watercolor illustrations of facades of Montreal buildings featured on the cover of the local full-color television weekend magazine; she felt "modern", (she was one of the younger instructors, likely in her late twenties, and exuded a sexuality that the other male students picked up on.) Usually donning a tight sweater and jeans, her explanation of graphics techniques were clear and superb; her patience and compassion shown through. How lucky I was to have this stable of professional artists and designers as teachers. Another notable teacher was a short, stout woman who took great delight in scratching away at our projects as she attempted to assess and grade them individually, and publically; she lined them up, side-by-side in front of the class for us all to see. After sometimes a week of intense and devoted "blood, sweat, and tears", with a sneer on her face, she would begin to scratch away at the stick-down lettering, or even chip away at the paint in areas of the piece. I understood that she was trying to give us a taste of the competitive nature of our career. Nonetheless, few of us liked her, and she in turn seemed to like none of us.

One of our photography teachers, a native of New York, introduced himself to us during our first class with him by walking into the class-room, noticing some spilled water on the floor and uttering his now-legendary phrase, "Hey! Who pissed on the floor?" Most of us looked at each other, not knowing whether to laugh or be shocked. His reaction was an accurate indicator (at least to myself) of his great humor mixed with fearlessness and great experience and knowledge. I believe he was consciously trying to "loosen us up" as well. He allowed me to "permanently borrow" an expensive 35mm. camera, which I subsequently and frequently used in the "real world" for years following college. He was the "cool" teacher, grey-haired, sporting a goatee, tall and slender in stature, and usually gripped his cigarette holder between his fingers and thumb in a devil-may-care pose and attitude. Almost always wearing an unbuttoned dress-shirt with ascot visible, and slacks, his semi-casual attitude helped take the edge of the competitive energy that permeated our classroom. At sixty-something, he was a new father, his young wife glowing and attentive to him at school functions. I'm still grateful for his great heart, humor, wit, and expertise at teaching us how to use the "stabilizer" when printing out photos.

Other instructors included a thin, nervous, (but amiable) illustration teacher, who was middle-aged, had a huge over-bite, and was very kind and patient; another one of our "Life Drawing" instructors insisted that we occasionally draw with our non-dominant hand, or without looking down at our paper, or with only one continuous line, again, not lifting our charcoal off the paper nor looking down at our work. She confessed that these techniques to "sensitize" were done to her, at the California art school that she herself had attended; I suppose we were meant to suffer the same exercises that she was subjected to; we would not be spared! She would often wear dark glasses, sport a tam, (or beret) a long scarf around her neck, knee-high boots, and she would strut around the classroom in a manner reminiscent of an "S.S." lieutenant, even holding in a similar manner a stick of some kind under one arm, propped in place with the same hand of that arm. She spoke in a manner that implied that we had no choice in her instructions. From her I gained confidence drawing nude models with charcoal, using the edge for sharp lines, and the side of the charcoal for broad, sweeping strokes. I actually learned how to "loosen up" thanks to her class, which I always looked forward to. Her name eludes me, unfortunately.

Music and Marijuana

By second year college, I was playing a lot of Cat Stevens songs on my relatively-newly-acquired steel-string, and nylon-string guitars. I was also writing my own songs, as well! This more or less caused me to put my magic-hobby on the back-burner for a while. I occasionally played coffee-houses and parks and recreation events, even after college.

I enjoyed "jamming" with one of three guys in my class, and then one day, after finishing a strumming-session at the back of our empty classroom, he asked me to join him in the stairwell. I followed him there, and then he proceeded to pull out a "joint", (a home-rolled marijuana cigarette) which he lit up and offered me. Thus, at age eighteen, I "enjoyed" my first "joint". To say "enjoyed" is not accurate: I actually felt nothing, as apparently was not unusual for a first-time smoker of "weed". Subsequent times, usually on a Friday afternoon, (and occasionally with our third-year "Photography" teacher) but usually with two other students, I partook of this dubious "past-time". We would then sit in the lounge, with the lights out, and enjoyed watching the hundreds of headlights and tail-lights of cars passing over the Jacques Cartier bridge; what an entertaining view, especially in the dark winter months! I remember almost falling backwards down the stairs of my parents' apartment building in my dizzy state, returning home carrying my huge leather portfolio; thank goodness for taxi-cabs.

My Introduction To Montreal Night-Life

It was one of my cousins with whom I went to my first bar in Montreal. Actually it was with him, and my friend Charles.

I remember eagerly-anticipating that night; my cousin and I were both newly-turned eighteen, the legal age for drinking in Montreal, and also the "magic age" which my parents had dangled in front of me for so many years: the year they said I was free to come and go as I please! I promised myself that I would never take advantage of this, adhering to my own, self-imposed limit of returning home by "around" midnight on the weekend, which in reality meant 1:00 a.m. My mother bought me a turquoise-colored "leisure-suit", at the time very popular with those aged over-thirty, but hardly popular, "hip", "with it", etc., with our age group. Nonetheless, I cherished and wore this gift from my mother, sporting my large, shiny-black platform shoes with the ensemble, for height. I sported my now-legendary "afro", tinted aviation glasses, with my beard and moustache. My cousin and Charles were less pretentious, each wearing leather jackets and medium-cropped hair. I recall my cousin sporting a black, silk, patterned-shirt beneath his jacket, with tasteful gold jewelry; I memorized and later duplicated this look, adding the popular "puca-shells" to my look, after all, my cousin would soon be returning to his home in Toronto; there would therefore not be any duplication. In those days, with his moustache and thin frame, my cousin resembled Canadian singer Burton Cummings, while I resembled Cat Stevens; Charles resembled himself; what a motley group we must have been! What added to the excitement of the night, was that we took the train, from near Charles' home, right into downtown Montreal, which was a comfortable and efficient way to travel. In future journeys into town, either Charles, or my friend David would drive us, as I didn't have my driver's license at the time, nor a vehicle.

I recall staring at myself in the window of the train the entire ride downtown, admiring my "look", nonetheless, my self-esteem and confidence was at a premium, and I soon discovered an inability to approach strange women to ask them to dance; my cousin, however, had no difficulties in this area. Perhaps I was more vain than confident. I enjoyed walking around downtown Montreal, for the first time unhindered and unsupervised by my parents; it was the beginning of a feeling of freedom that was to never end, no matter where I lived, except in Vancouver. The lights of the city, the feeling of joy and the sounds of laughter were ever-present in downtown Montreal's night-life: I remember a large, stretch-limousine with dark, tinted windows pulling up near me, stopping briefly to let it's passengers out. these passengers turned out to be a famous Canadian author wearing a tuxedo, his wife in a gown, draped in diamonds and jewelry, and their female companion sporting similar attire to his wife's. They entered one of the countless upscale bars that lined Montreal's

Crescent Street. Once, I accidentally bumped into a famous comedian, (from a Saturday night comedy show) who was visiting a mutual friend of ours at a comedy bar, (now long-since defunct) also on Crescent Street. What a glorious, glamorous city Montreal was, and still is. Mesmerized by the disco-lights and the alcohol, my cousin, myself, and Charles had a grand first time out, although I'm sure it wasn't their own first time out. We all returned triumphantly to our respective homes, confident that there was much more to explore in the future, with the possibility of dancing with, perhaps even bedding, a woman.

Strip-Joints And More Bars

Montreal is apparently infamous for their open and liberal morals, and this was proven to me continually as I frequented the dance-clubs and strip-joints of the day. Everything from a glamorous Paris and New York-based upscale disco with its disco-balls, smoke bellowing up onto the dance-floor, multi-colored strobe-lights and loud sound-system blaring "Love to Love You Baby", to a pub on Crescent Street and de Maisoneuve, a local "brasserie" with live bands, to a tiffany-lamp laden smaller club on Aylmer Street, another blue-collar/live-band pub on the outskirts of Montreal, even an upscale disco in an airport hotel that had a huge aquarium built into one wall, where you can sip on drinks, with people dancing in the water, looking over your shoulder; this was, after all, Montreal! There was the infamous "bunny club", (which I was too intimidated to visit) an upscale strip-club in the heart of Montreal, with silhouettes of naked women dancing in the windows of that establishment, similar to the women of the night sitting in the windows of the main street of certain sexually-liberal European places like Amsterdam and Germany. Yes, Montreal was, and still is, the "Europe of Canada", with it's world-famous "joie-de-vivre", or "joy-for-life"! One of my college sculpture-instructors had even designed the wooden, orgy-like and phallic-pieces in another club in Montreal, where the servers were topless. He proudly showed off his work to us one day over drinks, on a college field-trip into Montreal to that bar. That was only one of several other college field-trips that we were taken on by various teachers. In another class in which we were studying record-jacket design, another teacher took us to a record-store in Montreal which had an holographic image of a famous American rock-group rotating and singing with no audio. I never forgot this experience, as I can say that I saw the reality of three-dimensional holograms being used in the mid-seventies, at least in Montreal. How miraculous life seemed at the time. That summer, my foray to a nearby downtown Montreal print-house resulted in my successfully selling my full-color children's book to them! Based in Paris, they immediately loved my full-color mock-up, promising to distribute it worldwide, including schools, where the characters could be used for educational purposes. I was thrilled! Later on, when they informed me that I would have to fund the entire project myself, my joy turned to disappointment, but I never did give up on that project, self-publishing numerous versions of the book, even as recently as this year! By the way, it's available as a Kindle book or hard-copy, on Amazon!

Combining my parents' relatively liberal perspective of strippers and the genre being "glamorous" altogether, plus my passion for discos, the summer of second-year college certainly was only the beginning of my forays into Montreal's exciting night-life!

"Gloria"

Gloria (just like everyone else in this book, was not her real name) was my platonic female-friend with whom I would frequent the clubs and discos of Montreal. She was rather tall, and large-framed, so we must have looked quite the contrast. Hanging out with her gave me an automatic dance-partner, and took the pressure off me of trying to "meet" and dance with strange women. Gloria also occasionally introduced blind-dates to my friend David, who chauffeured us around: Gloria lived with her parents in a suburb just north of Montreal.. What great fun we all had dancing; I also chose to be Gloria's "confidant", as she confessed certain sexual liaisons with older men.

It was my friendship with Gloria that introduced me to the concept and possibility of actually having a platonic relationship with a member of the opposite sex.

On some nights, me and "the boys" would trek to one of the legendary bagel shops which had line-ups around the corner at 3:00 a.m.! We'd take our precious brown paper-bags each filled with a dozen hot, freshly-baked dark and/or white-seed bagels, baked in a huge wood-burning brick oven; we devoured them on top of Mont Royal, amongst the lovers in cars facing the "lookout"; I thought it amusing that our car's windows were fogged up because of the bagels' heat, the smell of the freshly-baked doughy-treats running rampant throughout the interior of David's vehicle, while adjacent vehicles were fogged up from heavy breathing and the interior of the vehicles smelling of sex.

Second-Year Romances

Second year college was a time of discovering "romance": first, there was "Heather" whom I met at a college dance. She was short like I was, and also sported an "afro" hair-style. Like myself, she was Jewish, but unlike myself, she was from a wealthy European family. She and her mother, father, and two sisters lived in a Montreal suburb, a mere few blocks from where I lived, but it might as well have been on the other side of the world! They resided in what one might refer to as a "mansion"! Her parents seemed to like me, and Heather introduced me to a couple of dance-clubs in downtown Montreal, one of them located at the underground shopping-hub of the city. Montreal had an entire infrastructure beneath the surface of downtown Montreal, almost a second "downtown" of stores, upscale boutiques and restaurants, all accessible via the subway or "Metro"! Winnipeg has the same thing. The club on Aylmer Street (also long-since defunct) also became one of my favorite places to socialize, drink, and dance, long after we split up, because as time went on, we realized that we required more than just having height and afros! Through her, I met "Sarah" who became a good platonic friend, who also shared my passion for discos, dancing, and drinking! She even attended the marriage of myself to my first wife! When I visited Montreal from Winnipeg in the 1980's and wanted to go for coffee and drinks, her older sister would sometimes be available, who looked very similar to her!

"Louise" was my first non-platonic girlfriend, whom I also met at a college dance. She, like myself, was taking a break from dancing and drinking, sitting in the lobby of the school, having a smoke. We found after a brief conversation, that we seemed to have similar tastes in music and literature, so we began seeing each other; my friend David would "chauffeur" us, as she lived in the relatively far suburb, while I lived in the "Cote-des Neiges" area of Montreal. He was so nice to drive us to our dates! Occasionally, "Louise" and I would brave public transit in the middle of winter to see each other. In the end, after almost a year of dating, she moved in with someone else whom she never mentioned to me: she had apparently been seeing more than one person, unbenounced to me! This coincided in May, with the administration of my college encouraging me to jump-ship to "Commercial Art" for my third year of college; this, too, was an initial shock to me! The issue was, for me, that there was an immature "hierarchy" in college. "Fine Arts" ("Arts Plastiques") students felt that they were "better" than the "Commercial Art" students; the "Graphic Design" students felt that they were "better" than the Fine Arts and Commercial Art students, while the "Interior Design" students thought that they were "better" than all of us! In reality, of course, each required completely different skill sets. Even though I can now see the advantages I had of attending both Graphic Design and Commercial Art, at the time, it was a great shock and let-down to switch over, like a failure of sorts! This, combined with the failed relationship, resulted in me plunging myself into a mild depression and Anorexia for a year. My mum also pressured me about my relationship with Louise, who wasn't Jewish; my mum wanted me to marry someone of our same faith one day, even though I was taught very little about my own faith! All I knew of my religion were the meals served in conjunction with the various holidays. All I learned of the history, traditions, and rituals of Judaism I researched by myself, later in life for historic and spiritual context. My second wife also bought me, one year for Christmas, "The Idiot's Guide To Judaism", thank goodness! I know now, that Jews are not just followers of a very ancient religion, but we are a race of people, genetically different from gentiles. We're not better or worse than others, but certainly different. Most people still don't understand this, especially in western Canada, where some believe that Jewish people are "gypsies", or worse, that we are "going to hell" if we're not "saved" by faith in Jesus Christ! Unbelievable! If the historical Jesus existed, he would have been Jewish, of the "Levite" (or "Levi", as Jews call them) family, as science and archeology suggests. Jesus would have therefore been Jewish himself! How ironic! I myself, according to my father, am a "Levi"! More on all of this later.

Regardless, after almost a year, I had lost fifty pounds, taking me down from an overweight 165 pounds and size 36" waist, to 110 pounds, and size 28" waist! I was buying jackets in the "children's" section of department stores, unaware of my physical state, and the potential health-hazards associated with being so under-weight. All that I knew was that I was happy being as thin as my hero, Cat Stevens, sporting my afro, and beard/moustache; a fellow student was calling me "Cat" because of my resemblance to him, and my penchant for singing his songs. One day in August of 1976, (the summer of the Montreal Olympics) I "awoke" so-to-speak while viewing myself in a mirror at home: I suddenly saw myself for the way I actually looked, physically: dangerously under-weight! It was like I "'snapped out of" some trance I was in for a year; I was determined, with and thanks to my mum's help, to gain some weight by the end of summer vacation. I would make sure I would never again be over-weight, but merely weight-appropriate for my height and bone-structure. Regular milkshakes and three home-cooked meals a day resulted in me going up to 135 pounds and a size 31" waist, which I felt was close to normal, but nowhere near my previous overweight state. I was thankful, content, and happy to enter into my third, and final year of college. I felt so relaxed and happy, that I spent the rest of that summer drawing and illustrating my own personal projects. I was drawing again, not to fulfill some school-related project, or to achieve a high grades, but because I wanted to; I started to enjoy art again!

Third-Year College

Relaxed, confident and happy, I did much better in my new "Commercial Art" classes. Administration was right, I was more suited for this!
I did not succeed in finishing my third year, as I felt overwhelmed by the

death of my good friend and classmate's father. "Sandra's" father passed quickly and suddenly one day in the spring of 1977. I couldn't even attend the funeral; I had met and knew her brothers, mother, father, and her boyfriend; I felt too close to her to objectively and emotionally support her during this time, so I backed away from her in May of 1977, and from my college as well.

Post-College

I started looking for full-time as well as freelance graphic design assignments by June of 1977. I was twenty-one years old. The deal was that my parents would pay for college, but once I was done and had a "trade", I had to become "independent", which meant finding gainful employment and housing.

Every morning and every afternoon, I would go through the phone book, calling fifty businesses in the morning and fifty in the afternoon, who might potentially hire me. I was still living with my parents at the time, as we agreed that once I was out of college and acquired a job, I would move into my own place. The businesses that I called included advertising agencies, (yes, things were just like on the television program "Mad Men"!) printers, commercial businesses, etc., until I generated regular interviews, schlepping my huge leather portfolio on public transit, and wearing the only three-piece suits I owned, made of corduroy! One was black, the other one was gold-color. Imagine, travelling more than an hour each way, in ninety-five degree temperatures wearing a hot, corduroy three-piece suit! It was Montreal, so almost every time, there would be at least fifty people ahead of me in the waiting room competing for the particular position! I was told that on average, several hundred would be competing for the particular position, advertised in one or the other of two English-language Montreal newspapers. I began to generate some regular freelance jobs, but .I felt barely able to maintain my brand-new relationship with someone who I would eventually become engaged to. I was stressed!

The Fiancé

The girl I actually had a crush on, "Mary", whom I had dated only a few times previously, and who made a better platonic-friend than a girlfriend in any case, made a house-party which myself and my friends attended. One of these friends, "Jonny", called it "breaking the clique", or meeting a girlfriend's female friends. We had some silly terms for things back then in Montreal; "scoffing" meant "fressing" or eating food voraciously; I recall Jonny using that phrase a lot. I still have this vivid image of Jonny with a string of pizza-cheese dangling from his chin, as he flirted with our server at the neighborhood pizza-joint one night. The cheese swayed back and forth as he chatted with her, creating an hypnotic pendulum of sorts; perhaps he intended to hypnotize her into bedding him? I don't know. Nonetheless, I ended up dating "Kathleen" and Jonny ended up dating Mary! Unbenounced to Jonny, Mary was also dating another guy, "Harold". Kathleen and I would "double-date" with Mary, regardless of which man she selected that night. We all just enjoyed each others' company. Harold and Jonny didn't know of each others' existence. In the end, to spare Jonny's feelings, I informed him of Mary's "extra-curricular activities, which of course, he chose to not believe and to ignore. Denial is a cruel thing, and Jonny ended up being devastated. At least I couldn't say that I didn't try to help him avoid this heartache! He never spoke to me again after all of that. I considered Jonny to be a good friend, who passed some freelance graphic design work my way after college; his father owned a company that painted lettering and logos on large trucks; I was commissioned to do such a job for them, as they were somewhat overwhelmed with work.

Harold's father was very kind to me as well! He helped me to get out my resumes and promo-material during my campaign to win some newspaper cartooning contracts, once I was finished college. I was already drawing a nationally-syndicated cartoon-strip, (more on that later) and I was keen on doing political cartoons, called "Editorial Cartoons" for any and all newspapers throughout North America. Harold's dad suggested I use the "pen-name" of "Michael-U-Likey" as a gimmick, and allowed me to photocopy hundreds of samples, not charging me for the postage and envelopes required to get them out to potential markets, either. He was very generous, and doing well with his exporting business, based in Montreal West. I was of course, grateful for everyone's help, and their faith in me. Somebody from Montreal may be reading this right now, directly or indirectly involved with what I just shared, and I'd like them to know how grateful and thankful I am for all of the help in those early years of my career. Eventually, a small weekly newspaper whose demographic was the Jewish community contacted me, interested in my cartoons; I freelanced for them for a few years, providing them, for the fee of $50. a week, with a political cartoon. This was great fun, as I would do the cartoon a week in advance, trying to "predict" the following week's outcome of anyone of a number of political situations; Montreal, and Quebec in general, was a hot-bed of political uncertainty and unrest, with fascinating municipal, provincial, and federal politicians. How I loved caricaturing these characters, placing them in creative situations, mirroring metaphorically their political positions and situations. apparently, I was gaining a bit of a fine local reputation, thanks to these cartoons. At the same time, I was freelancing for an advertising agency, owned by a lawyer whose office was across the hall from my favorite Montreal magic-shop, located not far from my very first apartment!

All of this was going on for a year after college; I was also dating Kathleen at the same time., as previously mentioned. We enjoyed each others' company, and it was Kathleen who encouraged me to do more outdoor things, like going for walks, singing and playing guitar on Mont Royal, even swinging on the swings and going down the slide of our local park. She helped me to remember to be a kid again, as I was becoming too serious with all the recent changes and "traumas" of being out of school, and our losing our virginity. I even started to develop a healthier skin color, becoming tanned for the very first time. I must have looked interesting at the time, with my very dark skin color, afro, dark prescription aviator glasses and slender frame. I remember some former high school friends of mine running into me at the time, not recognizing me! This happened again years later in Toronto, circa 2000, when my current wife and I encountered a former high school acquaintance on the bus that we were travelling on; "Where's the other half of you?" she exclaimed, before leaping out of the bus and loping towards the next bus she was in a hurry to catch. We could barely react to this fleeting incident, merely turning to each other, our mouths agape!

Nevertheless, I suppose from behind, Kathleen and I looked like two males. One day, while lined up to go on an amusement park ride in Montreal, we heard two males mockingly say in French, "Voila, deux homosexuals!" We turned to look at them, and then we all laughed, as they realized we were male and female! I suppose that Kathleen's shorter frame, and shorter, dark curly hair, from behind, could have her be mistaken for a male; I never thought much about it before or after that time, but it made for an amusing incident to us.

Kathleen had a few good friends whom I met during our time together. One was Gillian, whom I recently reconnected with thanks to social media. Gillian was dating one person when Kathleen and I first met, but by the end of our relationship, Gillian was dating someone else, whom she eventually married and had children with. Today, Gillian is happily engaged to another male; she seems happier than I've ever seen her. Gillian reminded me of one of my aunts: like that particular aunt, she had a quick smile, a glint in her eye, the occasional sarcastic comment, but sensitive and loving. Smart too. Gillian also played the piano, and would sometimes accompany me when we visited her in her mum's suburban home. Once, Gillian wrote a poem which I put music to. I would sing and play my guitar, while she sang and played the piano. The man she dated near the end of my relationship with Kathleen was someone I went to high school with; I remember him wearing a "Kwai Chang Caine" costume (my hero from television's "Kung Fu") for Halloween one year. I watched him as he passed me in the hallway, even having a flute hanging from his shoulder;

How bad could he have been? I suppose Gillian eventually found out!

Another couple I formally met through Kathleen, was her friend "Sandra", who was dating another classmate, George. George was my oldest friend's cousin! This George had a very similar last name to Jonny's last name, but he was in fact cousins with my oldest friend! What a small world! George drove this cool little lavender vehicle. Another friend of mine drove a very sporty vehicle which had a classy "glittery-green" finish, long-horns between the back-seats and the rear window, and side-windows decorated with small stain-glass parrots. I loved that car. Of course, I loved my "first" car as well, one I used to borrow from Kathleen's brother: a green 1969 fast-back "Barracuda". In fact, it was this same vehicle I drove after earning my driver's license. I outraced sports cars and other "muscle cars" in Montreal. Hard to believe how easy it was to get my license back then. Yes, we had to pass a written exam, but only one student was picked from our driving class when we went to the Motor Vehicle Branch to take the driving test, and it wasn't me! I was so relieved.

Another activity/social event that Kathleen and I enjoyed almost weekly for a year, was to attend the video-taping of a nationally-syndicated television-show styled like a discothèque.

The Disco-Show

Since the Montreal "disco-scene" was very much part of our social activities, and with the "Bee Gees" brand-new soundtrack for the wildly-popular movie "Saturday Night Fever" recently released, we knew we had to attend this weekly taping. We also attended other television-show tapings, like a variety-show featuring a famous local singer. Two local comedians wreaked havoc on that singer's show! I remember a soon-to-be-famous stand-up comedian also on that particular show's roster, famous for his regular spot on the TV-show, "Soap".

The disco-show was a great opportunity to "strut our stuff" along with the other "beautiful people" of the Montreal disco-scene, and then to try to find ourselves later, on TV, among the dancing crowd. There were many famous local and international entertainers on that show, both live, in-studio, as well as pre-recorded. Today you can to a social media video site and look up the title of the show, where clips from those days still bring the past to life! There's even a clip of an animated commercial of which I can gratefully say I was a small part of participating in! I was one of the artists who drew the "in-betweening", and painted and "cleaned up" cels. I got these freelance assignment thanks to the boss of the animation company where I was co-drawing a nationally-syndicated comic-strip.

The Syndicated Strip

One of my proudest achievements occurred one year after college. I was deeply engrossed in my freelance graphic design career, and still relatively enjoying my new "fiancé"-status, after all, it was the natural progression for our relationship. All the while, my mother had fallen emotionally unwell when she learned who my fiancé was; she was still adjusting to having "lost" her only son to a new woman, after all, at least she was Jewish! But when she formally met Kathleen, who informed my mum of her last name, I could feel my mum's non-physical reaction. If there was an actual reaction, she would have collapsed with shock and disappointment. Kathleen's last name was the same surname as the local "mentally-ill" person whom she witnessed singing and dancing up and down her street when she was growing up in Montreal, after her families' emigration there. He was known to be schizophrenic, and my mum feared that if we ever did marry, our children might suffer from the same affliction. Kathleen's own mental condition, as well as her mother's, father's, brother's and sister's was called into question in my mother's mind, as a result of this knowledge. Subsequently, while dating Kathleen and coping with freelance work, I also had to endure my mum's hourly tirades and eventual deterioration of her own mental health. This is the reason I called a meeting with my mum's psychiatrist, out of concern for her health. My moving out of my parents' apartment now appeared imminent, not only because of the stress at home, but because of my newly-acquired freelance client, the animation company, which insured me a steady salary of sorts, doing what I had originally wanted to, having entered into college to achieve this! .My hard work and faith in myself finally paid off! An achievement that many never see by the end of their life.

One day, while actually relaxing in my parents' apartment for a moment, I "woke up" once again, so-to-speak! I suddenly remembered, after three years of college, and over a year of freelance graphic design, what I really wanted to do: be a nationally-syndicated cartoonist! Feverishly and passionately, I drew full-color, and black-and-white samples of my proposed comic-strip, about a wise-cracking baby, "imprisoned" in his crib. I mailed out these samples to hundreds of potential syndicates and newspapers throughout North America. After two weeks, I received a phone-call from a major newspaper syndicate located in Montreal! Newspaper syndicates, if they approve your comic-strip or one-panel cartoon, distribute (sell) them widely to as many newspapers and magazines that they can; the more markets they distribute to, the more money they and the artist make. Everybody wins. "Zelda" from the newspaper syndicate asked me to call my future boss-to-be, who owned the largest Montreal animation studio; he was also the creator/writer of the wildly-popular, Canadian syndicated comic-strip, and the owner of the largest collection of Walt Disney memorabilia! I was a regular reader of this comic, which was widely distributed across Canada, so needless-to-say, I was thrilled and eager to call him back. After an initial interview, we agreed that the original artist, (who was relocating back to his home city in Ontario) would train me in the same "Disney-style" he himself used for the characters in the strip. I went daily for the free training; during that time, I broke the second finger of my right hand in a cycling accident. This finger was now in a splint, and would require physiotherapy once the digit healed sufficiently and the splint was removed. Initially, I feared that this brand-new potential career was ruined, but I chose to ignore this minor physical set-back, riding my adrenalin and passion for cartooning; I continued the training, holding the pen or brush with all but that one finger. By the time everything healed, my brush-strokes were actually better, and more easily achieved; the loss of use, and then subsequent gain of the use of that finger actually made the drawings easier to do! similar to a technique one of my college teachers shared with us and made us do to make us more "sensitive": she made us draw only with the opposite hand that we write with for a period of time, in her class. When we switched over to the dominant hand, we could draw more naturally, with greater ease and finesse! This worked out even better than I had anticipated, with my drawing skills having developed to a greater level, but more importantly, to the point that my boss felt that I was "ready" to draw the strip. Because of the shock of "losing" the original artist, my boss decided to hire myself, plus another artist to draw the strip, in addition to the original artist's occasional participation, "long-distance" from Ontario. I was officially drawing a nationally-syndicated comic-strip! My dream had come true! I was also getting a fair wage per artwork which ultimately insured that along with my freelance work, and business from a suburban newspaper, a another French weekly paper, plus the ad agency, liberation from my parents was now guaranteed, resulting in the ultimate acquisition of my own apartment! The sun seemed to shine brighter; it felt and looked like a brand-new day. I was well on my way now, with my cartooning career. My heart soared!

The New Apartment

At Kathleen's dad's suggestion, he invited me to lease the basement-suite of the duplex next door to them; it was newly-available he heard, was also furnished, and only fifty-dollars a month...unheard-of for Montreal! A little too close for comfort to Kathleen and her family, but excited by the potential of my newly-found liberation from my parents, I inquired at the owners' residence, enjoyed a brief tour of my future domicile, with a handshake and first-month's rent sealing the deal! A note about Kathleen's parents: they were uneducated, but well-intentioned, sweet and loving; ethical, and hard-working, with her dad being a "jobber" (or middle-man between the printer and the client) for a neighborhood wholesale printing company! Across the street from them was the world-famous hot dog processing plant. All of this a hop-skip-and-a-jump from my parents' residence, and my new one! Naturally, I paid the printer a visit, with the hope that they could wholesale to me and any potential clients I might acquire, after all, I could provide both the client and the printing-firm with camera-ready (print-ready) artwork, thanks to my education and experience. I also mentioned Kathleen's father's name as a reference. They agreed! This enabled me to print up my first business-cards, which was a sepia (light-brown) silhouette of my afro and aviator sunglasses looming partially up from the lower left-hand corner of the card; in the middle of the card was my name, and phone-number. I was so proud and excited when I picked them up from the printer! A thousand cards for a very small amount of money! I could now give these out to potential clients and existing ones. All of this thanks to Kathleen's father, who I thanked profusely. My relationship with this print-shop lasted from 1978 until 1994, ending only because of my relocation to Vancouver, a little too far away from me to regularly visit them.

I loved my first apartment, and quickly made it "mine", although it was fully furnished. There were two large rooms, one, the living room, had its entrance from the side of the duplex; I enjoyed cleaning daily the lovely hardwood floors in this room, and although all I had for a kitchen was a small fridge/freezer and hot-plate, I enjoyed some of my meals there. I insisted on not bringing with my television, because I wanted no distractions; this was to be my "fortress of solitude", with only a radio/record-player/cassette-player combination to enjoy my pop music. It was here that I wrote many of my early songs, which have yet to make it to one of my albums! Virtually all of my early songs, except for several dozen of them, were written here, the rest were written at my parents' place, in my bedroom!

The back room served as my artists' studio, with a board resting on four paint-cans as my drafting table, and the floor as my chair! Believe it or not, some of my early syndicated cartoon-strips were drawn this way, until I bought a beautiful, handmade wooden drafting table from my boss. Owning this table made me further feel as if I had become truly successful, and it was also when I at the height of my visibility in print-media. I felt like a true professional, and took this table with me to my next apartment.

The Sub Place

After a couple of years with Kathleen, I began to tire of her.

We had absolutely nothing in common, and hanging out with her seemed bittersweet to me, as I knew more and more that the end of the relationship was imminent.

One late night we found ourselves in a local submarine sandwich shop (now long defunct) on Decarie Boulevard. As usual, we were talking about matters superficial, which we had recently grown into doing. Out of the corner of my eye, I noticed a tall, looming figure darting about, cleaning up and bussing the tables. I'm not sure if this person had also taken our order or not, but nonetheless, my attention was subsequently grabbed by this person obviously enjoying her task of mopping the floor! Around and around she hummed and sang, while practically using the mop as her dance-partner! She seemed to glow with a light of joy and happiness, and flashing a toothy smile at me, cautiously, respectfully, yet boldly asking me how everything was going, as she glided up to our table with her mop. "Great", I responded, while Kathleen looked sideways at her the way she did when she felt unsure of herself, smiling regardless. "What are you guys up to?" the stranger continued on with her inquisition. "Swimming! We're swimming!" was my sarcastic yet playful response. I could just read Kathleen's face which seemed to be saying "Please don't encourage her!" On our way out, I took the store's business card, while I slipped the stranger my business-card. Upon my return home, I felt restless, and couldn't get to sleep. I felt compelled to phone the submarine shop and ask "Hermiome" out for drinks and/or dancing that same night! I just had to! I had never felt such a joy and optimism from anyone before, and her very smile, her very presence lifted me up! Hermiome was still at work, and after her boss gave her the phone, I told her it was "me" and would she, could she come out dancing with me after work. It was 1:00 a.m. and Montreal was and still is the "city that never sleeps"! She immediately said "yes", picking me up in her 4x4 vehicle, which I climbed up into. I gave her a peck on the cheek, and she reciprocated! I hadn't felt so happy in years! "I'm so glad we're doing this!" I said to her; she said "Me too!" We danced for hours at one of Montreal's numerous discos, and then enjoyed dessert at 4:00 a.m. in one of Montreal's deli's. We just seemed to connect on every level: intellectually, emotionally; she too, like myself, was an artist, I learned that night! Eventually she returned me, safe and sound, to my basement suite, right next door to Kathleen's home. I felt so let down to say "good-night", (or "good-morning" in this case) but also felt paranoid that Kathleen might know that I had dropped her off and then spent most of the rest of the night actually having a great time. I'm sure I mentioned to Hermiome that I lived next door to my fiancé, but it didn't seem to bother her, after all, her boyfriend was away, hitch-hiking across Canada. I never met anyone so liberal and free-feeling; this also helped me to loosen up more and free up my own mind and heart after many years, so it seemed. I eagerly anticipated seeing Hermiome again, after all, she was only a friend, and for all intents and purposes, Kathleen had nothing to worry about.

My phone rang the next day, and it was Hermiome, wanting to see me again; I was over the top with joy! Nothing else mattered, but hanging out with her! With Hermiome, it felt like anything was possible, and that was turning out to be true!

Hermiome turned me on to a local comedy club on Crescent Street in Montreal, where I was introduced to some of her stand up comedian friends, including a soon-to-be-famous comedian who used a rubber surgical glove in his act, a Toronto-based comedian who at the time also sported an afro, and whom Hermiome said I reminded her of. When I wasn't with Hermiome, I was drinking and laughing on my own at the comedy club!

One day in early July of 1978, when I was drawing a cartoon for that syndicated comic-strip on Hermiome's drafting-table at her apartment, I looked up at her as she worked on some graphics for the comedy bar's menu and upcoming comedy roster. I said to her, "I'm going to do it. I'm going to break up with Kathleen". You must understand that my relationship, although completely platonic, was the most emotionally satisfying one that I had ever experienced; to have Hermiome just be my friend was more than enough, as we laughed and played together, having much in common. She too, was Jewish. She too, had an apartment in the Cote-des-Neiges area, about fifteen minutes from my apartment. Very convenient! Unlike my other relationships, all of my friends liked her, and she liked them: we'd all sometimes hang out, go for coffee and dessert; but it was always just Hermiome and myself who spent quality time together, often laughing about the same things. I declared, "I'll do it after my birthday!" "Isn't that unfair to her?" she asked, "You'll get a birthday present from her and then break up with her?" "No, no!" was my response. "It's not like that at all; it's kinda tough around my birthday, so when it's over and I feel stronger, then I'll do it." "Okay, you know what you're doing." she reassured me. I never felt more sure of these two things: my friendship with Hermiome, and breaking up with Kathleen.

Hermiome had confessed to me that she had recently experienced a traumatic personal family tragedy, from which she and her entire family were still recovering; this explained the request she made to have me help her move out of from her home with her mother, into her own residence. She could no longer bear the memories of what she saw upon her return from school one day, so she chose to attempt to sever those memories by moving out. She introduced me to her mother one day who seemed quiet but nice enough, and her famous uncle's parents, who were quite old at that point. The actor's eccentric mother, an octogenarian, would hide her hubby's pipe and tobacco in the dumb-waiter from time-to-time, and I got to witness the humorous results one day. Coincidentally, my friend, whom I had gone to high school with, and who was also Hermiome's cousin, bore the same name as her uncle, a very famous television and stage actor. Hermiome showed me old black-and-white publicity pictures of him one day, and this made me feel even closer to her. Her uncle's original 1960's television series was about to become a major motion picture, which I eagerly anticipated, being a great fan of the original series, and which was off the air since 1969.

I recall one night when I was out with Hermiome, and my friends "Franklyn" and "Gerald". We were enjoying dessert at Howard Johnson's in Montreal, when Hermiome and I got mischievous with each other, throwing ice cream from our sundaes at each other, flinging it with our spoons! Hermiome decided at this point she would get the "upper hand", and raising her entire sundae-glass, began to get ready to fling the entire contents at me; I tilted to the side, and the creamy contents spread across the carpet beside us in an incredible mess, narrowly missing Gerald! We though this was incredibly funny, and we laughed and laughed until our waitress approached us, a stern look on her face; immediately, Hermiome stood up, climbed over us in one motion, offering to clean it all up, which she did. I'm sure one of us made an obscene reference to the ice cream mess at some point, but it was all in good fun.

Hermiome also helped me get a few folk-music gigs for Montreal's Parks and Recreation events, and the audiences seemed to enjoy my music, which gave me more and more confidence to perform; I even played a solo-gig at a local college that year as well. Hermiome and I went to her cottage one platonic weekend. The cabin was a glorious structure which her architect father had designed. Large, looming beams overlooked the beautiful logs which made up the actual walls. It was my first time canoeing, then, and she also introduced me to the pleasures of cycling, which I did a lot, both with her and on my own. It was Kathleen who taught me to just let loose and play outdoors, even to tan my pasty skin, but it was Hermiome who introduced me to more physical exercise, even though I already daily did calisthenics; for these things I am grateful to them both.

When I finally broke up with Kathleen, Hermiome was there for me, as I was for her during her difficult time; she helped me to move into my new two-bedroom apartment I was going to share with, a former classmate of mine, Georgie.

Georgie and I initially seemed to have much in common: he was my friend Mary's cousin; we had David in common as a friend; he and I attended the same grade-school until grade four, after which time he defected to a Ville St. Laurent school; we were both top-five students, enjoying a somewhat friendly competition back then; we both enjoyed astronomy, and he owned a telescope, through which he once had me gaze upon the rings of Saturn! There were, however some major differences, which would eventually turn out to be fatal flaws: this was his first apartment, and I was a "seasoned" individual, "free" from my parents for some time; he went to university, while I had finished college a few years previously, and I was enjoying the work-force; he went to bed promptly at 10:00 a.m., my evening only began at that time, as I prepared to leave to go dancing all night! One time I had walked in at 7:30 a.m., heading for the washroom, as he exited from his bedroom, hair disheveled and sporting a bathrobe; "You just coming home?" he asked knowingly, "Yes!" was my hurried response as I barely made the bathroom-trek. I had come home on public transit and apparently you can't drink beer, you can only rent it! On one occasion, he bought some items for the apartment without first consulting me, demanding my half of the money for it; this pushed my buttons, so we argued about it, and then I refused to pay for half the cable, since he insisted that his television remain in his room. Of course, I enjoyed the wonders of television when he wasn't home! At that time, I had an active social life, which included seeing Hermiome occasionally; Hermiome stopped by my bedroom to check up on her former stuffed creature "Carrot" which she had given me as a "house-warming", and the next morning Georgie had left a note on the wall of our kitchen, which separated our rooms; it read, "Were you out for another night of debauchery? I heard Giggly-Hermiome who kept me awake all night!" I laughed to myself while reading this, but honestly, I don't know if he was serious or not! I remember one time when his parents were visiting him: they enjoyed a private conference in his room with his door ajar; curiosity got the better of me, and I just happened to walk by on my way to the washroom, glancing through the door's opening: there sat Georgie on his bed, his mother beside him, cradling his head in her arms, as if to comfort him. This struck me as being odd, especially for a twenty-something year-old man.

One night, I was enjoying a stand-up comedian at the Crescent street comedy club with my friend "Cynthia"; Georgie walked in, knowing that this was my main "haunt", and approached us. Pleased and surprised to see him in a bar, (as he didn't drink booze) I introduced him to Cynthia. Cynthia was a McGill student from New York, and one of the brightest and sarcastic people I've ever known; she would frequently entertain me, playing piano in one of the halls of McGill, where I would visit her. We'd then hang out at a McGill pub, where we would enjoy playing pinball, eating pizza, drinking beer, (she was amazed by the higher-alcohol content that Canadian beer had) and dancing to "The Time Warp" from "The Rocky Horror Picture Show". I frequently enjoyed her cynical observations, one of which she made this "night of Georgie"! Immediately after approaching me, without even acknowledging Cynthia, he pulled out from his knap-sack a recently-purchased cardboard box with a cellophane window on its front: it was a "Napoleonic Replica", a miniature detailed model of a soldier that may have fought in Napoleon's army; he intended to paint in full-color detail, this soldier, including the moustache and side-burns; understand at this point that the model stands only three-inches tall, so this paining task would be of gargantuan proportions! As a professional artist, I admired his patience, and skill at doing this, as he had previously and proudly shown me his one-thousand soldiers, all painted, and in a military formation on a table in his room! This also through me aback somewhat, though. apparently this must be what he used to "indulge in" fairly regularly when he'd shut his bedroom door, turn off the light, (which I could detect from the crack under his door) and then proceed to blare the "Eighteen Twelve Overture" until its trademark canon-climax, including, I suspected, his own! Nonetheless, after proudly displaying in the bar the soldier to myself and Jane who insisted on being included in all of this, he proudly exited, leaving Cynthia and I blankly staring at each other. Her subsequent comment: "Is he that insecure that he has to carry around miniature soldiers to defend him if need be?" We both laughed.

That night, upon my return home, at approximately 2:00 a.m., Cynthia called me, and not wishing to disturb Georgie's sleep, I promptly took the phone into our hall-closet, which was situated directly in front of his bedroom door. This well-intentioned strategy was to no avail, as partway through my phone conversation, there was a knock at the closet door; I excused myself to Cynthia, and hung up, determined to place the phone back onto its table, directly outside and to the right of the closet, against the wall. Keep in mind that the lights in our apartment were turned off, again, so as not to disturb Georgie's peaceful slumber. Imagine my surprise, when Georgie began whipping me with a towel in anger, as I exited the closet! I began to run, laughing, as he chased after me, continuing this whipping action with the towel; he was angry, apparently, actually and seriously angry! Apparently I had disturbed him, despite my valiant attempts at the opposite. Cornering me against a wall, with his hand around my throat, all I could feel was his hot breath as he was mouthing some angry words, I assumed; his facial expression displaying a similar rage which my own mother had shared with me years previously. I was scared. Thinking quickly, I responded with a calm, parental tone: "Georgie, I'm really disappointed in you!" He backed off, shoulders dropping, head now hung, the flaccid towel now hanging from the palm of one of his hands. "I'm sorry", he said, as his whole demeanor changed; "Can you please ask your female "friends" to not call you at this hour?" Relieved at the sudden turn of events, I agreed. Reluctantly.

Soon thereafter, one early morning as I was shaving, there was a loud pounding at the bathroom door; I could feel his rage again; "What now?" I thought. Slowly, confidently, I opened the door, insuring that I had a puzzled, as opposed to worried, expression on my face. He started yelling at me, "Do you know that you tap your razor twenty times every morning on the sink, and flush the toilet three times too? Tapping! Tap, tap, tap! The flushing is driving me crazy! And the bath-tub! Look at it! Its filthy! Why don't you clean it?" I decided to utilize the parental-tone which worked the last time; I later learned that I was inadvertently using a psychological technique from "Transactional Analysis"! "Hey, guy, calm down, you'll make yourself sick; here, sit down and have something to eat." He responded well, and then it dawned on me: our room-mate time was coming to an end, or would soon have to end.

During this time, Hermiome's boyfriend returned from his hitchhiking journey across Canada, so I backed away somewhat to allow them some space to either re-bond, or to break apart. I continued to platonically see Cynthia, who also bore a remarkable resemblance to another platonic female friend of mine, "Joan". Both were somewhat overweight and had shorter, dark hair, which framed a rounder face. Both wore tight black turtleneck sweaters and tight blue jeans. Joan was also a musician, who sang folk-songs and played guitar like myself. The two of us once visited Heather, and all three of us sang and played guitar and piano, as we all enjoyed similar genres of music! Whenever I would go out with either Joan or Cynthia, I'd take them to the Crescent Street comedy club, or the McGill pub, which they also enjoyed. In retrospect, I was probably risking them running into each other, but we were all in a platonic relationship, so I didn't see that there would be any problem. One night, when I was waiting to meet Joan in the lobby of McGill to go to the pub, I was also with a few male pals, the aforementioned Franklyn and Gerald, plus their friend "Dick". I'd been going to bars with these guys, who except for Dick, lived in my neighborhood. Franklyn sported an afro and moustache, looking unerringly like Gabe Kaplan; Franklyn had ten pairs of identical shirts and pants, hanging in the closet of his room, which was at his parents' place. His desk was neatly organized, including the small electronic organizer he possessed: in alphabetical order were the names of the women he was dating, including some sort of ranking system, their phone-numbers, and other details. After he shared this with me, I began to feel uneasy about our friendship, after all, he was unemployed, considerably older and still living with his parents! Furthermore, I didn't remember him from high school, perhaps because he was several years ahead of me. Years later, I heard that he became an accountant and lived and worked in Toronto. Gerald was thinner and smaller in stature from Franklyn, with an unusually narrow face and head, also sporting a darker, but closely-cropped afro then myself or

Franklyn. He too lived with his widowed mother, and was older. He often sported a rain-coat, I suspected encouraged to do so by his mother. He had a strange sense-of-humor, sometimes also yelling obscenities at passerby's from his vehicle when we were out. Dick was the shortest of all of us, small and fit, with a sort of a shorter, "David Cassidy" hairstyle. He wore designer shirts and jeans, and drove any one of his father's cars, which belonged to the "business": what business, no one ever spoke of. Some nights he'd pick me up in a corvette; other nights he'd pick us up in a Cadillac. It felt good to pull up in front of McGill in these expensive cars!

"The Winnie Girls"

One night when the four of us were at McGill to try to meet Jewish girls attending "Israeli Dancing", one of "the boys" said hello to someone named "Roxanne". She was one of the "Winnie girls"; apparently they were holding out on me: who or what were these "Winnie Girls"? Roxanne looked different from most Jewish Montreal girls, and with good reason: she was a Jewish girl, fresh out of university, from Winnipeg! She sported a blonde, "Farrah Fawcett" hair-style, red-checkered or plaid blouse, and tight jeans. Small in stature, she stood as if she was used to riding horses, legs a distance apart, with a stride reminiscent of Matt Dillon! She spoke softly. I immediately felt as if I needed to protect this small woman from "the big city"; little did I suspect that we would someday marry! Nonetheless, she more or less ignored me, walking off to do something more important.

Eventually, I met the two other "Winnie girls", consisting of "Rayna" and "Christine"; there was apparently another "Roxanne" whom I might have met briefly, who was also from Winnipeg! I find it interesting that I had spent my whole life in Montreal, never meeting anyone not from there, and suddenly, it seemed, I had struck "prairie oil"! The boys and I mainly engaged in social activities with Rayna and Christine, whom we'd hope to "break the clique" with, if possible, as they were returning to Winnipeg, and again, our friendship was purely platonic. Christine was dark-haired and the taller of the two "Winnie-girls", with a pleasant but cynical air about her; Rayna was shorter, with dark, curly hair framing her face; she to, was pleasant, somewhat sarcastic, (which I enjoyed) and sweet. Years later, I learned from Roxanne that both of them were always determined to marry doctors or lawyers, bearing a specific amount of children with them as well. It made me wonder just how pre-conceived relationships can be! Nonetheless, with the boys and Winnie-girls as my main companions now, I felt fulfilled, especially with my work which continued well. I began to dread returning home to my room-mate, however, who by this point, had established a sort of adversarial relationship.

The Birthday

Georgie's birthday was coming up soon, and I decided to try to smoothen out our friendship. I decided to order him a birthday-cake, which I drove home from the bakery with on my bicycle one day, miles and miles from our apartment. I steered with one hand, while holding the cake in its box with the other. It was quite literally uphill all the way! Finally I arrived home. I entered stealthily, after all, I had no idea if he was home or not, and gingerly placing the cake down on the kitchen table to catch my breath, I then opened the fridge door; reaching for the cake-box, in-between the table and the fridge, I "fumbled the ball", so-to-speak, dropping it on the floor! Imagine: I so carefully drove miles and miles on my bicycle, handling the cake-box as if it were a baby, and then two feet from its destination, I drop my precious cargo! Fortunately, no harm befell the "baby". The next great task, no less difficult than this one, was to actually coax, lure, convince Georgie to accompany me to the McGill pub that night, where some of my stand-up comedian friends were performing, and were also aware of my room-mate's "special day". Of course, Georgie initially refused, insisting that staying home and painting his soldiers was what he preferred. I pleaded with him, asking him to accommodate my wishes to "do something" for his birthday, and so, with great trepidation, he agreed nonetheless. He asked if "giggly Hermiome" was attending, stating that he preferred not to see her; fortunately for him, I wasn't in contact with her at that point, for reasons previously stated, and so, no, there would be no Hermiome. "Will David be there?" he asked me. "Yes, I said, "He's picking us up and taking us there." was my response.

We arrived without incident eventually, and Heather greeted us, whom I had maintained occasional contact with. She had never met Georgie before, and immediately disliked his manner and sarcasm towards her, which was evident from her facial expressions. Cynthia was there, but distant. Finally the time came for my friends' show to start, which, surprisingly, A seemed to enjoy. He also partook of his birthday cake, which we skillfully unveiled, lighting the candles as well. I felt proud and relieved that the evening was coming to a close, and that all of this would be shortly forgotten. To this day, I still don't know if Georgie actually enjoyed the event, or if he was merely going along with things; regardless, I felt it was the right thing to do!

A Relationship Develops

Somehow, after running into the "other" "Winnie-girl" regularly at McGill, I decided to take her aside and strike up a brief conversation to see what she's all about. I suppose my curiosity was getting the better of me, and again, I was getting bored with my current social circle, which appeared to be going nowhere fast. Roxanne was on summer vacation in Montreal, after just recently completing her Bachelor of Social Work at a Winnipeg university. In time, I learned that she had "free" accommodations at an upscale apartment, inhabited by a nice, Jewish, Montreal dentist. She often spoke about the "neurotic" bird that was this fellow's pet, and eventually came clean about her living arrangement after we started to date; the "ring twice, hang up, and call again" was initially suspicious, but it wasn't until she insisted on coming down, and not being escorted back to her apartment that my curiosity was really piqued. It was David who offered the somewhat obvious possible situation that Roxanne was in. Why she chose to not initially tell me the truth, I to this day don't know; perhaps it was her mid-west values, which dictated the secrecy of an out-of-marriage relationship; in retrospect, this was probably the case, as she kept our living arrangements a secret from her parents after we relocated to Toronto together! I even "had to" get a second apartment, where I had to appear to live when her parents came to visit her in T.O.

Nonetheless, our relationship developed into a committed one, as she moved out from the dentist's condo, getting her own room in a charming "turn-of-two-centuries-ago" boarding house, where we both ended up night after night for a month, until we both surfaced to reassure our friends that we were still alive.

Georgie immediately did not take to her, and made salacious comments about our sleeping arrangements, forbidding her to stay over at our place! She nonetheless and persistently chose to be kind to him, the two of us having made an ice cream sundae, which we left on the floor just outside of his bedroom door; without a "thank-you", or even a word, the door slowly opened, upon which time a hand stealthily slithered out from the door-crack, quickly clutching the sundae-glass, and removing it to the depths of his room, the door shutting behind this all.

Perhaps it was because he felt insecure about our friendship; perhaps it was because he feared he would lose a room-mate; I suspect that it was for all of those reasons, that he made our life difficult, hurling sarcastic and judgmental barbs at us both when she was visiting us. Perhaps it was because I had had enough of his judgment and sarcasm some months before meeting Roxanne, that I had hurled a condom, filled with a bit of beer, blown up and tied at the end, into his room and onto his bed. Perhaps it was the sardonic tone he spoke to me with, that I chose to return home with several female friends, all of us somewhat inebriated and giggling, as I pretended to have to speak with him in the middle of the night; when he agreed, we all barged in, turning his light on, so that all those present might enjoy the sight of a man quivering in his bed, sheet pulled over his pajama-clad body, hair disheveled, and sporting a disgusted facial expression. Perhaps it was my immature reaction to his unyielding, inflexibility. To this day, I still don't care; it makes for great stories, however!

This action was probably the beginning of the end of our friendship, as well as my room-mate status. What he feared the most, was becoming a reality. Roxanne was basically the straw the broke the camel's back.

It was one night, when Roxanne was over, and Georgie was making himself something for dinner, that the "last straw" happened. As he sat down to enjoy a sumptuous dinner, the aluminum, tubular chair-legs which held his portly frame gave out, screws flying everywhere as he tumbled to the kitchen floor in the blink of an eye! There was "King Georgie", "de-throwned"! Neither Roxanne nor I had prepared his chair to do this, which, of course, he accused us of doing; but honestly, we did not! This was a prime example of "karma", I suspected.

Decisions, Decisions!

It was December of 1979, and Roxanne was preparing to return to Winnipeg for Christmas. Already there was a light dusting of snow on the ground, and a chill in the air.

One of two major Montreal newspapers went under after many years that fall, the increasing cost of newsprint at the time, plus the growing popularity of its competition spelled the end of that paper; unfortunately, that failed newspaper was a major subscriber to the syndicated comic-strip I was drawing, which as a result of the paper's failure, meant the end of the strip as well. No problem, my Political/Editorial cartoons were still being published in several local weekly papers, but my major freelance Graphic Design client, the advertising agency, too, was going under. I would have to scramble quickly to pick up the slack so that I could continue to support myself!

A Revelation

There was an alternative plan. With my social life having drastically transformed with the "Winnie Girls" also returning to Winnipeg, my growing disenchantment with my room-mate and social-circles, I thought, "Why not relocate with Roxanne (if she was willing) to Toronto? My Toronto aunt and uncle would keep us with them until we obtained gainful employment, and Toronto, being mainly English-speaking, would suit Roxanne's criteria for finding work in her chosen field of Social Work within a large, Anglophone community. (She couldn't speak French, which she believed hindered her chances of working in Montreal; what most people west of Quebec didn't realize back then, is that although the majority of Quebec, although Francophone, also contained several million Anglophones, making the odds of finding gainful employment within an

English organization very high!) Regardless, I had visited Toronto previously, and liked it, so I was confident about finding work in animation, cartooning, advertising and Graphic Design, with a few years of work experience already under my belt from another major Canadian city. (Montreal) Roxanne agreed to this, from her parents' home in Winnipeg, as did my aunt and uncle. I broke the news to my parents, who were always mostly supportive, especially when I appeared to be sure of myself and my decisions. Now all I had to do was do some short-term freelance graphic assignments to earn enough airfare to go; my parents agreed to move my stuff out and store it until I called for it. all that was left, was to find someone else to replace me as Georgie's room-mate, as I would never "bail" on him and leave him in a lurch.

I decided to find a new person for Georgie first, before breaking the news to him. I placed several classified ads in the now only-English newspaper in Montreal, to no avail. I spoke with everyone that I knew, including Dick, Hermiome, David, and many more, and yet none of them were interested, nor knew of anybody searching for a room-mate in a two-bedroom middle-class Montreal neighborhood. I felt it important that I inform Georgie of my plans at this point, which of course, was met with a less than enthusiastic response. "I knew you would screw me!" he exclaimed, panicked and angry. "Look, guy, I asked everyone I know, and even placed classified ads in the paper", was my response. "I don't trust anyone else!" was his retort. I saw where this was going. I would have to move, then periodically send him my half of the rent for the remaining six months of our lease, if need be. My part was $350. Not an insurmountable task, I thought. Little did I know that it would take me close to a year after relocating to Toronto, that I could in reality fulfill my self-made obligation. I felt that I had already done my part to try to replace myself as a room-mate, which was really the only legal obligation I needed to prove to avoid any legal problems with Georgie, this advise having come from a lawyer-friend of mine. I decided not to worry about any of this for now, but instead, to focus on earning my airfare and organize myself further for my move.

It wasn't hard in those days for me to earn quick cash for some sign-work for local businesses. I merely walked up and down a nearby major street, "Victoria" with my portfolio in hand, and within a couple of hours, I had some assignments from a few retail businesses that would more than pay my way to the "promised land".

Double-checking with Roxanne and her progress, along with my aunt and uncle in Toronto, we set our arrival date as being January first, 1980. To me, the start of a new decade symbolized new beginnings, and a potential bright new future, leaving behind the 1970's and all of which those memories and accomplishments held.

The night before I was to leave my beloved Montreal, I held a party to end all parties, inviting everyone I ever knew at that point in my life who was willing to attend, and I got very, very drunk, deep down not really wanting to leave my city, the place of my birth that I still enjoyed and marveled at every day. Georgie looked on at me, arms crossed, as he stood chatting with David. Hermiome, as usual, was the "social butterfly", while Heather chatted with her newly-found confidants. Sarah appeared cheerful, with our mutual female friends in attendance. I recalled another party I had organized at Georgie's parents home, while they were away. It featured most who were attending this one, with one exception: I was unavoidably detained, so Georgie, David, and Charles were forced to make due until I arrived with Kathleen. Like this party, I got exceptionally drunk, not wanting to deal with Georgie's negativity. As Georgie, David, Charles, and I held a "meeting" in his washroom, gossiping about the females in the next room, and shortly after my "grand entrance", I chose to lean back while perched on a clothes hamper; assuming that the multi-colored "wall" behind the hamper was solid; I found myself suddenly looking up from within the bath-tub, the shower curtain having deceptively masqueraded as a wall, and now I was sitting in the bath-tub, while Georgie, David, and Charles looked at me, laughing along with me.

Yes, those were fun times. But there was something different about this night. The decisions, promises and obligations were set, and there was a vague feeling of queasiness and anxiety in my heart on this night. I don't even recall saying "goodnight" to my guests that night; perhaps I blocked out the potential feeling of "mourning", I don't know. Nonetheless, with guitar-case in one hand, and suit-cases in the other, I awaited my flight to Toronto from Dorval airport the next morning, my head pounding from the night before. I had a vague feeling of impending doom; had I made the right decisions to leave my room-mate and commit to this virtual female stranger? Better yet, I was leaving my home-city for a "life" of potential and infinite possibilities; but possibilities don't pay the bills. Who really knew me there, from a business perspective? Would my gifts, talents, and experience be readily accepted in this "new land"? Would my ambitious nature be enough to establish myself as I did in Montreal? All of these doubts vanished as the announcement sounded, and after having checked my luggage, I boarded the plane with optimism and eager anticipation of my new life.

3 TORONTO
1979-1981

January 1st, 1980, heralded in not only a new decade, but also new challenges for myself.

My uncle was waiting for me at Pearson Airport when my plane from Montreal landed. Roxanne had already arrived from Winnipeg, sporting her now-familiar, hippy-ish knee-length, fur-lined-and-trimmed coat. She seemed smaller than I remembered, even though it was only a few weeks since we had said goodbye in Montreal. My uncle helped us load our bags into his trunk, but I insisted on handling my precious guitar myself. As we approached the city from the airport, I remember, while sitting in the front passenger seat, the looming, impending city. Truth be told, the "big-city lights" looked magnificent, with the full expanse of hope before us. At that point in my life, I still marveled and glorified the fast-pace and glitter of a large city, after all, it was all that I ever knew! To me, the big-city meant endless opportunities for making money doing what I loved best, (I still had the lure of millions of dollars and a Rolls Royce by thirty in my mind) plus great dining, world-famous arts and culture, with a well-dressed, hip, and sophisticated populace. These were not just my expectations, but in fact, what I took for granted about Toronto. This city, like many other cities in the rest of Canada west of Quebec, would prove to be an education and a test of my patience and compassion. In short, I would quickly have to learn to "go with the flow" with an open mind, and without judging, or be disappointed, miserable and perish. "Accept or reject" would have to be my philosophy. This would also apply to my personal relationships.

We arrived in a northern suburb of Toronto, where my aunt, uncle, and cousin resided. Torontonians would be the first to reject the term "Suburb", for you see, "North York", "Willowdale", even "Mississauga" and

"Scarborough" were "cities" in themselves, no longer referred-to as "suburbs" by Torontonians. I had a sense that Toronto was in the middle of a growth-spurt and evolution, and thus, they were suffering from growing pains, as more and more immigrants were re-locating there. This largely English-speaking, white, fair-haired and blue-eyed population was struggling with their own non-judgment and flexibility, as a great many Quebecers were also emigrating to "Toronto The Good". I must have looked quite the sight there, as I confidently, perhaps even arrogantly made my way around the city via public transit. I remember a snarky bus-driver's reply to me when I asked him if his bus stopped at a "Metro", early on; in Montreal, the subway system was referred-to as the "Metro", while Torontonians called theirs the "subway"; too, they referred-to their city either as "T.O.", and/or "Metro Toronto", so when I asked "Ralph Kramden" if his bus stopped at the Metro, he sharply and sarcastically replied, "What??" Perhaps it was because he had heard this questions countless numbers of times from ex-patriot Montrealers, whom Torontonians resented for some reason? Perhaps because of my darker skin and afro, he assumed I was black? Up until that point, I had never encountered so much outright prejudice and anti-Semitism until my arrival to this fine city. Perhaps he hated French people, and because of my question, made certain assumptions? Perhaps he'd been a bus-driver in this city for too long? Nonetheless, I asked him again, as I clutched the vertical steadying-bar with one hand, and my portfolio with the other. "Do you stop at the Metro?" I asked of him again. "Oh, you mean "subway"!" was his reply; by then I thought he was just an ass-hole, trying to give me a hard time. "Yes, I do." he finally informed me. Over time, I realized that a big part of Torontonians was their sardonic humor, a kind of tongue-in-cheek, dry-wit, done with a straight face. I eventually adapted to this, and grew to love it, it becoming a normal part of my day-to-day verbal expression. I had to learn to temper it, lest I hurt or offend the softer-skinned western-Canadian populace.

I loved learning the ways of Toronto's subway, frequently riding it to pass the time. The fact that part of it ran underground, and part of it ran high above ground, fascinated me, for I was only familiar with Montreal's underground Metro system. As well, the breaks of Toronto's subway cars squeaked loudly, as the sound of steel-on-steel also continually jangled my nerves; Montreal's Metro cars had large rubber-wheels, and the trains "whooshed" away, faster than Toronto's system, on their tracks in a futuristic fashion. The trade off, was that at least once a year, there would be a fire in the Metro system, usually caused by the rubber tires igniting! Toronto's system did not have this problem.

The Burbs

Roxanne and I quickly settled into the basement of our temporary home in northern Toronto.

My aunt and uncle also owned a miniature, long-haired Sheltie named "Princess", a noisy, miniature-collie-like-affair, which continually begged for food, subsequently upchucking the rich treats, ultimately causing a crises resulting in family chaos, fingers pointing at each other, blame being hurled for Princess' discomfort. One day I returned to their home after a trying day of looking for work, when a dinner plate whizzed by my head, narrowly missing me, and making full-contact with an adjacent wall, the expensive Chinaware breaking into numerous pieces onto the floor. This was meant for my uncle; they were in the middle of a fight, when I happened in! Roxanne was with me, and she merely stood motionless, eyes wide open, mouth agape, at this interaction. I would eventually learn how emotionally and verbally unexpressive her parents were, often bottling up their anger and issues. I wondered which was worse? Doing and saying things you might regret later, (or as they say in the west, "You can never take back what you've said"!) or holding things in resulting in illness, mental and emotional issues, or worse? Nevertheless, I was no stranger to this sort of thing, as I was raised to be expressive, in an environment of my parents yelling at each other and myself; never for one moment of this did I ever doubt that my parents loved each other or myself; it was just our way, and apparently other people's way, too. I completely "got this", and wasn't panicked by it, but I did feel as if they should have their privacy during these outbursts of emotional expression and release. We slinked down to the basement, where Roxanne explained to me that my uncle and aunt might have had enough of us being there. (it was four weeks already, and we were given six weeks to establish ourselves) I agreed. After numerous interviews with Toronto animation studios and ad agencies, I had two concrete offers: one was doing graphic design at an upscale porno magazine, (this greatly interested me, and I even studied in great depth the sample of their magazine which they gave me) or being the Layout Artist and Editorial Cartoonist for a major suburban weekly newspaper: no contest1 I would say "yes" to the newspaper! Roxanne took a weekend/overnight job at Canada's first group home for mentally-challenged Jewish adults. The time was right: with potential jobs at our fingertips, we would look for that "perfect" domicile, thus freeing up my aunt and uncle from any more tension and lack of privacy, after all, their townhouse was relatively small, and their son, my cousin, was also living there.

Pears Avenue

We inspected, then we were inspected, and then we finally took this "perfect domicile", which was to be in the form of a furnished, studio apartment above a Krishna restaurant and an upscale bar, not far from Hazelton Lanes in downtown Toronto. It was in a beautiful hotel, a place for newly-divorced or separated over-forty adults, we soon discovered. Downstairs, the bar, once-a-month, became a "magic bar", which was right up my ally, so to speak! I had recently returned from Montreal, and while visiting my parents, opened up my old "Pandora's Box" of magic tricks, and so I had "caught the magic bug" again! One of the local magic clubs held their events at the bar, and I was thrilled to attend and watch. Just down the street was a lovely magic-shop owned by a Groucho Marx lookalike; I loved his sardonic wit and charm, plus his low-key presentations and demonstrations in the store. I frequented that place several times weekly, secretly bringing home more and more tricks, which I cleverly hid behind our couch. Other nights of the week, (especially when Roxanne was at the group-home) I enjoyed the humor of the aging bartender and his heavy British accent downstairs; he reminded me of characters from a TV-show from my youth, "The Pig and Whistle", so I felt right at home in this friendly, neighborhood bar.

I loved my new job at the suburban weekly newspaper. The commute was exhausting but necessary, taking an hour by public transit to get there, then an hour to return to downtown Toronto at night. This was the general routine for most working people in Toronto: take hours to get to work, and hours to return to your suburban home. I recall hearing the "clack", "clack" of hundreds of high-heeled shoes, echoing in unison throughout the subway, which felt apprehensive to me; why couldn't even just one person step differently, out-of-rhythm, from the others? I found it both eerie and disconcerting that nobody ever thought to do this.

I loved our neighborhood, which consisted of upscale and trendy places, where you could buy a week's worth of groceries for $15., but this was after all, 1980. Most of all, I loved an after-hours burger joint near Bloor and Yonge Street; one would be served by very "artsy" and friendly types, the dark green walls displayed large, black-and-white "Film Noire" type images of actors, with one part of each photo colored red. (usually the lips, or a tie) The menu was something else! Sexually suggestive descriptions of the various burgers added a clever and humorous touch to this hip place. It took less than a year to establish ourselves in Toronto, and I felt right at home!

Roxanne decided she wanted to visit Winnipeg for Christmas, which we proceeded to do; of course, I couldn't "stay" at her parents' home, as she had once brought home a boyfriend from New York, with great turmoil and scandal ensuing; as well, her sister had recently been dating an "older man" from New York, with whom she was living in Israel. Her parents were highly suspicious and pessimistic about this union for no reason in particular; "Does he have any kids?" her mother nervously asked. The truth was he did not. She and he eventually married, spawning several children from the relationship. December 8th of that year, the world changed permanently with John Lennon's assassination. We learned of this first when our neighbor, who worked in the fish department of Loblaw's, gave us the news. Our head spinning, we spent some time mourning this, as we had just bought his new album, "Double Fantasy", which we greatly enjoyed. Just as it seemed that Lennon found peace for himself, this tragedy occurred. The snow outside our window seemed a little deeper and a little bit colder.

Nonetheless I felt quite fulfilled with my freelance cartooning work, feeling like I was on track with my life, and with nineteen eighty-one just around the corner.

Winnipeg: First Impressions

Nonetheless, we arrived at Winnipeg's airport, close to Christmas time of that year. The flight was pure magic, with fluffy, marshmallow-like clouds billowing beneath the plane, with a bright-blue sky above. A smooth, turbulence-free journey highlighted, for me, this flight! The airport appeared deserted, save for a lone, tall figure looking out mournfully at the bleak, cloudy winter's day. We took public-transit to Roxanne's parents home in New Tuxedo, as there was nobody to greet us at the airport upon our arrival. I thought this to be rather strange, since their second-daughter was coming in for the holidays; nonetheless, we approached her folks' home.

A great wood-and-stone affair, this multi-level mini-"mansion" proved to feel as empty as its occupants! Indeed, as she gave me the grand tour, we made our way into a sort of "waiting room" off of the dining-room area. All of the furniture was covered in clear plastic, (not unusual for older Jewish people to do to keep their furniture "clean"; Alan had clear plastic over the couch his parents gave us for our own abode!) but more importantly, I had never felt any place feel so "empty", almost blood-chillingly cold"! The minus-forty temperatures had nothing to do with it; it was as if no-one had ever set foot in this room, nor the entire house for that matter; it was more like a tomb, or something shrine-like, like a museum that no-one had ever visited. I never forgot this first impression. Suddenly, the front door shut closed, and I heard a comment about bags getting in their way; it was her parents, returning home from a brisk walk in the area.

The Parents

They both seemed short to me; he, grey, short curly hair, with a hooked-nose hanging over thin, pursed lips. His eye-brows, curled upward, meeting just above the nose, revealing a somewhat nervous and suspicious attitude. His and her face both somewhat weathered. They both sported coats of a material and pattern I wasn't familiar with. It turned out to be a "Cowichan Sweater" from B.C., the now-familiar style being somewhat popular in some areas of Canada. Her blue eyes nervously darted from side-to-side, grey, curly hair framing a face that reminded me of a Dr. Seuss character, especially her half, hesitant smile. Pleasant enough, they directed all comments and conversation at Roxanne, ignoring me completely until she introduced me to them. Immediately, he drew the curtains so that no-one could see me visiting their home. "You've brought home men before", was his comment to Roxanne. I felt right at home!

I stayed at Rayna's parents' home, which proved to not be unpleasant either, after all, I had a bed, my portfolio and guitar, and my newly-acquired local weekly downtown newspaper which I had picked up during a brief stop to Winnipeg's version of the Eaton Centre, complete with underground shopping, which reminded me much of Montreal's downtown core. Feeling inspired, I paid a visit to the newspaper's offices, and the owner/publisher.

"Sal" was a displaced American living in Winnipeg with his wife and two daughters. He was partners with another person, who owned a half-dozen or so community papers in Manitoba. Sal's "baby" was this downtown weekly newspaper, and we hit it off immediately! His quirky sense of humor jived with mine, and the fact that he was Jewish, eccentric, talented, and a good businessman were traits that I could both admire and relate to; his feelings were likewise! He loved my cartoons, and thought it interesting that I was drawing cartoons for a Toronto paper of the same name as his paper; he agreed to my proposal: he would pay me $50. for 52 one-panel "Gag Cartoons" called "Out To Lunch" which he would publish weekly in his paper; if I wanted, after a year, I could send him another 52 for the same fee. I was over the moon! Again, feeling relaxed, combined with inspiration and an "ah-hah" moment resulted in me accomplishing things that I loved and desired to do.

At that point, not only did I have regular freelance cartooning work in T.O., but I was also being published in Montreal, Toronto, and Winnipeg!

Later on during my visit to Winnipeg, I found myself wandering around the downtown area, much of it feeling familiar to me, although I had never been there in this lifetime. People seemed open and attracted to me, smiling as I entered stores, including a comic-book store on Portage Avenue! Roxanne introduced me to some of her friends, including an alcoholic male who worked a steady government job, but lived in his mother's basement. I liked "Brian" for his quick-wit and sense-of-humor, and something he would someday say to me would further inspire me to relocate to this amazing city. I call it amazing, because it had a proliferation of culture and the arts, which made me feel happy and hopeful for some reason. It was ethnic and culture-filled, hopeful and optimistic like my beloved Montreal, but unlike Toronto, which I liked for other reasons, mainly its size and endless opportunities; the relative openness of Torontonians was also impressive for a big-city I thought.

Roxanne took me to a trendy restaurant in the Osborne Village on this trip, and I to this day remember with fondness the friendly and hip servers, along with the scrumptious milk-shakes served in sealing-jars! Coffee was served in a similar fashion, but with a cinnamon-stick in it! This was an exceptionally novel and expanding and evolving town I felt, and I was lucky to have "discovered it" thanks to Roxanne. I had a good feeling about this place, like I was "meant" to be here, because even with my poor sense of direction, I was able to intuitively navigate the city. Even my future father-in-law made efforts, eventually, to help me to feel at home during a family gathering: he enthusiastically grabbed my portfolio, displaying it to everyone and saying, without actually knowing what a Graphic Designer is, "He's a Graphic Designer!" An elderly male family member said to my future father-in-law sarcastically in Yiddish, "Others are descending, while others are coming up". I immediately responded in Yiddish back to him, to his great embarrassment. I was a force to be reckoned with, and "nobody would fool with this big-city boy" I thought to myself. This attitude would eventually create some problems for me in the future, hindering my happiness and full enjoyment of life. But more on that later! One of the family members asked me at this gathering, "So, what do you think of our city?" to which I honestly, enthusiastically, and with love answered, "It's quaint!" Someone shouted out, "Quaint???" I explained that I thought this was a good thing, and that I really liked the city. The unintentional damage was done, and I quickly gained a reputation (at least among this small crowd) for being a "big-city snob"; I knew I wasn't, so I really couldn't care less. My mistake of not remembering how fragile and sensitive the locals were would too, affect to a lesser degree, my status there in the future. The time came for us to return to Toronto, and resume our life; this made me happy, too.

The Second Year

Most of 1981 went well, and as we were approaching mid-year, my job came to an end, and a sudden proliferation of cockroaches and rats spelled the impending end of our tenure at hotel on Pears Avenue, whose rent was

$350. per month: I would not suffer the same fate as my parents, who endured for too long living in a middle-class neighborhood over-run by these same creatures; there wasn't enough room for all of us! Roxanne took a brand-new job with the City of Toronto's Welfare Department, her duties as a Social Worker was to include surprise visits to tenements in Toronto, to uncover potential welfare fraud, but to also encourage other people to apply for social assistance, when it otherwise might seem a bit daunting for them to do so.

I however, had great difficulty keeping a position in Graphic Design, due to lack of earlier full-time experience in the trade: I lacked certain exacting skills necessary for the technical requirements of the trade, because I started off in Montreal mainly doing illustrative work, rather than acquiring the more technically-demanding jobs in order to build up those required and exacting print-house skills. I managed to hold onto several full-time jobs for no more than two weeks at a time in T.O., including a brief tenure at an ad department; there, I was "Junior Layout Artist", under the direct supervision of a female not much older than myself, originally from Winnipeg! She didn't fit the picture of the middle-aged male ad managers of the day, but was pleasant enough. I met my future friend "Stefano", the copywriter, with whom I chose to socialize for many years to come, long after losing that job. We enjoyed an occasional after-work beverage or two at the nearby Eaton Centre's watering hole, whose hot fudge sundaes I enjoyed with a passion! Funny enough, one of the ad agency's clients that Stefano and I worked for was a major Canadian drugstore chain, owned by a certain Jewish family, which would soon become significant for me. I was forgetting at the time that I wasn't doing what I truly loved and which I believed I was meant to do, which essentially was cartoon-related. Returning daily to our new apartment near Bathurst Avenue in Toronto from interview after interview, I started to become exhausted and discouraged. I needed a vacation!

I took short day-trips to look for cartooning jobs for papers just outside of Toronto, again to no avail. A brief vacation to Niagara Falls yielded little results, as far as relaxation was concerned. I began to resent the city for not automatically providing me with employment the way Montreal did. My parents encouraged me during long-distance telephone conversations, emphasizing to above all, "take it easy" during my quest. I followed their advise and through this advise, I gained a significant temporary job.

The Recreational Park

The previous summer of 1980 was a magical time, in that I acquired one of my all-time favorite jobs doing caricatures for visitors and tourists at a major local recreational park. Just as I had acquired the syndicated comic-strip during a completely relaxed and "ah-hah" moment, so too, and in a similar fashion, did this job "come to me"!

One day, Roxanne and I decided to "take a break" and check out the park. Finally feeling more relaxed, I noticed many large orange umbrellas peppered throughout the park! Under each one was a caricature artist, drawing someone sitting in front of them. At the time, the sign said, "Small $5., Large, $10." There were great line-ups for these drawings, so curiosity got the better of me, and I looked at each artist's drawings. There were also many "Portrait Artists" offering full-color chalk-drawings of visitors, framed, if requested, (and paid for) by beautiful, decorative wooden frames. I knew that I could draw these quick, black-and-white sketches, so I asked one of the artists how she got this job; she gave me "Sam's" phone-number and address in Mississauga, seamlessly resuming her drawing!

Calling Sam the next day with an inspired "fever", I obtained an interview with him and his wife that same day. Knowing in my heart this was right for me, I passed the test of drawing her wife and her rather large protuberance in an inoffensive manner, which, Sam later told me, was the key to the whole thing. That, and being prepared with about a dozen or so themes/hobbies/jobs that the customer would likely wanted to be drawn as. Sam asked me to report to him at the park around 10:00 a.m. the next day, and the rest, as they say, is history! Despite the rainy weather, and having started my season with them in July rather than the usual May opening, I managed to outdraw the other artists that summer, having apparently (according to Sam) grossed more money than the other artists! I merely did my job, as quickly and pleasantly drawing my subjects, receiving cash-payment from them, then keeping 60% of the day's take, Sam and his wife (she was one of the Portrait Artists, I soon learned) keeping the 40%. I figured out that they must have netted (after paying the park their split and/or rent) $200,000. for the summer. Quite a brilliant business they had established over many years!

Aside from this, during the year, my friend, a very pregnant Heather visited us from Montreal, with her husband "Bob"; this proved to be a brief but enjoyable stay. Robert and his friend stayed briefly with me at my extra home, the basement suite off of Bathurst in North York, near the Hassidic synagogue. Interestingly enough, like my first apartment in Montreal, it too was owned by an elderly Jewish couple, and it too, was a furnished two-room abode costing me only $50. per month: the perfect "get-away" when Roxanne's parents visited us. I quite enjoyed the privacy, as well as having my own space to do the (finally!) many poster and illustration/cartooning-related assignments, including an Editorial Cartoon for a weekly paper; little did I realize that I would eventually be working at the Winnipeg equivalent of this paper of the same name, and that this would take me to Winnipeg permanently; more about that later.

A potential client called me, one of Roxanne's friends, and ended up providing me with ample and regular freelance cartooning assignments. Eventually I was interviewed by a small community paper about my upcoming "Cartooning and Gag-Writing" course at a huge north-end community centre owned by the same family that owned the major Canadian drug-store chain! This course successfully provided me with a steady income, besides the freelance cartooning. I was still drawing my Editorial cartoon for Montreal's weekly suburban newspaper, and so I began to set my sights on steady freelance assignments from the Winnipeg market.

At this point, I was enjoying a "life" in T.O., enjoying our Bathurst-area shops and bars. Next building to us, in the house, lived a famous Canadian actor, whom I spotted on several occasions driving his black Rolls Royce out from his garage; was this a reminder for me that I'm on track, and to not forget my goals? How grand and majestic this vehicle appeared, and how out-of-place he appeared in the driver's seat, his waist-length braided grey hair punctuated by his torn jeans, bare feet, and shirtless frame! Nonetheless, he and his two small children, played and danced in the park in front of our apartment building. One night, I enjoyed him singing at a corner bar; he was improvising with the Jazz-music, "I'm a gnome; I'm a gnome; I'm a Metro-gnome!" This reminded me of several years before, at the Crescent Street comedy bar in Montreal, when the soon-to-be world-famous comedian came out dressed in a monk's outfit, complete with hood, potato-chip bags pinned all over his costume; he sang, "I am the Chip-Monk, yeah, yeah, yeah!" In another segment, he would come out in a diaper and baby-bonnet, talking in a high-pitched voice; I also enjoyed the rubber-glove which he blew up, stretching it over his head. But some of you might have already seen this numerous times on television; I had the honor of seeing him no more than six-feet in front of me, still trying out these routines early in his career.

Comedy

I even tried my hand at stand-up comedy myself that summer of 1981, in Barrie, Ontario, just north of Toronto.
Answering a classified ad, I found myself somehow successfully passing the test, and being included in a comedy line-up that featured a soon-to-be, world-famous major comic-star himself! Orangeville just happened to be "Jimmy's" home-city, and what a night that night proved to be. Amongst a bar filled with mostly-drunk rednecks spewing racial comments at me, (again, my darkly-tanned skin and afro deceptively and unintentionally camouflaged my Jewish background, which might not have been readily accepted either. I had images of rifles being drawn at me, which foretold a

potentially unpleasant set of circumstances to follow!) Nonetheless, I managed to get through my set, largely unoriginal, and to which I can thank one of my stand-up comedian friends for! Another comedian followed me, and then the featured performer, who just prior to being introduced, touched up the zits on his twenty-one year-old face with a make-up stick. His subsequent performance was unforgettable, as his tall, lean frame bent and gyrated, contorting his rubber-like face as he sang like Jim Nabors, Elvis, and many others. His impression of the "Amazing Kreskin" was spot-on, and accurately caricatured. I had no doubt that this person was destined for greatness, which proved to become true, many movies and a TV-show later. His former relationships, especially one with a famous blonde and her son, are legendary. The blonde has since moved on to dating and marrying a member of a boy-band, who also currently stars in a television cop-show. After the show, we all enjoyed sharing a marijuana cigarette, this now-famous comedian improvising and creating new characters on the spot. I remember him impersonating Edward G. Robinson as a ghost, saying "Boo, boo! I'm scary, see?" with Robinson's voice. Before we realized it, morning had dawned, and we all returned to our regular day-jobs and lives again. I decided from that moment on, I would never do stand-up again, but that I would "hide behind" my magic-tricks and/or my guitar. It was safer.

The Neighborhood

I loved our neighborhood, what with "Casa Loma" a brief walk around the corner to; one day we took a tour of this "mini-castle in the city"!
Nearby Loblaw's (located behind the subway station) had some new products called "No-Name Brand", which consisted of cut-rate anything and everything! It amused me to see yellow-boxed condoms near yellow-boxed frozen french-fries; imagine a whole box of frozen fries for twenty cents! I monitored the situation, and each week the prices went up by a dime.

I had enjoyed a busy cartooning freelance-season, which enabled me to accumulate enough spending-money for a spring trip to Winnipeg. There was a natural progression once again, which appeared to suggest that Roxanne and I get married. after all, we had lived together for two years, and I believed we knew each other quite well. Despite some indiscretions, we both trusted each other, and we felt ready for the next step: a "commitment", which I thought we had any way! I bought her an engagement ring on credit to "seal the deal" so-to-speak, and we began to move forward with more plans. "If it doesn't work out", I thought to myself, "We can always get a divorce."

Winnipeg

I'll never forget my spring visit to Winnipeg, which proved a bright and happy occasion.

This was to be a more or less "scouting expedition" for myself, to follow up on my previous visit's hunches about Winnipeg. First thing was first; after staying with Roxanne's parents this time around, (we were now officially "engaged", so staying there was fine, just not in the same room as her!) we paid my local weekly newspaper and Sal a visit, after all, I had another year's worth of cartoons for him. As soon as I informed him that we were getting married that fall and moving to Winnipeg, he assured me that, upon our relocation to the city, I would have temporary part-time employment with his paper as paste-up artist and Editorial Cartoonist until I found more permanent employment! I was over the top, seeing this as a positive confirmation of our impending move. Roxanne felt the same way! While visiting her friend Brian and giving him this news as well, I asked him how he felt about my doing magic shows in Winnipeg. I had accumulated at this point a sizeable amount of stage and close-up illusions which I secreted behind our couch! My goal was to do Mentalism (a la Kreskin) and magic there, to at least earn back the money I had spent at the two Toronto magic shops! Besides that, I loved magic, and I felt that there were many potential venues for me to perform in Winnipeg. He snapped, "We already have a magician here, "Bingham Fey"!" "I see", was my reply. I was non-plussed; "We have a magician already"? What sort of place was this, that wouldn't welcome several, if not dozens of magicians, jugglers, clowns, and other variety entertainers to their fair city? Were they so crammed with entertainment and culture that there just plain wasn't any more room? I later checked the local phone book, and sure enough, found only one magician listed under "Magicians"! I asked Roxanne about Bingham, and if she knew of him; apparently, they were friends years before, until he set off to "back-pack it" through Europe. He told her that on this little trip, he had performed at street corners for spare change, thus gaining more experience. This explained (or justified) why he promoted himself by boasting that he "toured Europe with his magic shows"! Not exactly a lie; "What a clever sales and marketing person he must be", I thought to myself, quickly deciding without doubt that the city had room (whether it knew it or not) for one more magician! It was settled then for sure, between Roxanne and myself, that we would marry in Winnipeg and relocate there! Upon our return to Toronto, I would work hard and make as much money that summer at the recreational tourist park towards our relocating to Winnipeg! I had a great feeling about it all.

Summer 1981

I turned twenty-five the summer of 1981, and I couldn't complain, as that summer I grossed $10,000. for caricatures drawn between mid-May and end of August, with my May-start assured. I also learned that one of the best "assigned" spots (which were first-come-first-served) was in front of "Kelly's Bar"; I made sure I beat out the other artists by being there right at opening each morning, securing that spot. During the day, (10:00 a.m.-5:00 p.m.) I would gross on average $50-$100; from 7:00 p.m. until midnight, I grossed $200. additionally! Very few artists were willing to work past 7:00 p.m., so I in essence, had a monopoly. It was both exhilarating and exhausting, and I loved the routine of getting home on public transit to my North York basement suite by 1:00 a.m., (Roxanne returned to Winnipeg that summer to get everything together for us, including getting us a rabbi for the wedding, and our first Winnipeg domicile together) rising and making it back to Ontario Place by 10:00 a.m., six days-a-week! I was quickly burning out and I knew it, but the amount of cash being "thrown at me" was hard to resist; my competitive nature also loved the fact which was shared with me by Sam, my boss, that I was their leading grosser; there was no stopping me now! Not even "Arnold" would get in my way!

"Arnold"

Arnold V. was a retired, short, 300-plus pound caricature artist, who had his own customized and reinforced folding chair! This chair was guaranteed to hold his great weight, which also forced the chair legs approximately six-inches deep into the concrete around him! Arnold would frequently fall asleep at his post during the day, his blue fishing hat pulled over his eyes, causing him to miss, no doubt, some opportunities to make a buck. He had worked for Sam for many years, and was held in high esteem and respect. enjoyed his European accent, which reminded me of Montreal..

On my way, daily, by public transit to the large recreational park, would sit Arnold, on the "final stretch" to the park, and daily, I would smile, greet him, then dash off the train, speeding to the entrance to the park exactly by 10:00 a.m., where my spot would be guaranteed. He was the only other artist who tried to get to this spot before me, and never succeeded; he always ended up securing for himself the next-best spot. No-one was going to stop me from making as much money as I could before relocating to Winnipeg, after all, what were the odds of their being the same opportunities for me there as this? No: I would work hard and buy as much magic as I could before moving! Speaking of magic, I was invited by the owner of the nearby magic-shop I frequented daily now, on my way to the park, to come to the "magic bar", maybe perform with some of the "boys" from the local magic club; I was excited and flattered!

The Toronto Magic Club

I had never "mixed" with other magicians before, so this was exciting! If I would have known that I was to be in the presence of such "magic royalty" as the internationally renowned "Eisenthold", (magical inventor and author) I would have been more nervous, or even declined the invitation. Nonetheless, there I was, performing magic near the make-shift stage beside the bar. I performed a floating ball routine, and also a dancing cane routine, in addition to other magic-tricks; I was so nervous, that I hid my hand behind the bar frequently during the times in my routine that required I wear a flesh-colored gimmick on my thumb! I got through it, and received much accolades and encouragement from this true "brotherhood" of magicians. Later, a well-dressed, white bow-tied and tuxedo-clad Spanish-speaking magician shared with me a far smoother way to "force" a card on someone; his method was completely smooth and far more deceptive than the standard methodology! I performed a "card-to-wallet" routine for him, and endured a good-natured mocking look from Eisenthold, in response to the cheaper plastic wallet I used for this illusion. Subsequently, I always made sure that I owned only the best leather gimmicked magic wallets that money could buy on the market. I truly felt like I had a "home" with these professional hobbyists! This left such a positive impression on me, that I gauged all future magic societies on this one, and thus, I was always disappointed with the other ones after this. The club frequently passed along smaller shows my way, and this helped me to gain more experience and confidence! I even passed along a birthday party show to Eisenthold, as I was to relocate to Winnipeg shortly and had no time for it. He graciously accepted, thankfully.

David's Father

That summer, my friend David's beloved father passed away from cancer. I had met him on many occasions throughout the years, and I was shocked. Stricken by grief, I cried and cried when David gave me the news by phone. Perhaps this was the "last straw" of a stress-filled summer: The lack of sleep and over-work combined with failed plans to get our apartment furniture shipped to Winnipeg by a certain date was finally getting to me; it was August 1981.

I cried and cried until I had no more tears to cry. I sat alone in our darkened bedroom near Bathurst, boxes upon boxes lined up throughout our apartment. My glasses were placed on the floor. I shivered, even though it was ninety-plus degrees out there. I began to shake, sob, then cry again. I felt overwhelmed for the first time in my life; I finally couldn't cry any more. Words came to me in my mind, I could see them so clearly, and a tune; I automatically wrote and wrote a song on a scrap piece of paper. The song was called "Time Travelers", and some of the words were, "We are time travelers, traveling through space..." These words, which I packed away in one of the boxes, would prove to be extremely significant shortly.

My energy renewed, I managed to successfully finish off my summer at the recreational park, and ship our belongings off to Winnipeg by our due date, which the movers guaranteed me in writing I thought it amusing that I chose "Mayflower Movers" for the job, representing in some way my landing upon "new shores" to start a new life; I thought to myself, "I can tell people I arrived in Winnipeg by "Mayflower"!"

Another "amusing" thing that came to light for me during my time at my North York basement suite, was when David came to visit me there; chuckling at my door, he said to me, "Guess who I was just visiting?" I had no clue. "Georgie! He lives just around the corner from you!" I was floored! Georgie had no idea that his "arch enemy", the man who barely escaped his clutches and law suit over the rent, lived a few steps away from him! It was Toronto after all, and it was rare to run into the same person twice in any given year, but Georgie? My parents would say in Yiddish, that it was "finster (or black/dark) in front of my eyes!" David did spill the beans to Georgie, who subsequently mailed me a lawyer's letter; I scribbled "moved" on the envelope, returning it to a nearby mail box. I never heard from him again.

The summer was growing old, and the day came to fly to Winnipeg; I bid a fond "adieu" to Toronto for now, a place I grew very comfortable and happy with in only a couple of years; as our plan was for me to gain a couple of years of practical full-time Graphic Design experience in Winnipeg, I reassured myself that we would return to Toronto in a couple of years again to work full time. Something deep down said that that was not to be.

4 WINNIPEG
1981-1994

Two days before I was to wed, stressed and burnt out, I made it to Winnipeg, staying at my future in-laws' home on Driscoll Crescent. I was given the itinerary from Roxanne almost immediately upon my arrival: tomorrow would be my Bar Mitzvah, since the traditional rabbi she had commissioned for officiating was required by Jewish Law that I would have had this done already during my thirteenth year. "No problem", I thought, as I looked down at the slip of paper that contained the phonetic pronunciations of the Hebrew words I was to say in front of a congregation consisting of strangers, namely, her family. "How intimidating as well as potentially humiliating", I thought! Nevertheless, I felt this was a way to honor my background and to also respect my future wife's wishes, let alone adhere to Jewish Law. I enjoyed the "dress rehearsal" the same day that I landed in Winnipeg, being ushered into Roxanne's parents vehicle along with herself and the Rabbi; it all seemed rather theatrical to me and ritualistic, (I loved tradition and rituals!) what with the opening of the curtains at the synagogue, revealing the "Torah", or scrolls containing the ten commandments. On the rabbi's cue, I was to lift a corner of my prayer-shawl, kissing it and then placing this "kissed" corner to the Torah, which was paraded around for the congregants to "kiss" as well! I was shown how to "follow along" with a beautiful metal pointer as I supposedly read the text at the front of the congregation, at the "pulpit": in actuality, my phonetic "cue cards" were placed on top of the Torah's ancient scrolled text, but the illusion would be perfect from the congregants perspective. "Interesting that it was all "illusion" to fulfill religious obligations", I thought to myself. Nonetheless, the rehearsal went well, after which time the rabbi mumbled in Roxanne's direction with a wink, "positive reinforcement", upon which time she gave a knowing smile back in his direction. This disturbed me somewhat, causing some mistrust in my mind to be planted.

At the successful conclusion of the actual ceremony the next day, everyone threw candies at me, to my shock and surprise; I wasn't "warned" about that part; I smiled politely, nervously making my way back down to my seat, my prayer-shawl and "yarmulke" (skull-cap) having been gifted to me by Roxanne. What came next was something I wasn't "prepped" on.

The "Baptism"

A "baptism" or purification of us both at a "mikvah" (body of water) was also required by Jewish Law, before the rabbi would marry us. The thought being that we would have to be both "cleansed" of the past, and thus "renewed" before consummating the marriage. Besides the rehearsal for the Bar Mitzvah upon my arrival, there was also a counseling session with Roxanne and I in the rabbi's office or chambers. Little did I realize that in actuality, he was going to give me a post-hypnotic suggestion for a series of responses and experiences that would be induced during the baptism.

While sitting in his office, he proceeded to shut the blinds, creating both a somber and a peaceful environment. Returning to his seat, he began, "Let us meditate." I lowered my head, closed my eyes, and began to concentrate on my breath. I followed closely his words, which were uttered in a somber and relaxed manner as well. He gave us a visualization of packing up all of our troubles and sadness from the past into a nice, neat package, tying a bow on it. Then, continuing, he suggested that we open a window in our home, carefully placing this package in a garbage bin just outside, letting it all go, as we place the lid on the can. He further led us verbally to a beach, making sure we looked out at the body of water in front of us during the visualization; he then invited us to slowly imagine ourselves walking towards and then into the enticing sparkling water that lay before us. He gave the suggestion, then, that we feel the warmth of the sun on ourselves, creating a warm, loving protection. Roxanne had previously informed him that I didn't swim, and that I also didn't enjoy placing my head underwater, thus the following visualization was added: he had us imagine that we both dunk our heads quickly beneath the surface of this beautiful body of water which we were already waist-deep in, and then, quickly rising up, that we look again towards the bright, warm, loving, and reassuring sun. I could see this so clearly in my mind's eye, that it, like the throwing away of the package, moved me to tears! I felt refreshed and renewed in this waist-deep water now, with a "knowing" of bright-new beginnings ahead of us. Soon enough, he had us "come back", as he opened the blinds again. I felt cold and calm, almost refreshed and renewed, in the same way that I felt after crying at the news of David's dad's passing! I was shivering slightly. The rabbi had accomplished something special, I felt, and I began to have a deeper respect and admiration for him as a result of this. I turned my head towards Roxanne, to see how she was, but she didn't give me a glance. "Did she feel anything during this?" I pondered. Regardless, the next day was to be my Bar Mitzvah, followed by our wedding ceremony the day after that.

The Wedding

My parents arrived the night before our wedding, along with my friend Sarah, who flew in from Vancouver especially to see me. We had not seen each other since our old "disco days" in Montreal in the seventies! She looked beautiful, and I felt reassured by her presence. Both she and my parents stayed at a hotel near the airport, where the reception was also to be. Roxanne and I had a mutual friend from Toronto, "Wilfred", attend our wedding, and to also stay at the hotel. David was unable to fly in for the occasion, although I wish he could, as he was my oldest friend, and both he and Sarah knew each other from our many escapades in Montreal. Sarah sarcastically asked me if Georgie was going to attend. Looks like I had my parents, my aunt and uncle, Sarah, and Wilfred representing myself, while Roxanne had her parents, (her sister, brother-in-law and nephews were unable to fly in from Israel) plus two-hundred other guests and members of her family. I felt somewhat outnumbered! We had a small "family dinner" at one of the fine dining rooms at the hotel the night before; attendance consisted of myself and Roxanne, mine and her parents, plus Sarah, Wilfred, and my aunt and uncle. Roxanne's dad made an attempt at a joke that night at the dinner table, and in response, my aunt sarcastically responded, "Very funny, Freddy!" He didn't understand her intention, so he gave her a broad smile back! She continued with multi-layered conversation, rather clever, which showed me just how sophisticated my background was, as opposed to my future. This made me feel sad, queasy, and somewhat anxious and trapped. I didn't want to "Become just like them after a while", as my dad had warned me would happen, so I resisted adapting to the "ways" of Winnipeggers (or "Winnipeggians" as I initially called them) lest I "lose myself"; this was the beginning of my eventually (and unhappily) adapting to an ever-changing environment which was to come, particularly in Vancouver; but more on that later. After dinner, Sarah insisted that I spend "My last night of bachelorhood" in her room. I obliged, and enjoyed reminiscing with her about times and people passed, while she undressed down to her underwear, dancing around seductively to music that played on in the background. It was the disco-tunes that we so loved dancing to in Montreal long ago, but that was in the past; she was married now, (her husband whom I never met, did not fly in) and I was to wed the next day. I honestly still don't know to this day whether she finally wanted to break our long-standing platonic-status, or whether it was simply my own guilt, plus my broken heart at her having rejected my advances early on in our friendship, but regardless, I did nothing, and the hymen of our platonic-status remained intact. At that point, I just wanted everything to be as it was in the seventies, with her and myself on our way to the Aylmer Street dance-club to dance, and then to the burger-joint for a late-night burger, but it was too late; the bittersweet reality was that everything had already changed for many years, and as someone once said, "You can't turn back the clock". This made me feel sick inside, with a feeling of mourning something that no longer existed, and yet was standing as plain as day before me.

I held onto a small portrait of her, taken by a photographer at the wedding, for many years, which I kept in one of my photo albums. Her beautiful blue dress and winsome smile reflecting a knowing glimmer in her eyes. Her trademark edge-brown-tinted dark hair framed her face. Years later, too, I was to spend some time with her and her hubby after I relocated to Vancouver.

Later that night, as we all wandered around the hallway delirious with drowsiness and fatigue, my father gave a leering glance towards Sarah behind her back, while giving me a wink at the same time; I wished I could tell my dad how I truly felt about her, and the recent "missed opportunity", but I simply shook my head "no" towards him; I'm sure he sensed my disappointment. During this same meandering around, my mother kept muttering things about Winnipeggers being "farmers" in front of Roxanne, which embarrassed me to no end; we may have all been feeling this way (particularly those of us from the east) but it was still rude to rub their faces in it, I thought! What a crappy attitude I had, but I justified it by suppressing it long enough until I gained my working experience in Winnipeg, upon which time we would return to Toronto. "If the marriage didn't work out, well, there was always divorce", I thought again, as I had previously thought. What happened to commitment? Faith? All of this I would not learn in Winnipeg, but later on in Vancouver in my late thirties and forties. I was so immature! Roxanne didn't know what she was in for, but then again, neither did I.

The Mikvah

The next day, the time came for the cleansing/renewal ceremony at the mikvah, which was to occur at Bird's Hill Park's large body of water. To this day I don't know which lake this was, but it was big! I later learned that Bird's Hill Park is the site of the world-famous Winnipeg Folk Festival, which unbenounced to me, I was going to get involved with in the future. Nonetheless, Roxanne and I drove the rabbi up to the location, and we parked. Standing at the edge of the body of water, we disrobed down to our bathing suits, the three of us walking into the knee-high water; The rabbi stood before us, and after saying a few words, some in Hebrew, cued us to dunk our upper torso down into the water and then up again. I did it immediately and without thinking. there were stood, and I automatically began to turn my body towards the sun, feeling a warmth and a reassurance, in addition to a feeling of new beginnings, as if our bodies were drying in the sun like rocks on the shore after the tide came in. I was moved to tears, and again, felt shivery like I did after David's father's death. Cleansed, renewed, and exhausted. Years later it dawned on me that some of these experiences in the mikvah may have been planted by the rabbi during our "counseling" and meditation; a part of me also knew that the rest of it was some sort of genuine spiritual experience, my first conscious one at that! This was only the beginning of my journey, which continued on to a greater degree during the wedding ceremony.

The Wedding Ceremony

The time was nigh, and it was "show time" the next day! The rabbi had given us the basic structure, blocking, and staging for this, which was to occur at my father-in-law's home, weather permitting outside. Four o'clock was the time of the proposed ceremony, and it was three forty-five already! Where was the rabbi?

Finally, he arrived, taking control. He had Roxanne's four cousins each hold the poles supporting a makeshift "Chuppah", (wedding canopy) while he placed Roxanne and I in front of him, under this canopy, the idea being that it unites man with God during the ceremony. The four holding the poles (broom handles, actually, supporting a large bed-sheet) reminded me of the people who held the casket at Kathleen's uncle's funeral, of which I was part of as well; I likened both events to family uniting during a ritual. My aunt and uncle stood nearby, as did Sarah, Wilfred, "Freddie" and "Winifred", (Roxanne's parents) and some other members of Roxanne's family. My mother and father stood directly behind me, and I could "feel" my mother's presence there. The rabbi stood before us, book in hand, dark sunglasses shielded his eyes from the sun, but also shielding us from seeing his eyes. I felt shut out! This was how I usually "connected" with people, through their eyes and therefore their soul, but this was not to be for me today, at least not in the manner that I was previously accustomed to. He began to speak of this beautiful day, and how the singing of the birds punctuated everything; at that moment, birds suddenly chirped and twittered, as if they were part of some great cosmic orchestra! He raised an arm, speaking of the breath of life being the wind, and a large gust of wind nearly blew my yarmulke off, let alone blowing away the canopy. We all stood rigidly as the great wind subsided. I felt that something more powerful than us was present and at work. What was really going on here? I was both moved and humbled with the Unseen Power that was making Itself be seen through nature, and the rabbi's words! Perhaps the Unseen Force was nature Itself? Little did I realize that in the future, this "metaphysical philosophy" would become such a huge part of my life. How could I ever imagine at this point, too, that one day I would be a metaphysical minister, aspiring to create during wedding ceremonies as an officiate, even the slightest spiritual effect and reaction of that of the rabbi's ceremony. The capper was this: he began to utter the exact words from the poem/song I had written back in Toronto, still packed away in one of the moving boxes! "We are all Time Travelers", he began, "traveling through time and space." I was truly shocked, moved, and any sort of metaphysical theories I had held up until that point were confirmed at this moment, and all at once! I was convinced (and never did lose that conviction ever since, not even for a moment) that we are part of something greater, something loving, humorous, and certainly "on our side". This "something" was letting me know of its presence, reassuring me. I have since kept myself open to signs such as this, as a reminder that sometimes we just have to trust and have faith that we are not always the "driver", and some sort of "Higher Intelligence" is really steering, occasionally allowing us to drive for a bit; should we veer off and into a course that might not be in ours (or others) greatest interest, then we are steered "back on course". This was proven to me countless numbers of times, when I might have berated myself for making "wrong decisions" (more on Vancouver later!) and sure enough, this Higher Intelligence" enabled me to make the most of my decisions and actions, with the best possible outcome occurring regardless! I'm not encouraging anyone at this point to consciously take self-destructive actions, but I know this for sure: if you trust your heart and not mull things over too much logically, and then make decisions based only on what your heart "knows" up to that point, (not what you think you should do, or what others would want you to do) then the best possible outcome results. If it, in the short term, does not appear to "work out", then it becomes a learning thing, and should you repeat that same action, then there's no pity for you, you knew better! I believe the "Universe"/Higher Intelligence gives us a "pass" if we don't know any better, and through cause and effect (karma) we learn better than to take the same actions the next time. The trick is patience and compassion with ourselves during a "learning curve"! Our best, if we allow it, will always shine through regardless of us getting in our own way, helping us to achieve more than we expected!

Regardless, we then exchanged golden rings with Hebrew characters on them translated as "I Am Yours, And You Are Mine", symbolizing the three-way bond with God. Regardless, the time in the ceremony came when we had to each say "I do", and it was my turn; I'm positive I heard my mother insist under her breath, "Don't do it!" upon which time my father nudged her with his elbow; I could feel both of them flinch during these actions. Others in attendance insisted that this didn't happen; did I imagine all of this? Were those guests being kind? To this day I'm convinced that it did actually occur! Next came the point in the ritual where the groom stomps on a glass wrapped in fabric, which I did. I was told that rather than a glass, a light-bulb was used to guarantee that the sound of breaking glass would occur. The breaking of the glass is to remind us that amongst joy should also be the remembrances of the Jewish peoples' historical catastrophes. The ritualistic, yet spiritually-moving ceremony was complete! All that remained was for us to duck inside to sign the Hebrew wedding contract, created especially for the occasion by a scribe, and drawn with ink and nib on parchment. We were shown where to sign our names, and it was done! We had survived the ceremony. Soon to follow was the reception at the hotel, and I couldn't even begin to imagine the melee that was to ensue there!

The Reception

We all made our way to the specified banquet hall located at the hotel. It is all still a blur for me, even more so thirty-four years later.

I recall a long, main table, elevated upon a platform, where Roxanne and I, seated side-by-side, faced towards our guests' tables. On either side of us, also at this long table, sat our parents, aunts, uncles, and cousins. I remember at one point the Baked Alaska being brought out, huge flames trailing behind it. I remember nothing of the actual meal itself; I remember my mother feeling anxious and uncomfortable; she was sensitive to energy and "vibes", so no doubt this strange mixture of people was beginning to get to her. What I remember the most was the odd feeling that we were attending someone else's wedding, since we had both previously attended plenty of other ones; it was hard to fathom that all of this was for us! Eventually the band arrived; actually, two bands arrived simultaneously, one of them in error! The one band's leader had failed to ever confirm their attendance, assuming all was well, and without the usual and obligatory contract! The other band was fully engaged, with signed and confirmed contract for the engagement. Apparently after receiving a quote from the first band, and then subsequently hiring the second band, no-one took the time to cancel the first band, informing them that they would not be engaged for this event. I felt it was rather sleazy of the first band to argue with my father-in-law about this, but nonetheless they were "encouraged" to vacate the premises "or else".

The music and dancing ensued.

We were informed that we had to dance to the first song, which I recall was Kenny Rogers' rendition of Lionel Richie's "Lady". I felt awkward and uneasy, not just because everyone was watching us, but mainly because it all just felt "wrong" and/or "phony". Something deep-down was telling me something, but I chose to ignore it. As we danced, I saw out of the corner of my eye my mother slapping Roxanne's friend Brian, and then chasing after him around the circumference of the room; my father followed quickly behind, I could tell he was trying to calm my mother down. Was this evening to be filled with drama after drama, crisis after crisis? What a great way to start off my new life! I remembered at that point the fellow who was sitting in the reception-area at the City of Winnipeg office just days before where we had to drop off some paper and blood-work. He squeaked, "Quick wedding, quick divorce!" His manner and appearance was not so different from one of the citizens of the fictional town of "Mayberry", complete with plaid shirt, denim overalls, and tanned, sun-worn complexion. I also recalled for some reason at that point the middle-aged salesman, who approached me awhile ago while we shopped for my tuxedo at a major department store in downtown Winnipeg: he sported a green-plaid sports-jacket, yellow shirt, bright-red bow-tie, and broad, toothy-smile framed by his short, graying curly locks. His voice reminded me of the cartoon character "Goofy" as he enthusiastically led me to the somewhat limited assortment of choices of tux. I kept remembering the tuxedos worn by the Toronto magicians: slick and sleek, with narrow bow-ties; all of the bow-ties here were broad "butterfly" bow-ties. I noticed during a walk along Portage Avenue, (the equivalent to Toronto's "Yonge Street" and Montreal's "Rue St. Catherine") a proliference of older model "Valiant's" and Dodge "Darts" driving slowly down the street, a far cry from the "Lamborghinis", "Ferraris'", and "Porches" of Montreal and Toronto! The majority of the jean-wearing populace here were all wearing generic, high-rise baggy jeans as well I noticed, apparently newly put on sale at a local "Kmart"; I really missed the sleek "Jordash designer jeans of Montreal and Toronto at that point! All of this suddenly flooded my mind, as I wondered if I was making a mistake, leaving "the big city" for a somewhat smaller, more provincial but friendly town. Roxanne rolled her eyes, and we both ran to intervene between my mother, father, and poor Brian, his overweight and "over-alcoholled" body perspiring with a vengeance, his red face expressing genuine fear, while his chest heaved in and out attempting to grasp at some oxygen. "He insulted me!" exclaimed my mother, as my father attempted to console her; "Is this true, Brian?" I inquired of him. "I only said that her dress looked tight!" was his honest response. "Oh, oh", I thought to myself; you never comment on my mum's appearance unless it's a huge complement, warranted or not, as she prided herself on her manner of dress, as did many Montrealers, after all, New York and Montreal led the fashion-scene in those days! The situation was quickly extinguished, all parties returning to their respective corners, unhappily, but peacefully. My dad spent the rest of the evening leaning his back against a wall, face towards the heavens, while my mum "licked her wounds", holding onto his arm the whole while, looking down at the floor with self-pity. In their eyes, the evening was ruined; in my eyes, I felt badly for them, and really couldn't care less about Roxanne's alcoholic friend or his real actions or intentions. Everyone else was dancing, drinking, and having a great time, it seemed. No-one ever spoke of this incident after this night.

Later in our room, Roxanne and I counted our "booty"; all the checks that we had received as wedding gifts totaled to more than $10,000., a goodly amount in those days, and enough to buy ourselves some brand-new (and expensive) bedroom furniture. As agreed, we would spend one night at my in-laws, after which time we would leave for Florida on our honeymoon. I couldn't help but remember what had happened during our ceremony, and I was still stunned by the metaphysical manifestations that had occurred in those moments. It made me both excited and restless, permanently optimistic, knowing that no matter what, there is some sort of plan, some sort of cohesiveness to this life; a sort of interconnectedness with others and Infinite Intelligence or God, and this has stayed with me even to this day. If anything, this is what marrying Roxanne gave me. All I could think about was the feelings that the metaphysical experience had left me with. I later learned that the rabbi. was a student and teacher of the Judaic mysticism known as the "Cabbala", and not the "New Age" version practiced by some, including the famed singer "Madonna". The teachings of the real "Cabbala" involved studying the meanings and sounds of the individual letters of the Hebrew alphabet, including the words they formed and their individual and collective sounds and meanings, among many other things. A lot of the "New Age" beliefs were watered-down and misinterpretations of the "Cabbala" as well as other far eastern ancient texts. This explained the knowledge and power behind the rabbi's words during our ceremony, and I began to respect him even more as a teacher and "man of God", later attending during the more significant Jewish holidays, his "alternative" congregation which consisted of many Jews who were also Buddhists, Sufi's, and more.

Regardless, a little while later that evening, as Freddie helped me load our luggage into the trunk of the car, he said to me in a rough, bullying manner when he knew that no one else was around, "You better be good to her!" Taking offense to this, and not to be bullied by anyone let alone him, I replied, "Don't f_k with me; I have plenty of "family" too, and they take care of me!" He backed away, and never again tried anything of the sort again. I couldn't care less whether he liked me or not; I had worked hard to get to where I was, with respect from people far more "important" and influential than him; I also couldn't care less how rich he was, with several "Million Dollar Realty Sales" plaques on the wall of his den. I would study his sales techniques, as it was obvious to me that an entirely different approach in selling myself here might be required. In time, I learned that friendly small-talk was a necessity. In Montreal and Toronto, it was quick meetings, a "this is how I can make you rich" sales-pitch, "these are my skills and experience", a handshake, and you're done! The pacing here was slower, friendlier, and less stressful for me, to be honest. It seemed that almost anything and everything I had to offer in Winnipeg would be met with curiosity, respect, and acceptance; this proved to be true over time.

The honeymoon was quick and merciful, and it was then that I fell in love with Miami Beach, Orlando, Disney World, and Florida in general! the quick pace, and large Quebecois population with mob undertones reminded me so much of my beloved Montreal. I loved tanning outside at the pool, cooling myself with iced drinks and finally relaxing after the busiest summer in Toronto of my life, and the stressful and hectic arrival in Winnipeg, which all seemed like a distant memory to me. Roxanne enjoyed shopping, particularly at the "163rd Street (I believe) mall"! I was taken aback at the sight of the armed security guards that patrolled the mall, replete with high-powered rifles and hand guns! What did they know that we didn't? Thankfully, there were no "incidents, and we never found out! It was late in August of 1981, one of the hottest times of the year there; I made a mental note to return during the cooler, winter months when the cost of airfare would be considerably less as well! We enjoyed the tropical foliage and palm trees, a first for me, but not for her, as she had seen plenty of those during her previous trips to Israel.

Like Montreal, there was also a largely visible black population, which also made me feel "at home", as my two neighborhoods where I grew up were predominantly black and North African. Everybody seemed to "shuffle along" slowly in this over 100-degree heat, the elderly population somehow managing to survive it all. I suppose that everyone was used to this climate, and I too enjoyed and still prefer this sun and heat to snow and cold, or nine months of rain!

What great magic-shops there were as well! I recall one in the "Sears" mall, famed magician Paul Diamond's magic-shop, where I purchased my wooden "Joanne (a.k.a. "Gwendolyn") The Duck"! My personal favorite shop was one in a mall: "Biscayne Magic" was the shop's name, owned by three younger, peer magicians. I loved the layout of the store, the assortment of tricks/stock, and most importantly, the progressive "vibe" there. I bought "Mind Control" then, demonstrated by the skilled and charming "Andree".; I still do this Mentalism effect as part of my close-up routine to this day! I'll never forget the impact the trick had on me: it was simple and impossible! How could Andree have accurately predicted which color I would choose? It was a puzzler for sure, and only cost me a few dollars, a minor investment, since I have made back my money invested a half-million times!

Disney World was truly magical as well! I felt nauseous after riding "Space Mountain", the world's most terrifying (if not longest) roller coaster ride! The highlight for me, was of course, the proliferation of magic shops there, Disney World's (and Disneyland's) trade mark! Their shops were small, with commercial and simpler tricks designed for quick-sales to tourists, so all that I really enjoyed of their magic-shops was the "small-town" feel, and colorful displays. There was nothing there for me that a professional magician could want or use that I can remember. The Mickey Mouse ears were something else, which I quickly bought for the two of us; I would use the ears for years in my magic shows as part of an original routine I performed at kids' shows. This routine was published in a magicians' trade journal a few years later!

Overall, Disney World was the highlight of our honeymoon, with its colorful street-performers and cartoon-characters roaming the main street; a beautiful fireworks display topped off a visit that I would never forget, returning several years in a row during subsequent Winnipeg winters! Two weeks seemed like too long a time to be there, so we also promised ourselves that if we returned, we would break up the trip with a visit to the Bahamas, which we did do the following year. The Bahamas, (we stayed in Freeport) with their relatively quiet environment, and lush with foliage, tall trees, conch-shells, and extraterrestrial-like flowers, (apparently the television series "Star Trek: The Next Generation" brought in Bahamian flowers to achieve their futuristic, other-worldly atmosphere) made the perfect getaway from Florida! I saw many signs advertising magicians at the numerous hotels and gambling casinos, and I made a mental note of this, to perhaps catch a show there in the future. During another trip to Florida alone, (Roxanne was visiting her relatives in Israel at the time) I took in a great stage show with Andree, later meeting one of the performers, the famed magician Norm Nielson, whose famous "floating violin" routine I got to see first hand, thanks to the front-row seats we got because I tipped the doorman $50. During another segment of his routine, Nielson produced coin-after-coin seemingly from thin air; he managed to "drop" one of his coins, which rolled off the edge of the stage and right into Andree's lap! He knew her and her famous magic-shop, so this was no coincidence! Andree made me feel quite at home in Miami, which I hoped to someday move to, for its potential of my doing magic-shows, and for its cosmopolitan feel and faster pace; besides, I loved hot, sunny weather, let alone the Atlantic Ocean: quite a far cry from Winnipeg's arid and cold climate, virtually void of bodies of water save for a few lakes. The Bahamas, with its tax-free shops, numerous places for me to perform at, and British Commonwealth government, also presented a natural and potential progression from Winnipeg for me one day, I believed. Andrea even offered, when I was ready, to sponsor me to the states! I never took her up on that, which I regret somewhat to this day. Nonetheless, everything has a rhyme and reason to it, so I trust that everything evolved as it should, and/or was meant to, as you will see further on.

The time came for us to return to "reality", as the honeymoon was now over, and we had to return to Winnipeg, and our jobs and life there.

The Jobs and Charleswood

Roxanne had secured a co-op townhouse in an area of Winnipeg called Charleswood for our first   residence. The wooden, rustic-looking townhouses and apartment houses were surrounded by a beautiful forest of trees, a few steps from our domicile. It was mostly peaceful and quiet, despite the children and families that lived there. She had secured this while I was still in T.O. wrapping things up.

Part of our agreement about relocating to Winnipeg was that we were to use her long-in-storage car, (a Valiant!) as I made it perfectly clear that I wasn't going to stand at a bus stop in minus forty degree temperatures. Toronto and Montreal were entirely different matters, as their weather was less cold and therefore more tolerant. I would eventually crash the car upon a return from the Bahamas in February of 1983, as I was still adjusting to Winnipeg's winter driving conditions. I ended up buying an almost identical Valiant from a mechanic who had kept it well-tuned. I even ended up doing a magic-show for his little girl's birthday, in gratitude for him having sold me such a good car! I did this show on crutches, (as I did with many other performances over the next six weeks) until my broken ankle had mended; this broken ankle I had incurred during my car crash; a horrible scar on my face eventually healed as well, thanks to the dozen or so stitches applied by the emergency ward doctor! The other thing was that my intuition (a hunch?) was that I would be performing magic shows, which would require a vehicle to transport my props. Nonetheless, we were now a one-car family, and I was to drive her to her full-time job every morning, where she worked for the City of Winnipeg in a similar capacity as her job in Toronto. I would then drive myself to my part-time job, picking her up on my way home at the end of each day. This worked out fine. I continued drawing cartoons for that downtown Winnipeg newspaper, and my first Editorial cartoon for them created a stir, which also made the National News! Apparently, cartoony stereotypes of women, accepted in those days for many years and, pardon the pun, broadly, were considered "sexist" by then-Winnipeg standards! Women protested outside the doors of the paper, there was radio and press-coverage, in addition to the National News paying the editor a visit! I only heard of all of this from him, as this happened on one of my days off. The front-page cartoon depicted a sexy blonde-haired woman in a tight blouse, short mini-skirt, and knee-high boots, referring to her boss of a rival newspaper as "poopsie". This reflected a recent scandal wherein a female employee was having an affair with the well-known editor of a rival newspaper. My cartoon raised eyebrows as well as raising havoc in the eyes and minds of many of the people of the city. I kept thinking to myself sarcastically, "Welcome to Winnipeg, Michael!" Eventually the brouhaha died down, but left me with some resentment over the "backward-thinking" to all of this, after all, I was drawing generic, caricaturey-women like this for years in Montreal and Toronto papers. I made a note to be more sensitive so as not to offend in the future. In an editorial that the editor wrote for the following week's paper, he referred to Winnipeggers as "thin-skinned", and had me draw a cartoon of that same woman holding a tray with his head on it, her boss looking on in the distance lovingly. At least the city was far more familiar with the cartoonist "Likey".

Eventually, after three months of part-time employment with that newspaper, I applied for a full-time job I saw in the newspaper, for the advertising department of a major grocery food chain; the position was for an illustrator, which was right up my alley! I succeeded in acquiring the position, and I loved it! My responsibilities included organizing the filing-system containing previously-drawn ads and illustrations, plus laying out, pasting up, and doing brand-new illustrations for the then-fledgling chain of "superstores", a sort of "Loblaw's on steroids". The company owned a dozen other local grocery-stores. They were in direct competition with the major drug-store chain I worked for in Toronto, and also with a major American grocery-store chain.

I adapted quickly to my environment, which consisted of my supervisor, "Frank" the ad manager, who seemed to spend more time during the day tinkering with the huge, blue computers, the female (his assistant) whose name escapes me right now, (she was all-business and a little uptight for a twenty-four-year-old I thought) several drafting tables inhabited by the junior layout/paste-up artists responsible for the various smaller grocery stores, my section, which consisted of a long, low filing cabinet, my desk, my drafting table, and a clear, hanging "divider". Towards the back of this office was a door leading into the camera-room, operated by Harry. Harry was a twenty-two-year-old engaged-to-be-married male with a wicked sense-of-humor. He would repeatedly hide beneath and behind the table upon which I would place my illustrations for him to shoot down to a certain percentage, which I would then paste-up into the "superstore" ads; his hand would dart out, grabbing mine, resulting in me letting out a loud, startled yell! We became quick friends, him succeeding in startling me each time, him and I playing practical jokes on a few select privileged co-workers. One of these fortunate few was "Ralph", a serious, nervous, twenty-four-year-old Jehovah's Witness; Harry got me to sketch a miniature demon hiding behind one of the product illustrations to be placed by Ralph into one of his ads. This demonic manifestation was only visible to those who knew where to look, but we fully expected Ralph to somehow notice it before he inserted it into his grocery ad, and the subsequent photographing for newspaper proofing, but he never did! To this day, and as far as Harry and I knew, the ad made it to print, the leering "horned god" peering from around the diaper package!

One of my other co-workers was "Hal", a thirty-something artist who formerly had the position I was currently occupying. Hal was a personal friend of the ad manager, and so had seniority; before my arrival, he requested from Frank an easier, less-stressful position within the department, so Frank "demoted" him to layout/paste-up artist, which required far fewer responsibilities. Hal was tall, and walked stooped over somewhat; his longer hair and moustache made him look like Frank Zappa, and his sardonic humor and quick smile made us both quick friends as well. Harry and I would occasionally go for a beer or two on the weekends, while Hal and I once went to a dance club. Hal seemed good-natured and non-judgmental, whereas Harry's humorous and satiric view of people kept me in stitches both on the job as well as away from it. One Monday, Hal didn't show up for work. He had apparently been in a car crash on the weekend while having fallen asleep at the wheel. He eventually returned to work, minor scarring on his face.

Magic in Winnipeg

After a month in Winnipeg, I decided it was time to look for part-time work as a magician, in addition to working as a graphic designer.

One Saturday night, Roxanne and I went "cruising" by various bars and restaurants in downtown Winnipeg. I stopped and got out where it felt "right", approaching the owners or managers of the various establishments; I was armed with close-up magic tricks in the "close-up case" I had fashioned from one of our cutlery boxes! On the top of this case was a "red-velvet, padded close-up mat", attached to the top of the case with Velcro. Roxanne had sewn the mat herself. The second establishment I approached was definitely interested in my services. They were a European-born, late-twenties, husband and wife team who co-owned "October's", this after-hours restaurant/lounge. He ("Jerry") was a denturist by day, and she

("Rhonda") ran a clothing boutique out of their home in New Tuxedo, not far from my in-laws. His mother was the "money" behind this little venture, and she was very pleasant and obviously an astute judge of character! Friendly and ambitious, Jerry and Rhonda were familiar with magic being used as a marketing tool/draw in larger cities in North America, and I was about to re-ignite this craze in Winnipeg, unbenounced to me! They agreed to my proposal of my receiving $50. a night for doing a small stage/platform show at midnight on Saturdays, preceded by walk-around close-up magic. I was very well received by the patrons and management! I was very excited about having acquired my very first magic "gig", not to mention being the only local magician (at that time) performing regularly in a restaurant/bar! I loved interacting with the audience, and if I so much as deviated from my regular stage tricks, they would come up to me later, asking "why didn't you do the "Coke Bottle" trick?" I honed my stage presentations at "October's", gaining more and more confidence as a performer. Replicating the magician's trick I saw at "Kelly's" bar in Toronto, I would produce at close proximity one of my doves, which I also kept as pets and included in my stage shows. This stage show was largely a "Mentalism" (fake mind-reading act), culled from Kreskin's show I saw live in Montreal when I was fourteen. I would "read" audience-member's thoughts from the platform, announcing correctly they, or their families birthdates, pet's names, etc. I would follow up by inviting someone on to the stage to assist me with an "experiment" in "Thought Perception": I would ask the audience-member to grab a group of cards from a random, and well-mixed pack of cards, and then, averting my gaze from their packet, and with my back to them, I would call out correctly the dozen or so cards in their hands! I followed up with several other magic illusions, including my trade-mark "dancing cane", segueing to "cane-to-silks", (the cane visibly melts in the blink-of-an-eye to two silk scarves) and finally ending with a double dove-production. I would occasionally vanish or transform the birds to something else, utilizing a gaudy, multi-color box; in the future, I would place the two birds into a large, attractive cage, the walls of the cage collapsing to reveal a large bunny rabbit, which was also a pet! (I raised/bred my own rabbits, which wasn't hard to do considering their considerable skill at multiplying!) I would end my show by visibly vanishing a full bottle of "Coke" with the flash of my wand! Some shows I wouldn't work with the doves, depending on my mood and energy-level. The music for my cane and dove routine was piped through a "ghetto-blaster", or portable sound system which I brought to the club.

People would ask for my business-card from my first night there, and I quickly garnered shows away from the club, including children's birthday parties! I kept to the same fee that I was receiving from "October's" for a magic-show consisting of four TV-dinner trays, doves and rabbits, not knowing that I was seriously under-pricing the other local magicians, who would do a trick or two in their stage shows, and receive $120. for their act! I realized this a year later when I witnessed one of these older, more mature magicians doing a show at a major department store chain in a suburban mall. As I gathered a couple more steady restaurant jobs, other magicians began to visit me at these locations, to see this "young upstart" who was taking the city by storm! I was also honored to eventually be invited to speak at one of the local magicians' gatherings, which I will talk about shortly. At this point, I was working full-time at the ad agency, and doing magic Friday, Saturday, and Sunday evenings, plus days on the weekend; this would eventually catch up with me, as I began to "burn out".

The Winnipeg Magic Club

The time came for me to do my presentation for one of Winnipeg's magic clubs, and I was nervous. Who was I, at this tender age of twenty-six, to speak in front of this mixture of both seasoned professionals and hobbyists? Nonetheless, I graciously accepted the invitation, and I arrived at the run-down hotel on Sherbrook Street in Winnipeg, drunks falling near me, and narrowly missing me, as I entered the lobby of the hotel! Roxanne and I looked at each other, as we took the elevator up to the room.

These magicians seemed to be an eager group of individuals, and as I entered the hotel room, I was greeted by a certain bespectacled, red-haired male who ushered me in; it was Bingham., Roxanne's friend whom I had written of earlier. They exchanged brief and polite greetings, and I then looked around the room. One good-looking, curly-blond-haired male, simply looked straight ahead at nothing in particular, his fingers busily rolling coins across his knuckles and back again; he had an apprehensive and insecure air about him, but I felt good about him! This would turn out to be "Jack", who became a good friend of mine, and whose lovely wife was expecting a baby; Jack was the local, major North America corporate restaurant mascot, garnering a huge salary (more than $100,000. a year!) for appearances throughout Manitoba and Saskatchewan. He was an amiable, honest, and hard-working magician, whose magic mall-show appearances I had enjoyed whether he was the mascot or Jack. He was also a collector of rare and older magic, which I loved looking at upon visits to his home. Present at this gathering as well, was a young escape artist, who would eventually gain worldwide recognition with his numerous television specials; and even today, at fifty-something, he's still going strong, "always escaping", which was also his former tag-line. Present as well was a young dove magician, his claim-to-fame would be his gold-medal award-winning dove act; he was the first magician to ever receive the gold medal honor by the International Brotherhood of Magicians major competition in the 1980's or

'90's, I forget which decade it was; today, he lives in Las Vegas with his wife and children, and still earns a living doing large magic illusion-shows on cruise-ships! Another, somewhat aged magician (now deceased) was also present, and he was an inventor of smaller, close-up magic tricks and novelties for sale to other magicians; yet another aging, chipper magician (also deceased) was also present amongst many others this night. This white-haired, mustachioed magician was reminiscent of old-time magicians on vaudeville posters, the kind of magician who wore a full tuxedo; he had started, with another U.S. magician, the world-famous "International Brotherhood of Magicians", which, along with "The Society of American Magicians", (founded by Houdini in New York in the 1920's) is the oldest magical society in the world! What an illustrious past Winnipeg has and still has, with famed magician Doug Henning, and today's Darcy Oake both hailing from Winnipeg as well! Darcy recently won the great honor of first place in "Britain's Got Talent" television show! What is it about Winnipeg which breeds such world-class entertainers who move on to world renown? My theory is the people of this city are very supportive, and very open to the arts, more so than any other city I've lived in, in North America, even my beloved Montreal! Winnipeggers nurture and encourage the local artists and entertainers, and are generally excited and enthusiastic and open to receiving anything new and different, whereas Montreal, also the Canadian leader in arts and culture in my opinion, almost take for granted their world-class artists and entertainers, who perform in world-class venues and on television throughout Europe. Toronto has plenty of well-paying venues for their artists to perform in, and Vancouver? Well, we'll discuss Vancouver later on.

My performance and lecture went well that night at the hotel, and I did attend a few other gatherings in the years to come, but only if I felt I had something to offer them that night.

Apparently I had brought much more to Winnipeg than I had realized, as upon my departure from Winnipeg for Vancouver in 1994, the local club honored and recognized me for bringing magic to many venues such as lounges, bars, and restaurants in the 1980's and '90's, as well as for producing and hosting the longest, regularly-produced television show containing magic, in the world! (nine years) Apparently I was also responsible for the club inducting their very first female member, my friend "Noreen", a school-teacher and fine magician in her own right! I was both humbled and moved by the magic-club treasurer's words, as I graciously accepted the gift, too, for my contributions, of a beautiful hard-cover magic book. All I ever wanted was to perform magic a lot, any time and any where I wished to, and Winnipeg was so accommodating; I bought my two Winnipeg houses thanks, in part, to my magic income, the rest garnered from my magic shop, graphics, cartooning, journalism, and caricatures. But more on all of that later! Winnipeg's magicians, and the population in general's acceptance of myself will forever remain in my heart.

My "success" as a professional magician in Winnipeg continued to grow, as I began to gather agent-upon-agent, each one paying me more and more for a show, or for drawing caricatures at corporate events. A local balloon-store in Winnipeg gave me my first professional shows, also creating for me my clown character of "Scribbles The Clown", (in the 1980's) whereby for a fee, (originally $50. per-our paid by the store, and eventually $250. an hour through a now-defunct major talent agency!) I would draw caricatures at special events, malls, and corporate events, plus country fairs and at schools. Their balloon-store logo was drawn by myself, (which was used until recently until they were bought out) on their store awning and website; they were the largest wholesale suppliers of balloons in North America, and also started the "Balloon-a-Gram" craze! I'm forever thankful to the original owner for his support in the early years of my career; he also funded Bean Bummerson's first major Winnipeg stunt, and a few subsequent ones: like Houdini himself did in 1920's Winnipeg, Bean hung upside down from the local newspaper's building, restrained in a straitjacket which he eventually freed himself from during genuine danger to himself; Bean made national news the following year when he failed to escape from a well-documented potential coffin-escape from the depths of the freezing Red River, press and media present; Bean's limp arm dangled out of the box's trap-door, as he remained inside, unconscious! The box was raised up and out of the river by a crane, and then lowered on to a dryer, safer place, Bean subsequently driven to the hospital in an ambulance. Many years and attempts later, Bean never again failed at any of his world-famous escapes.

Two years into working full-time at the ad department while simultaneously performing magic shows evenings and weekend, my tenure mercifully ended, as I was eventually replaced by technology; in this case, I agreed with my boss: a brand-new, $200,000. laser scanner would churn out dozens of product pictures a minute, rather than me slowly and meticulously sketching them and/or using pre-drawn file materials. The investment would more than pay for itself, and as I left the ad department's daily two-year routine and financial security, (Roxanne and I visited several more times Florida and the Bahamas thanks to our jobs) I went through a sort of "mourning phase" at the loss of my job, more than any other job I had been released from.

I created and registered my fledgling "Likey Graphics" business, where upon I subsequently decided I would never again be heartbroken in this manner, working for anyone else but myself: "There was no such thing as job security", I concluded, vowing that I would never jeopardize my emotional or physical well-being for a company that might eventually let me go; no, I preferred "controlling my own destiny" as much as I could!

Besides, I was now earning in my spare time, (evenings and weekends) the same amount of money that I was earning at the ad department full-time! Things were still growing with my magic shows, as I began to accept shows during the day and during the week also, adding caricature jobs to my resume, which gave me more versatility in the eyes and minds of my agents. In some instances, I would be hired at a great hourly rate to draw caricatures at a corporate function, which another magician would do a show or two! "The Kids' Fest" became one of my agents, and they gave me relatively stress-free gigs; the "Kids Fest were very "cool", earthy, and compassionate, and they, along with another major local talent agency (and his highest-paying jobs at $200. or $350. for a magic-show, or $200.-an-hour for caricatures!) provided me with more than a descent living. Len, (now deceased) the owner of the talent agency, had also previously created "Breakfast With Santa" for major department stores throughout North America, but now the local department stores were his clients, and he included me for a number of years in these early Saturday-morning Christmas shows; grateful for them, of course, I remember rising early in pitch darkness and preparing myself and my rabbit for a Saturday and Sunday day of shows, "Breakfast With Santa" usually kicking off the season. I recall, at 7:15 a.m. every Saturday morning in December, starting my car; it only started thanks to the fact that the oil, and interior car-warmer was connected and plugged into a convenient electrical outlet, for you see, it was the way of Manitobans, lest the engine-block crack from the extreme minus-forty winter temperatures! Upon my first trip to Winnipeg, I wondered why there were so many electrical outlets available in mall and restaurant parking lots, with electrical cords dangling out the front of car grills; were all the vehicles here powered electrically? Was I witnessing the world's first "electric cars"? No such luck, as I quickly learned the necessity of "winterizing" one's vehicle for the impending season. Come to think of it, I remember some Montreal vehicles parked, with an electrical cord running into the nearby house; now I knew why! I enjoyed, despite the 8:00 a.m. start, "Breakfast With Santa", as the pressure wasn't entirely on me, and I was part of a "troupe" of musicians that played Christmas songs, as well as (usually) one other variety performer doing there show, beside myself, then the "bringing out of Santa" (usually somewhat slightly "inebriated") for the kids and families to enjoy as they sat eating their breakfasts, all included with the registration-fee; what a brilliant business-thing that agent had started!

Other memorable agents who handled me as well were Patrick R., (deceased) and his friend, Terry. Pat entertained weekly for many years in the lounge of a hotel in the St. James area of Winnipeg; I was to perform in this same hotel monthly for ten years as part of a Medieval feast/dinner theatre which started for me in the early 1980's (a year after my migration to

Winnipeg); this same hotel hired me to paint caricatures of famous stars all over the walls of Pat's lounge, re-naming it "Faces" lounge in the early 1990's. I loved performing magic at those feasts.

More

In the early '80's, after losing the ad department, but gaining "October's", and before the St. James-area hotel, much was going on! While healing from my car crash, I decided to give full-time employment another chance, and so I applied for a Senior Layout Artist position for a major U.S. grocery-store chain's ad department. Not only was my former "superstore" ad department their biggest competitor, but both bosses from both corporations golfed together! I never knew what to make of this; were they covertly sharing company secrets? What was actually going on behind the scenes of these multi-million dollar corporations? My curiosity was extinguished when, after several months of drawing dozens and dozens of generic ad layouts for the U.S. grocery-store's newspaper and flyer ads, they let me go. I realized years later that they employed me just long enough for me to draw these layouts which they're still using to this day; I had outlived my usefulness, I suppose, after the two-hundredth ad layout, apparently! This didn't bother me at all, as I was extremely busy nights and weekends anyway, performing magic shows for numerous private and public functions.

I was on the verge of getting my long-running television program in 1985 (unbenounced to me) by way of renting a Planetarium's auditorium, (later on I'll elaborate on this) and the even longer-running medieval feasts, but after an interview at the corporate headquarters of a chain of themed Winnipeg family restaurants, my spirits were even further lifted with the acquisition of yet another client/steady gig, the restaurant "Gabby's"! (now long-since defunct) The management of the corporation envisioned me dressed in western garb, and sporting the name "Doc Holliday"; I was to visit tables and do magic for the patrons right there, close-up, under their noses, making sponge-balls appear and disappear, selected playing cards rising up and out of the pack, and so forth. I agreed to this concept, and my tenure at "Gabby's" lasted well over a year, while I continued at "October's", birthday parties, and corporate events. I was also given the opportunity (at the same fee of $50. nightly) to create a mini-stage performance in the lounge for Sunday-evening dinner: "Kiddie Cabaret" was born, which I would eventually elaborate on employing clowns and mascots at the Planetarium's auditorium; but more on that later! In actuality, Montreal Magician "Magic Tom Auburn" (now deceased) had done magic in the 1960's at a local Montreal restaurant with a similar family-themed title; I just had to pay tribute to one of the inspirations from my youth! I loved the patrons to "Gabby's", and apparently they loved me, as business began to really bloom, the "Wanted: Doc Holliday" posters with my likeness on it having attracted the attention of the media, with a brief but glowing article about me and "Gabby's" appearing in one of the major papers. Magic was flourishing globally at that time as well, and I recall miming my magic-tricks at tables with such songs as Steve Miller's "Abracadabra", "You Can Do Magic", and "It's Magic" playing over the P.A. David Copperfield had just "vanished" the Statue of Liberty on one of his numerous television specials, Doug Henning's magic specials were also mesmerizing audiences too. It seemed that magic was everywhere, even a Florida radio-station called itself "Magic", and I was lucky enough to "cue" into this trend, without any conscious marketing or planning: I just was doing what I loved!

This was the first time (but not the last time) that a newspaper other than that "downtowner" Winnipeg newspaper would print some promo material for me! Future newsprint stories included several by the late Gene Telpner, and a certain "Miss Mo", noted celebrity journalist who seemed to enjoy my style of shows, and would almost always follow my magical antics and local appearances. On one occasion, we were dining at a north-end restaurant specializing in pirogues, (potato-filled creplach) when I inadvertently caught Mo's eye (who was also dining there that night) as I was doing some magic for our server; I had never met her until that point, nor did I know who she was, but her winsome smile and glint in her eye encouraged me to approach her table and do a trick or two for her! She sent a bottle of wine to our table in return, and the final result was a very complimentary mention of myself in her next day's newspaper column! To this day I'm grateful to her for this, and she continued to mention my future local endeavors, including the St. James-area hotel's opening of their new lounge, "Faces"! For this incredible opportunity of painting those hundreds of caricatures on the lounge's wall, I am grateful to the former management/owners! Indeed, incredible publicity and a great credit on my resume!

Another amazing opportunity that happened for me during this period to add to my notoriety was my acquisition of the position of "journalist" with a local newspaper marketed at the Jewish community.

That Jewish Newspaper

I'm still grateful to the late owner/publisher, who had enough confidence in me to hire me as the part-time writer/columnist. Before that new owner, the newspaper had enjoyed decades of local notoriety. I had previous advertising copy writing experience, in addition to having my cartoons published for many years in several other Canadian newspapers, but I had never really been a "journalist" per se! I would go on to write for several years a feature column for them called "Around Town", essentially a "who's-who" of Jewish performers and their activities! I was even allowed to draw my own banner for the column; they would later commission me to draw cartoons and other headers for the paper, which I did, again, gratefully and enthusiastically. I believe I received $50. per column, or artwork, which I believed was fair for all.

The owner (my boss) personally gave me journalistic tips and techniques initially for the writing of my column, including answering the 5 "W's": who, what, where, when, and why, and I added "how"! My first column, in my eyes, would be an introduction of myself, as their new writer, which I believed was the "right" and friendly thing to do, besides, I wanted to create a sense of intimacy and have readers accept me as a "friend" in their eyes! The day that the first column was released was a surprising one; I came home to no less than twenty-four voice-mail messages on my machine! They were all messages left by the same "anonymous" female person, who hurled personal insults and abuse; she accused me and my column as being shallow and self-benefitting; I had liberally peppered my Montreal/Toronto background and credits in the article, hoping that that would lend some credibility to me; I can still remember an incident in Toronto during an interview with the CEO of a corporation, who, upon having read my resume and viewed my portfolio, lifted his head up, looking over his glasses and said, "Do you think I'm impressed with you being from Montreal?" This same CEO wreaked of alcohol and had initially asked me what my "background" was: anti-Semitism amongst certain demographics in T.O. (and I later learned in other Canadian cities) apparently ran rampant; either that, or he also suffered from mental illness. I began to ponder the words left by the anonymous female caller now, who proudly left her phone number during her messages. Was she mentally ill? Why was she so defensive and abusive about my photo with my tux on the columns' header? She had accused me of "gloating about my wealth and Toronto background" by wearing the tux; in reality, I had no other promo-photo of myself, so I gave the newspaper one of my magic ones! Shaken, hurt, and offended by all of this, I told Roxanne I was going to phone the caller back and retaliate; Roxanne advised against this, as she suggested that my role as journalist for that newspaper was also a "P.R." one, since I'm also representing the paper as one of their writers, and I should choose a more diplomatic approach, and "handle her" the way I might "handle" a drunk or a "heckler" in my shows! I agreed, and while I was on the phone with her, as she continued to hurl the same sort of abuse at me, Roxanne was listening on the extension, offering me "cue cards" of suggested answers and diplomatic responses. Roxanne, being a Social Worker, was an "expert" on psychological matters and "handling" "situations". I remember studying her many university text-books which had lent me on those subjects, including "Organizational Behavior", "I'm O.K. You're O.K.", and several on "Behavioral Modification", all of which I had voraciously devoured and subsequently employed, still to this day!

This all seemed to work, as the woman on the other end of the phone became both confused and placated after thirty minutes; her anger subsided, and we ended the conversation in a somewhat friendly manner. Several years later, this woman formally introduced herself to me at a Jewish function, shaking my hand and sincerely apologizing profusely for those phone-calls several years previously. I think she realized that I had "proven myself", and/or that I wasn't the "immature Torontonian" she initially thought I was. I really couldn't care less at that point, but I feigned sincere appreciation for her apology , which I accepted.

A similar thing occurred earlier on in my career in Winnipeg, when I phoned a certain entertainment agency's office, speaking with the CEO, who was also in charge of hiring entertainment for the major event which they put on annually at an immense park north of the city. Immediately he said, "We already have Bingham Fey, who's performed at this for years!" That sounded familiar, but I persisted, "Why don't you come down and watch my show, and then decide?" I suggested. "He replied with, "What political party do you ascribe to?" Confused and a little offended, (this reminded me of the drunk, Toronto CEO who had interviewed me years earlier) I replied proudly with the particular political party which I supported. (and still do) "Well I'm a "Plotskian" was his proud response. There was silence at that point. I had no idea what being "Plotskian" meant, but I suspected that it had to do either with socialism or communism, as there was several socialist parties there. I so wanted to say at that point, "So?" But I held my tongue. He made every excuse for not coming down to see my shows, and made excuses as well for his female business-partner to come down to the Planetarium's auditorium as she was "Too busy". Somewhat dismayed and resentful at his close-mindedness, I thanked him, hung up the phone, and continued on with my day. Years later, once my television show was on the air for several years, this person (still CEO of that entertainment agency at the time, but now since retired) approached me at an event marketed to children with his son, and said, "We both enjoy watching your show!" I thanked them both and went on my way.

I wasn't always snubbed by famous locals.

For years, the puppeteer, ("Darren") still a close friend and mentor on my television program, coaxed me to contact a certain children's television-show host who hosted this TV-show five-days-a-week. Still skittish from the previously mentioned misadventures, I avoided the subject, choosing instead to let things occur as they're "meant to", as things had previously. I would eventually (and literally) "bump into" that T.V.-host at a mall, while I was at the height of my confidence and popularity of my television-show, but more on this later!

At this point, I was tired of occasionally rubbing people "against the grain" with my enthusiasm and aggressive eastern sales-style, (had I not learned from my father-in-law anything about a slow-paced, friendly-banter approach?) which only some appreciated, such as the manager of a suburban shopping mall, who quickly picked up on my enthusiasm and admitted her kids watched my T.V.-show. I ended up working at the same restaurant as one of her kids, doing magic at a local family restaurant and bar, but more on this later. This lovely and progressive woman agreed to almost any and every promotion I suggested organizing, including "Magic Week", celebrated throughout the world (except in Vancouver!) and commemorating the death of Houdini every October 31st, and even a "Psychic Fair", which was starting to gain in popularity elsewhere by the time I left for points west. This suburban shopping mall was another contract I was lucky to have obtained, after being booked by an agent to do some shows there. I, after several years of being sure that the agent was no longer handling that mall, approached the management, as she seemed to be bright and on the ball. We immediately connected, and this too was the beginning of a fruitful long-term business relationship. I noticed that I seemed to succeed in Winnipeg, with those kinds of bosses and managers: there was something about them, a glint in their eye, enthusiasm and optimism. The ones I didn't seem to connect with appeared to need to be coaxed, lacking in enthusiasm, energy and vision; fortunately, there seemed to be more of the former types in Winnipeg, and Manitoba in general. Except in two rural Manitoban towns.

Over two summers in Winnipeg, around 1988 and '89, I acquired a contract through a certain kids' festival, of a government-funded touring program. This program, whose name escapes me, booked for various agricultural fairs throughout Manitoba variety entertainers and musicians, if they passed an audition. Myself and my "Kiddie Cabaret" show, (and the next year, my "Magic Circus" show) were booked at fifteen towns both summers to appear at their fairs. A company van and credit-card for gas was also provided, and myself and my troupe were excited to be part of this. That first summer, it was myself, (as M.C.) Roxanne as a clown character painting faces and participating onstage in "Clown School" skits, (we had been performing a lot together previously, both for corporate functions and malls, after the infamous Planetarium's auditorium had provided us with a TV-show, which we based this live show on) and several other clowns in this top-notch variety show. Both summers, we were met with enthusiastic and outstanding responses, except for two of the fifteen towns! Having lived in Vancouver now for twenty-five years, I finally have figured out was what going on (or not going on) back then: in the two towns' audiences, we were met with fearful facial expressions, very little applause, in fact a great reserved or repressed expression, and general feeling of discomfort from them! Walking around before and after those shows, the town's inhabitants would look at us out of the corner of their eyes, in some instances holding up their arms as if to "ward off the vampires"! I was frequently exposed to these kinds of responses throughout Vancouver areas, (still to this day) even without my magic costumes! The reason I was told by other Manitobans, was these two towns were part of their "bible-belt", or area of religious adherents. That explained the responses we received back then: the "magic" (albeit not real, of course, only for entertainment purposes and purely illusion) was against their belief system! In Vancouver, I started off doing psychic readings in an effort to pay down debts accrued during my relocation the that fine city, to no avail: they were more concerned in trying to figure out "what I was", and "what background", as they had little exposure to easterners, let alone Jewish people. I was faced with a lot of "discomfort" back then in B.C. after I first arrived, being called various names, but more on that later. The point was fear born out of a lack of exposure to many things, and that was the explanation for the behavior of the folks in those two towns. Little did I realize that was foreshadowing a great mistake I would make in 1994; but I believe you can almost deduce at this point what that was! Nonetheless, we're still in Winnipeg at this point, and all the great things that city (and province) afforded me.

Oddly enough, after several years of writing my column and doing cartoons and illustrations for that Jewish newspaper one of my cartoons they commissioned from me for an article about immigrants, caused a stir...not since that downtowner's apparent "sexist" cartoon did I make such an impact on this sensitive populace! The good-natured but satirical cartoon depicted people on a boat, reaching Winnipeg's shores; one of the greeters on shore saying, "Velcome to Vinny-peck!" Although this was approved by the editor, it was quickly met with a cold, nay, hostile reception! People in droves phoned the Jewish newspaper complaining that it put down immigrants either already living in Winnipeg, and/or arriving! I was apparently "making fun of the way immigrants spoke", which of course was not my intention! Good-natured satire is not meant to humiliate or put down anyone or anything; I forgot how sensitive ("thin-skinned"? not my words!) a populace can be. Perhaps I should have included as one of the boat's passengers a voluptuous, knee-high boots-wearing blonde? Letters to the editor expressed the same sentiment: my cartoon was critical and insensitive towards immigrants. Of course, the paper dismissed this all, asking critics to lighten up and laugh it off too: cartoons are meant to be satirical, and surely my cartoons are never meant to hurt, only to illicit laughter! Saved again!

The Medieval Feast

This was yet another thing I enjoyed with a passion, and which I acquired within my first two years in Winnipeg. The medieval feast which we performed at the St. James-area hotel was a miniature "Medieval Feast". The structure of it was generally this: The "Lord" (or "King") m.c.'d the show, introducing various acts which included myself performing two ten-minute magic-shows, one in the first half of the show, the second show in the last half of the show; a "minstrel" who sang and played several audience-participation songs, (British "Music Hall" upbeat, raucous songs, as true medieval songs were not upbeat nor commercial enough!) examples being "I'm Henry the Eighth, I Am", "Black Velvet Band", and "Drunken Sailor", again in the first and second halves of the show; the "Lady" ("Queen") would sing one "feature" song in each half, an example being "Danny Boy"; the jester or "fool" would play embarrassing, small jokes and stunts on unsuspecting female audience members, such as "sneezing" on someone's neck, but in actuality spraying water from a glass of water he held, and shoving his "jester staff" (with a rubber jester-head at one end, and a red-rubber devil's head at the other end) under another female's rear end as she sat at her table; people would be called up and put into the "pillory" or "stocks", head and hands firmly locked into place, as the "hag" in the show might kiss them, (usually a male "victim"; plus several other stunts, and audience-participation songs sung by us all as an ensemble, between the various courses, or "removes": an entree, main "remove", (usually roast beef and chicken) and then dessert. No-one was allowed to use or have cutlery, and big bibs served to keep things as civil and clean as was humanly possible! The jester would invariably "find" (really plant) a fork at someone's table, encouraging the audience to shame them by shouting in unison, "Fork you!" This was an outstandingly successful dinner-show which I was proud and honored to be a part of, some of the cast becoming my friend, and the "Lady", acting as agent for the show, would book it at other venues with a different name, such as "Lady Martha's Medieval Feast", for us to perform it at; some venues included army bases, the Irish Club, and some small-town fairs. She felt entitled to do this, as she had originally started it and performed in it for several years before the St. James-area hotel got a hold of it. I auditioned for it after seeing a classified ad in the newspaper requesting a magician for an ongoing dinner-theatre show. Because I didn't know that it was for a medieval feast, I showed up in full "magical regalia" including tie and tails, and of course, my doves "Puffy" and "Fluffy". During the audition, and upon being "produced out of thin air", Fluffy chose to fly a short distant, making himself comfortable on the bald head of the person auditioning me! I felt embarrassed and apologized profusely, not knowing that this person was the jester of the show, himself having a twisted sense-of-humor, and later on teasing me to no end about this incident. It was confirmed, I was hired to be the regular magician in this soon-to-be long-running show!

The management of the hotel wanted us to premiere the new show during a private function for the media, and it was amazingly fun!

As I went table-to-table warming the audience up with some close-up magic, one fellow at a table grabbed my sponge-balls, shoving them into his mouth! He then returned them to me and I carried on, making him the "hero" of the trick, as he was obviously there with a date he was trying to impress. I later learned that this fellow was a famous radio and television celebrity, who years later insisted that I be on the television premiere of his late-night talk-show; our mutual agents frequently booked us on the same roster of performers, and he was usually the host, or "master of ceremonies"; fellow performers would include other famous local performers and celebrities.

The feasts started off being four times a month, then twice a month, and in its last few years, once a month, always packing the banquet room of the hotel. Once a year, the hotel would book us to do a show with the local police taking up one-third of the room, an infamous biker group comprising the other one third, and the remaining third of the audience, seated between the police and the bikers, consisted of "civilians", or "regular" people. Needless to say, the bikers were always the most rowdy, and therefore the "best" audience, playing along with everything in an uninhibited manner! The Lady of the feast and the fellow who played the jester, and myself, remained in the group for the entire thirteen year run; the original Lord had quit after a few years, then passed away; his replacement was the most popular one, who stayed with us for most of the years of the run of the show. Recently I was informed by the Lady via a long-distance phone-call that he had passed away. I cried, and then was informed that two other original members of the feast had also passed! The original piano-player also played for The Royal Winnipeg Ballet, and so he wasn't always available, replaced occasionally by one of two "minstrels", who played guitar, accompanying us all in those rousing songs! My personal favorite minstrel was an instrument builder who played his self-constructed "cittern" (lute-shaped English guitar) which he also built for my own live shows, which were medieval-themed as well. He (who I occasionally chat with on Facebook) is still going strong, specializing in building harps nowadays; he built singer Loreena McKinnett's harp which she toured with in the 1980's, and his instruments were always featured in some local folksy music retail stores' windows, and across North America. The feasts lasted thirteen years, and were cancelled when we all demanded more money; (we had never asked for, nor did we ever receive raises during those thirteen years!) A new cast replaced us, consisting mainly of young actors; the feasts were eventually cancelled altogether after a year or two. I was honored to always be a part of this illustrious group of local, legendary performers in Winnipeg! I also got the chance to wear my various medieval-themed costumes, which I loved so much. I would bring my love for things medieval to my television show "Magic Mike's Castle" eventually.

I'll never forget one particular feast, and my very first personal encounter with a particular local mime/actor, who would eventually prove to be a good friend, and confidant! During one performance just before the halfway break, I kept "feeling" the stare of an audience-member from the back of the room. This intense staring continued until I finally decided to "zero in" on whomever this person was, so I glanced in his direction near the end of my set, and 'lo and behold, it was the mime I had witnessed a few years before in Old Market Square! Seeing any street performers at that time in Winnipeg was a rarity, which is why his performance stood out for me; I never approached him, but on this night, that was to change! Just as I was walking off to applause and towards the exit, he stepped right in front of me, hand outstretched as if to shake mine, and with what I perceived as an arrogant air, he said to me, "Hi, I'm Allen!" to which I replied dismissingly, "So what? I'm Magic Mike!" as I continued to walk out the door, not giving any of this a second thought. He was conspicuously absent upon my return for the second half of the show, so I assumed he and his date had left. That was all I saw and heard of him until one day, when I attended a meeting of the local "Society of American Magicians" branch in Winnipeg, "The Magic Circle 7" which unbenounced to me was at "Allen's" studio/home, in an old heritage building which also housed various government-funded arts and cultural organizations and societies, located (once again) in the Old Market Square district of Winnipeg. This area always reminded me of "Old Montreal", or "Vieux Montreal", what with its centuries-old buildings and cobblestoned streets; Old Market Square is also called "The Warehouse District", housing trendy bars and restaurants in renovated heritage buildings, again similar to Old Montreal, and Vancouver's seedier "Gastown" area. Nonetheless, after this meeting, Allen and I would get together for nachos and beer at a commercial spaghetti restaurant nearby, (long-since relocated) or beers at my local family restaurant/bar. One of the things I still admire about him, is his shear nerve: he was always his own person, never relying on bureaucracy, government funding of any kind, nor did he ever have a credit card, until he left Winnipeg for Vancouver. He taught magic, juggling, and mime, (his claim to fame was being mentored for a day by a world-famous mime) and he also did the odd escape stunt, subsequently garnering local publicity. His goal was to become a "street performer", which he accomplished after relocating to Vancouver. I admired his independence and discipline, being completely self-taught. He could just as adeptly play and sing the blues with a piano or a Dobro (steel-body guitar) and harmonica, as he could perform magic silently as a mime, juggling as well for the quarters tossed into his hat.

I now recognize and acknowledge that that takes a certain strength and faith, standing on street corners, performing for your next meal and rent! Until the last several years, rather than be grateful that he allowed me to stay with him in North Vancouver until I got on my feet, I actually resented him for his coaxing of me to relocate to Vancouver, which seemed to become my personal and professional undoing; but more on this later. I have recently learned from him that he has cancer, which scares me, because he might eventually become someone within my peer group who passes; mortality? I'm not yet ready to think about that at my tender age of sixty-two, there's too much left to do; with the recent passing of another peer, a Yoga teacher, our friend and neighbor, the real message of "enjoy the here and now and everything you've got" keeps swimming around in my head as a result; perhaps the Universe is trying to pound that attitude/philosophy into my head using Allen as well!

Allen is now (as of this writing) age seventy-two, but his thinner frame and sharp, optimistic eyes and curly hair project a youthful image, far younger than his actual age. His trademark hat always present, be it a "Pork-pie", "Derby", "Newspaper Boy", or wool-hat, I pray that I'm as active as he is over the next twenty years! Nonetheless, during those late eighties/early nineties years in Winnipeg, he and Darren, (whose background and childhood was also as traumatic and "of the streets") became my trusted friends and entourage.

Darren was always there for me, even when I believed I didn't need anyone, including on the occasion of my separation, when he supervised my move to the Corydon and Stafford apartment, helping me physically move my things, but also offering morale support and surprise visits to my new domicile. He'll to this day share the story of when, on one of these visits, he smelled something burning, upon which time I said, "Oh, that's my hamburger from the quickie convenience store...I'm heating it up in my oven!" Allen just today reminded me of one of his visits to our Lanark Avenue home, upon which time he approached my rabbit's cage; fearing his sudden movements might startle the rabbit, I shouted out, "Don't touch the bunny!" He says it more hilariously, with a sort of stutter. I have Allen to thank for his loyalty (as is the case with Darren) and friendship, and for being an inspiration for his dogged determination and romanticism. He was previously married several times, in all cases, truly loving his wives I believe. One of those relationships produced his twenty-something year-old son of the same name as himself. He and his ex-girlfriend, "Mary Jane", also still stay in touch as well. I'm not sure of the status of his relationship with "Little Allen's" mother, however. Yes, I think fondly of the good times I shared with Allen and Darren.

The Lanark Home

Roxanne had secured a position with the federal government. This was a secure and permanent position, involving much paperwork, and regular follow-up visits to seniors in her case-load. She was responsible for assessing whether seniors were eligible for certain benefits, and for making sure that existing clients got everything that they were entitled to, in addition to the regular monetary payouts. She would regularly find one passed away in their home; one was found crushed by their own stove when they were likely looking in the oven, which fell on top of them; another senior had "vanished", neighbors reported, until Roxanne paid a visit to her home; Roxanne found the person had rolled over and off of her bed, lodged between the wall and the bed, they eventually perished without a sound! In time, Roxanne would daily check the obituary ads to see if any of her clients were gone. I thought this to be quite macabre and depressing; she began to carelessly leave her tea cups around the house, and her clothes piled up on the floor beside her side of the bed. It was getting harder and harder to live with this apparent apathy; she even thought she had hung up the phone after a conversation with someone, carelessly leaving that business-line off the hook for hours! She couldn't care less when I confronted her about this, and her cups. Further, she started, after five years of marriage, demand children, which we had never previously discussed. She insisted that our children were to be raised as adherents to a particular religious following, and I didn't like this; I always believed that I would raise my children respecting their background and heritage, but that they would be given an education on various religions and spiritual beliefs so that they could make their own decision; I eventually realized that she wasn't as broad-minded as I originally thought she was, and I wasn't sure what to do about this, five years into our marriage! Why didn't we discuss this during the two years we lived together in Toronto? I might not have initiated the engagement altogether; that plus a few "indiscretions" in Toronto during that time made the relationship less palatable, but I eventually got over it. Still, some mistrust existed on some level of my mind.

My father-in-law informed us of a house in the River Heights area which he had insulated, and that it was coming up for a private sale shortly; he knew the entire structure from roof to concrete-slab base, and felt that it would be a smart investment/first home. We went for it!

Our credit approved, and a lawyer engaged for the sale, we left our rented Charleswood townhouse, and soon found ourselves the owners of a certain Lanark Street bungalow, near Corydon Avenue, in Winnipeg in 1983. The purchase-price was $40,000., and today, that same house is worth more than $400,000! We kept it until we divorced in 1991. The home was a three-bedroom bungalow, built during the second world war. One next door neighbor was a retired spinster teacher of British heritage. Her wonderfully sarcastic sense of humor resonated with mine, and one day her priceless comment about having seen a "polka-dotted rear-end with huge red shoes entering our home through a bedroom window" made me laugh and laugh: I had locked myself out of my home, discovering this only upon my return from a "clown-gig"; of course, I had no other choice but to break into my own home this way, my rabbits looking on in disbelief!

The Planetarium's Auditorium

Early on in Winnipeg, before I had any agents, or regular gigs, and when I was still working for that downtown newspaper, I answered a newspaper ad for a children's theatre group requiring a magician for some shows that they were planning on producing.

The producer and owner of the group, "Adrian", provided me with free and crucial training in stage-craft, movement, and timing, and I am still grateful for this knowledge, which I still put to use to this day!

This series of three magic-shows, each forty-five minutes in length, were to be at the Planetarium's auditorium, a venue which seated 200 people. I studied how he used the media to promote his shows in general, which cost him nothing. His motto was, "Advertising costs money, publicity is free", and I never forgot this as well. I decided to use my "pull" with the downtown newspaper to garner free publicity via articles I wrote about myself and this series, as well as all future Winnipeg public appearances, under a pseudonym. After Adrian retired, I felt it was okay for me to continue to rent on a monthly basis the auditorium, and produce my own shows, again promoting them through the same media outlets that Adrian used, in addition to that downtown newspaper! I called these monthly shows "Kiddie Cabaret", employing a guest variety entertainer, usually a clown, and/or in the case of my premiere show, a "mascot": The owner of the balloon store kindly volunteered to be in this premiere set of three shows, at 11:00 a.m., 1:00 p.m., and then 3:00 p.m. on that Saturday in 1984. The shows went well, and I certainly had enough magic to do three shows every month with different tricks each month; I also had at the box office, an autograph book for attendees to sign their names in, along with their mailing address and phone number, so that I could acquire a mailing-list for my promotional newsletters, which I proceeded to do after a few months. The shows which I produced without Adrian never made a profit, breaking even at best, but what great publicity this was for me, with other newspapers printing blurbs and articles about me, including that local Jewish newspaper, with whom I would get a job eventually, but more on that later!

"Kiddie Cabaret" was a great "ensemble" show, which featured little-known, but up-and-coming variety entertainers, mainly clowns who juggled and/or played musical instruments; one such clown whose name was "Cynthia", played drums and called herself "Boom-Boom", also because of some abundant attributes that nature had gifted her with. I got the original idea of teaming up with another clown, because "Gloria", a wonderful female clown at Winnipeg's summer outdoor city-wide variety stage-shows, made a wonderful assistant in those shows, and so was the true beginnings of "Kiddie Cabaret", featuring Gloria's clown character and myself! Little did I realize that several people in my audience at my Planetarium shows were from the local cable station, "CVW"! The Canadian Radio and Television Commission (C.R.T.C.) allowed each Canadian city a television station and channel where volunteer producers and broadcasters had access, (called "Public access" channels) under supervision, to television production equipment, including a studio, sound and lighting, etc. and could put together and air their own shows! My turn at this was at hand!

CVW

In May of 1985, I received a phone-call from one of CVW's Public Access managers who had previously enjoyed my Planetarium auditorium shows! I knew that this was the "big break" I was waiting for. She asked me if I would like to do a "one-off", 60-minute television special version of my "Kiddie Cabaret" show!

All my life, I hoped to have a regular television program, like Magic Tom Auburn had when I was growing up in Montreal. This looked like the perfect chance to do something like this. Armed with my resume, binders of live-show photos and newspaper clips, and a detailed marketing and program plan, (complete with minute-by-minute breakdown/structure of the show, which I would later learn was called the "Rundown") I entered the office of one of the very supportive managers of the station, including the program manager. They had that certain enthusiasm and glint in their eyes which mirrored mine, and we were on "the same page" immediately! Although this meeting agenda was originally about a one-time "special", they also accepted my proposal for an ongoing, 28-minute-long weekly television show! They loved the unique concept of "Kiddie Cabaret", and two weeks later, the "pilot" aired in mid-May of 1985, with the first official 28-minute-long "Merlin's Kiddie Cabaret" airing beginning of June, 1985! I had the support of Roxanne as her clown character, with her blue-sparkly "deely-boppers" (star antennas on her head), long, blue sparkly false eye-lashes, and (eventual) blue-and-pink "Care Bears" clown-costume. Roxanne's original costume was my "Scribbles'"-character black-and-white, polka-dotted outfit. My costume as "ring-master" and magician/M.C., was my black tux and tails, with silver trim, and "Arthur", a local musician and winner of a local song-writing contest, wore an Elton John-like set of goggles with windshield wipers on them, his balding head crowned with a red-plastic sun-visor; he wrote and audio-recorded very week an original children's song which he played on the show for three years! Other original clown cast-members included Roxanne's friend "Mary" as a winsome clown, my friend "Mitch" as a juggling clown, (I met him at one of those city-wide, outdoor stage events where I met Gloria) along with Gloria; Mitch and I had "toured" the local daycares with our own show previously!) the owner of the balloon-store dressed up for the pilot (but not subsequent shows) as a loveable, furry, cookie-munching blue character doing a "walk-on" and dancing with us during one of Arthur's songs. A mutual friend of Arthur's and mine, "Elijah", a musical genius who was musically-educated in Montreal, and who could also play a dozen wind-instruments, keyboard, and guitar, was in a famous local "Klezmer" band, also heading up his own wedding-orchestra, played songs with Arthur as "Big Ed", sporting a huge red clown's wig and over-sized sunglasses; a jumbo polka-dotted bow-tie completed his outfit! "Reba" the clown and "Polly" joined our ensemble, remaining for the duration of this show. The female who played "Reba" is credited for being the first person to take clowning into the kids' wards of hospitals as therapy for the recovering kids, and has since taken this to numerous U.S. kids' hospital wards. The show evolved over its original three years, (seasons) and I added Darren, who wrote the "Puppet Theatre" segment, was "Hoo-Hah" the clown, and gathered the "knock-knock jokes" for Arthur's segment, where his patients walk in and say "knock-knock", he says, "who's there?", etc. Arthur, Darren, and Roxanne also voiced the puppets for the "Puppet Theatre" segment, which was comprised of a unicorn, wizard, and dragon, later on "Desmond the Dragon", along with "Forgetful Lion" on my subsequent "Magic Mike's Castle" and "Magic Mike & Company" television shows. I had "inherited" Darren thanks to his brother, who regularly came to tapings of my show thanks to our mutual friend, a "New Age" "energy-worker", and massage therapist, "Francoise" It was a faced-paced show, utilizing "chroma-key" (a technique of "keying in") live, foreground images over pre-drawn background images) for the different backgrounds, and us running from one area of the studio to the other, during the "Bumps"/bumpers which bracketed the segments; these were colorful graphics I had prepared containing the names of each segment, the showing of the graphics and background music just allowing us enough time to switch costumes and studio-areas. The reason for all of this, was because we were doing this "Live-to-Tape", in other words, no editing! The technical staff from CVW were a pleasure to work with, part-time professionals and volunteers who truly made us look good. By my seventh season, and second incarnation of the show, "Magic Mike's Castle", editing, and even pre-recorded public service announcements were allowed, along with more professional "bumps"/shots of my castle. In the beginning of my magic career, I called myself "Merlin", eventually "Michael Merlin", then "Magic Michael Merlin", Magic Mike Merlin" and finally just "Magic Mike", which I was known as for the duration of my stay in Winnipeg! There was even an upscale pinball arcade in a suburban Winnipeg mall, started by a fellow magician/fan, which he called "Magic Mike's"! Needless to say, I would work with them somewhat, doing mall shows to promote myself and their store.

The "Kiddie Cabaret" TV-show format went for three seasons, until Roxanne and I separated, upon which time I lost most of my cast, who supported Roxanne; Darren segued with me into my new show, "Merlin's Magic Castle", voicing the two puppets, "Desmond the Dragon" and "Forgetful Lion". An aspiring actress and singer portrayed one of the castle's inhabitants, "Screwball The Clown"; she would do a walk-on, sporting minimal clown make-up and my old "Scribbles" black-and-white polka-dotted costume and its pointed-hat; pulling her pet toaster on a leash behind her each week, and subsequently singing to it, she was accompanied by a local professional folk-musician. This new format, literally put together in a week around my birthday of July 1989, had a chroma-keyed castle-interior background, as there was no time for me to build and paint the new set, which would come some months later; at the time, I was touring throughout Manitoba, dissolving my union with Roxanne, and dealing with temporary housing, which Arthur provided for me, my belongings and large props being stored in his huge shed in Charleswood. It was understood that I would find a new place to live in the fall.

The television program continued to evolve, eventually switching in the last three seasons of its run, to a non-medieval theme, and taking place during the present time, renamed "Magic Mike & Company". This came about as a result of my three-year, weekly appearances on a broadcast-television kids show starring a Juno-award-winning local radio and television celebrity. More on that shortly. Suffice it to say, his show supposedly took place in the present, not medieval days, in his set, an attic, so I felt obligated to adapt my own show with his in mind, for my public appearances. He also had a puppet-companion, voiced by the brother of a former cartooning student of mine, an extremely talented puppeteer. In fact, I had asked these two several years previously, to be part of my pilot, a re-vamped "Magic Mike's Castle" with brand-new and larger, Muppet-like "Desmond" and Forgetful", fashioned by this ex-student of mine, and voiced by himself and his brother; one of the musicians from the feast played the live music segment, and the entire affair was penned by my friend and floor-director of my current "Magic Mike's Castle", "Sandra", who is now a successful and famous horror novelist. We came very close to selling the show in a nearby town, where one of the province's major television stations was situated. They were interested, but then opted out last minute. I had a similar occurrence with a potential "Magic Mike Magic Kit" that a major corporation had approached me about! This corporation also owned the St. James-area hotel where the feasts were produced! We got so far as to agree on the percentage split, and which tricks would be in the kit; the corporation shortly afterwards declared bankruptcy, effectively not only putting an end to the kit, but to their name. They eventually re-emerged with another, similar name, but shortly went under again.

My careers nonetheless continued to flourish, which included my fledgling mail-order magicians supplies business, caricatures and cartooning, and magic-shows. Finally on my own in my own apartment on Corydon Avenue near Stafford, I was excited for my future. It was too bad that Roxanne and I had completely different goals, and that those differences had finally torn apart the marriage. I was confident that the right thing to do was to let her go so that she could pursue a permanent relationship that would include children, (I didn't want any at that point in my life) which was the main point of contention. Neither of us would budge on this, and she certainly deserved to have everything she wanted. Spirituality was another major issue, as I had recently received "Knowledge" (four traditional mystical, or "contact" meditation techniques) from a mahatma, (thanks to Arthur, himself a follower of his own teacher, a famous 1970's "Guru", Arthur having guided me in his direction) and this was the true, conscious start of my goal of experiencing "oneness" with "God", at age twenty-nine. I was always of the Buddhist/far eastern belief that God is within each of us, and I was determined to "know" and experience this Higher Consciousness, as I had been teased at experiencing when I was younger, staring at my parents' wooden floor, and leaving my body during my adenoids operation. Things metaphysical were around me now, which I could relate to because of my mediumistic mother and my own gifts, which I was experimenting with and attempting to develop at this point, also thanks to a friend's gift to me of a pack of Tarot cards. She was a Tarot-card reader at a well-established dessert place on Portage Avenue when she wasn't trying to break into show business; this establishment featured several readers, or "psychics". I was torn on the whole subject of "psychics," as the few psychics I had met were odd creatures; also, because I was a professional magician, and we as magicians are familiar with all of the techniques that the fakes, fraudulent psychics and con-artists use; Roxanne, a complete skeptic, had a cousin who apparently did fraudulent mediumistic readings somewhere at an establishment on Main Street, donning a kerchief and grabbing a crystal ball when a potential client would walk in. Yes, I was torn alright, but my heart said to continue on with my spiritual journey, practicing in my spare time how to read the Tarot by rote, as well as using my intuition; I believed that I was experiencing God through meditation as light, sound, my breath, and a secret mantra. I was feeling more and more fulfilled personally, professionally, and spiritually. I began re-reading my books on Zen, and I also started studying Wiccan practices which excited me because of my love of nature, including trees, stones and rocks, gemstones, and crystals, which the practice honors; the idea of "spell-casting" never appealed to me, but the medieval "trappings" of hoods, cloaks, and wands appealed to my sense of theatrics and stage magic, which I began to work into my shows; I even donned, thanks to that same friend's support, a beautiful dark-blue wizards' robe with waist rope-tie as my costume at one point, eventually moving onto bright red wizard costumes complete with silver sparkly stars and the compulsory 1980's shoulder-pads! I finally settled on a "Robin-Hood"-like costume, complete with brown leather hood, green-scalloped vest, brown suede knee-high boots, medieval belt and magic-sword named "Albion"; (after the prop in a 1980's British television series, which I was obsessed with, thanks to the "witchy" trappings and atmospheric music provided by an Irish folk-group.) I was feeling empowered, having finally found my onstage persona which was also "me": I'm convinced to this day that I had numerous past-lived during medieval and Renaissance times, hence my relating with, and obsession with all things medieval/Renaissance. The jester from the feasts was also instrumental in introducing me to books on making authentic period costumes, which I did do. Realizing that I wasn't a route to fame as she visualized it, my friend who gave me the cards eventually disappeared, marrying one of the techies from CVW and relocating to the U.S. somewhere!

A Cartooning Feather in My Cap

Another feather in my cap (in my Political Cartooning career) involved yet another weekly community newspaper.

A referral from Sam of the downtown newspaper (the mayor of Winnipeg at the time enjoyed my cartoons, and asked Sam for the originals, which Sam subsequently gave to him which he then had framed and put up in his office!) and this resulted in me starting to draw cartoons for "Val", editor of this new weekly community newspaper, at least new for me; we worked well together, often almost "reading each others' mind" as far as the visuals for that week's particular cartoon; she would give me the topic, or even punch line, and what I came up with almost always coincided with her vision! It was a pleasure working with this intelligent, well-read individual; she would also allow publicity stories for my magic career, as the downtown newspaper did, often publishing the stories under her own pseudonym! She even insured that I was commissioned to design the pink flamingo logo, for a local suburb's seventy-fifth anniversary! This logo appeared on T-shirts, hats, badges, and much more, and this was indeed a great credit for my resume as well. Val and I attended the gala celebration as well. A note: the pink flamingo was the suburb's "mascot", since the insider's joke was that many people in that suburb had dozens of plastic pink lawn-flamingos proudly displayed all over their lawns!

Another professional credit was my commission to illustrate a series of four or five books on Mentalism published by a major magic book publisher/retailer based in Calgary. This excited me for my love of magic and illustration, having to combine both for this project! I dealt with a Vancouver magician who headed up that city's branch of the publisher in the 1980's, which I enjoyed doing immensely, as he was professional and amiable! What a thrill it was to see those finished illustrations within the series of books! What a thrill it was as well, some years later, to actually meet the "legendary" "Michael Helstrom", during a lecture he gave at one of the local magic clubs. One of Michael's "claim to fame" is his still unparalleled wooden finger chopper, a totally examinable magic-prop which is actually gimmicked in a way that does not result in the amputation of a spectator's digit. Very clever indeed.

About The Three Separations

It came as no surprise, mainly due to the previously-mentioned differences in our overall life goals, that I left Roxanne; three times, in fact! One time being October of 1987, then October 1988, and the final time, (as a famous television comedian once wisely said, it "takes by the third time") October 1989.

Each time we reunited, with the promise of us going for relationship counseling and therapy, and making some progress each time. Unfortunately, and despite having worked out techniques such as "Non-Blameful Communication" and finding mutually-agreed-upon activities, and using the techniques from the book "I'm O.K. You're O.K.", in other words, "Transactional Analysis", I found that these were for me at least, temporary, band-aid solutions, and the bottom-line was, I had outgrown her. I wasn't even sure that I was interested in having her as a friend. Yet our social circle was completely unaware of all of this, we having previously hosted several work-friends parties at our home, and even a "goodbye party" for our friend Allen, who was relocating to Vancouver from Winnipeg. No-one suspected my unhappiness and growing discontentment with our relatively depressingly boring domestic routines. I felt dead, and her idiosyncrasies were quickly wearing more and more on my nerves. It wasn't her problem, I recognize, but the question was "how worth it for my soul was it to hang in there and make efforts to plaster the ever-growing cracks in the relationship?" At the time, I also had a "wandering eye", and so that each time we separated, I started a new romantic relationship, which almost always fizzled quickly. I left behind several good female friendships, and unknown to them, they were caught up with me in my dramatic, and addictive nature. All they were looking for was true love, and each time, they were disappointed by my flighty, irresponsible character. Perhaps I myself was looking for that "pot of gold" in them, some sort of similarities that only we shared, but I was always disappointed by this kind of thinking.

The last friendship, at the end of October 1989, around the time of my final marital breakup, was completely different! We were actually just good friends with a great mutual respect that I had not experienced with another female friend, except perhaps with Hermiome. "Victoria", myself, and her daughter (who bore a striking resemblance to me back then, what with our long, black hair and slim physiques) we apparently still do to this day, according to my present wife! Upon a recent business visit to Winnipeg from Vancouver, Victoria's now twenty-something-year-old daughter even wore the same kind of glasses as I used to, drove the same brand of car like we used to, and even to this day plays guitar, apparently owning a dozen or so! I too own several guitars!

In those days, (the late eighties) the three of us would walk around malls, and shop together a lot. Her then four-year-old daughter once called out to her mum, "Toys For Us, Toys For Us!" pleading for Victoria to take her to the local "Toys R Us"! They even attended a magic-show I did at a Winnipeg mall October of 1989, with a jealous Roxanne (I was ending my marriage with her that week) still in tow, and commenting to me, "What did you do to her to have her so in the clouds as she watches you perform?" Roxanne was overreacting, and for me, I was so done with her attitude; why couldn't a friend come to support me at one of my shows? Did there have to be some tawdry reason behind this? No, I was done, once and for all with Roxanne!

I would often be invited to Victoria's husband's parents' family dinners in Charleswood after the separation, and I was always made to feel at home. My favorite Indian cuisine was always served, which I enjoyed to no end! Victoria was one of the waitresses at one of my favorite watering-holes, a "blue's bar", just down the street from one of my favorite deli's. I had recently designed the business cards and T-shirts for that delicatessen, each bearing a caricature of the eccentric owner, "Uncle Steve".

Victoria also worked by day at a dental supplies business, with another female who would eventually be my future girlfriend, and with whom I would relocate to Vancouver with! It was thanks in no small part to Victoria's friendship, that I kept strong enough to not back down from my final separation with Roxanne! I'm grateful for our friendship during that time, to this day. She also introduced me to a younger female, hoping that this would turn into a long-term relationship post separation, but alas, the age-difference did get in the way. I ended up having her best girlfriend be my room-mate, and we shared my $600.-a-month rent at a large home on Grosvenor Avenue, after the Lanark home was sold. I loved this house, just a hop-and-a-skip from a metaphysical bookstore, and the always-helpful owner, who would occasionally give me little things from her store. There was (and still is) a very handy convenience store, which back then boasted being an award-winning franchise, for its decor and then-fledgling specialty coffee-drinks! Personally, I enjoyed their nachos and gyros, especially after a "night out" of drinking and dancing at either the blues bar, a local family restaurant/bar in my neighborhood, (ironically now completely renovated to house a chain of another family restaurant/bars!) and/or any of the three slightly-upscale family restaurants/bars which are now defunct! A note here, that the former had a location on Granville Island in Vancouver, when I first relocated here in 1994! Who would have thought?

This same former franchise, a location of which I would also frequent in the early nineties with my friend Mary Ann (she, by-the-way, was my friend Allen's ex-girlfriend; small world, huh?) Allen, as previously mentioned, relocated to Vancouver five years before I did, in 1989, leaving the recently divorced Mary Ann to date, and eventually marry a wonderful man! To this day, we are all good friends, including my current wife, communicating occasionally via phone and/or Facebook; Marry Ann even recently visited us to see her brand-new grandchildren! Years before in Winnipeg, and before her second son from her current husband, Mary Ann and her son by her first marriage came to a taping of "Magic Mike's Castle", for which I was grateful; they had apparently enjoyed seeing a TV-show taping. I am thankful for the friendship and support offered by both Victoria and Mary Ann during my third separation, without whom I may not have had the strength of conviction!

For whatever reason, (perhaps because I frequented one of their locations) that particular upscale family restaurant/bar (which also featured a soup-bar!) began to offer an alcoholic beverage called "Mike's Magic Elixir", which I don't believe I've ever tried! Flattering nonetheless. Unfortunately both of the aforementioned two restaurant chains are gone, replaced with two new ones.

What a Lifestyle!

After a night of dancing circa 1992-1993, I would return home from one or all of the aforementioned establishments, sitting on my couch and munching on those convenient store nachos or a gyro, eventually falling asleep on my couch while watching "The Kids In The Hall" at 4:00 a.m.

It was at this home, that my magic-shop quickly evolved over four years, from a mail-order business in 1989 to a "real" shop, moving from room-to-room, eventually ending up in the largest room of the six-bedroom, two-bathroom home, complete with several counters and shelves. The Winnipeg magic community was very supportive, giving me regular business, tandemly with the magic counter at a large, local toy store in the Old Market Square area of Winnipeg. This magic counter had a very fine selection of tricks, and was "manned" by very fine local magical enthusiasts. I expanded my mail-order department thanks to an idea given to me by one of the guests at my friend Hermiome's Montreal wedding around that time: a magic catalogue on video-tape, (VHS and BETA) sold through magicians trade magazines for a mere $5., and the real profits coming from orders garnered from the myriad of tricks demonstrated on the tape. I believe that I was the first magician to offer a magic catalogue on tape, circa early 1990's. Between my television show, the Juno-award-winning host's kids' TV-show, my live appearances doing magic or caricatures at $250. an hour, and my shop, I was at my peak of happiness and financial status, having just traded in my 1982 red Hyundai Pony for a candy-apple-colored 4x4 "Sidekick", which I just adored, and which would get me through the harsh Winnipeg winters with ease!

The Divorce

The natural extension of Roxanne and my one-year separation by 1991, was of course, the "Get". (Yiddish for the "divorce") Besides, the renewal of our co-signed mortgage on the Lanark home was coming up that June, and there was no way that I wanted to co-own anything with my ex; we would have to "go for" the divorce soon!

Of course, Roxanne tried to get me to pay for both the civil as well as the "Jewish" divorce, which cost considerably more. This "Jewish Divorce" was important and necessary for her, in case she remarried one day another Jewish person, which by Jewish Law, she could not do without the "Get". For me, it was not so important, and by then, I was living with "Katarina", a non-Jewish friend of Victoria's; both of them worked at that dental supplies business during the day.

The time came for the "Get", and Katarina was waiting for me in my car, outside the synagogue. Roxanne had paid for this divorce, while I had paid for our civil divorce, which I believed to be the "real" one, since it was a civil, legal one. I was soon to learn otherwise! A rabbi (not the one who had married us) stood before us, describing the ritual: we were to wait and watch as a scribe calligraphies a parchment in Hebrew, effectively stating that I am "rejecting" Roxanne. Then, this parchment would be folded up, and I would have to, using a ritualistic, ancient-looking knife, slice an "x" in the parchment, as Roxanne and I stood side-by-side, with the Rabbi presiding. This didn't seem so difficult, nor complex, besides, I hadn't seen Roxanne in more than a year, maybe even two years! She felt like a stranger to me at this point, and appeared different to me than I had remembered her. Regardless, while the scribe wrote, the rabbi asked that Roxanne and I sit in his chambers, beside each other to chat. We did. There was silence. As I looked at her, suddenly my mind was flooded with only the good memories of our union: when we first met, the honeymoon in Florida, laughs in Toronto with good friends, the move to Winnipeg and the start of our new life together. Overcome with emotion, I wept. She merely sat there, with a stiff upper-lip, in martyr-like fashion. Her coldness snapped me back to the present, and I remembered all the times I felt detached from her, with us having nothing in common; I remembered her indiscretions in Toronto, and how she once called me condescendingly and sarcastically, "A good little housekeeper"; I remembered her envy at my ability to earn the same salary as she was earning full-time, at something she couldn't wait to retire from, but part-time, and at things that I loved doing; I remembered that Friday night, when after five years of being married, I actually said "no" to her and the Friday-night dinner at her parents' home: I had had enough of cold, tasteless chicken and peas, never served with a refreshment of any kind, (I always had to ask for water) every single Friday for five years! Yes, I was grateful for her parents' efforts, but the ritual had become so predictable, down to the yellow "Jell-O" for dessert, and then during this, her mother declaring that once again, she had forgotten to serve the cole-slaw, bringing it out to show us in its over-sized plastic container, and then promptly returned to the fridge, where it may have remained until the following week, forgotten, and then again remembered, only to be returned once again to the fridge! Five years of this, with very little variation! Like clockwork every week as well, the four of us would retire to the family-room, where we watched, unwaveringly, "Falcon Crest" and "Dallas", which her mother appeared to enjoy. It was one of the few things that this woman appeared to enjoy in life, her anxiety-filled voice and facial expression still burned in my mind. All that was missing was the wringing of her hands, as her husband played the "together" and calm one of the pair. The whole relationship and their interaction appeared forced and mechanical to me, something that I hoped would never happen to me and whomever I was married to when I would be in my sixties! Nonetheless, I said "no" to Roxanne that night for the first time, standing up for myself, and the fact that I had a deadline first thing the next morning, and more than a hundred ad layouts to complete for a full-color, slick, sports magazine, published by the owner of the weekly community papers that I was employed by. No, this time I would not return home, bored and depressed at 10:00, and began my work until the wee small hours of the morning, only to rise early and hand-deliver the finished ad layouts to their office. I said "no" politely and matter-of-factly, adding that she would have to go, this night, by herself to her folks. Something snapped with her, and she began, with closed fists, to pound and pound on me, mostly my head and shoulders and back; this hurt more emotionally than physically, and also felt somewhat humiliating, so I grabbed both her wrists, and pushed her off and away from me; she called out, "You beat me up! You beat me up!" her eyes ablaze with anger and humiliation as well. I realized at that point that something was not right: not right with her, and not right with "us", and it was that night that I knew that we could no longer be; I had endured the pain and humiliation of some physical abuse growing up from my mother, I was not going to repeat a pattern. There were hints of Roxanne's potential for abuse, even back in Toronto, when I would act silly, and she would take a few "swipes" at me, to shut me up. I had ignored and suppressed these things, but tonight I was done; it was the beginning of the end, which mercifully ended five years later during our subsequent separation and finally here, in the rabbi's office.

Yes, I snapped back to reality, these past events overshadowing the good things in the union. I was strong again, and sure of all of this. With conviction, I said to her, "Let's get on with this, I have things to do today!" I also had in mind Katarina, who was patiently waiting outside in the car. Roxanne nodded to herself, with that familiar look which silently said, "Of course you do!" We exited the rabbi's chambers, the scroll already written and ready. Standing before the rabbi, we repeated the words in English that he prompted us to say, as he mumbled some words in Hebrew; the time came for me to slice that "x" in the folded parchment, and I did it, mercifully, with conviction, and with finality with each stroke! It was done, our marriage was over in the eyes of civil law, as well as in the "eyes of God". The ritual having concluded, we departed the synagogue.

I had never slept for so long in my life after this; upon returning home to my Grosvenor rental, I lay on the bed on my stomach, not awakening until twenty-four hours later! Dazed and disoriented as I looked at a clock and my calendar, I could barely believe that it was the next day, and then it dawned on me: there was a "spiritual severing" of the marriage, not just a legal, civic divorce, but a true severing of two people from each other, and the bond that united them made by God! This is what caused me my physical exhaustion, and that day I realized that this "Get" was the "true" divorce. I vowed to never put myself or anyone else through something like that again.

The Broadcast Television Kids' Show

Some time had passed, and I was feeling more and more empowered. It was the winter of 1991, and during a book-reading for children and drawing caricatures at a major St. James-area shopping mall, it happened! Despite my avoiding calling the Juno-award winning star of the kids' TV-show asking him for Darren and I to appear on his show, fate would bring us together, just as things that are meant to be happen despite ourselves!

The studios were right beside mall, and as he was hurriedly passing through on a break, I simultaneously turned away from my easel to go on my break, and "bam", we both ran right into each other! Immediately recognizing this as "fate" turning its heavy hand, I pulled out my business-card, saying to him, "I'd like to guest on your show, I could do caricatures and magic!" Smiling and nodding, he said, "You're Magic Mike, I know who you are, sure, here's my card, call me tomorrow!" He hurried off, his dimples and warm, receptive smile remained in my mind, as I also recalled the sparkle in his eyes. There we go again, all the signs: I was relaxed, "up" and happy, open enough for the next major turning point in my life to be received, loud and clear, just like the recreational park in Toronto, the syndicated comic-strip, and my TV-show! Even the downtown newspaper, the string of community newspapers, and much more I allowed myself to receive, thanks to me "working with the Universe", and "getting out of my own way"! Another miracle, although I never saw it like that back then! I was so closed to matters spiritual and metaphysical; my now close friend, Darren, a First Nations person, tried and tried to teach me and share things that are part of his culture, and which his grandmother, a "wise woman", had shared with him. What an honor for me, but I had no clue. He tried to get me to relax by going fishing with him, but I declined; he took me to one of the forests, Assiniboine Park, to relax and "feel" the energy, but again, I was so full of myself, that I blocked this subtle "feeling". We laugh about it today, but I must admit that I feel embarrassed at how close-minded I was back then! Others might justify it by saying that I wasn't "ready" yet. Nonetheless, I had acquired (or "given"?) a second television-show regular spot, this one on a "real", broadcast-television channel, seen throughout Manitoba and parts of the U.S. I was over the moon again! After my first appearance, (I drew a caricature of the host, I believe) I got invited back to do more drawing, and even do a brief "teach-in" segment. I asked him if I could do magic on his show, to which he agreed, resulting in me being one of his permanent, weekly guests to his popular show! The only other local kids shows more popular was a certain bearded children's entertainer on CBC, and my own, which ran a quick third, on CVW Cable 11. (formerly "CVW 13") I was now on two television shows, guesting periodically on other local shows, also on CVW 11. My show was starting to air three-times-a-week, and evenings, with the current , new episode on a Wednesday at 4:00 p.m. (against "Inspector Gadget", whom many kids chose over my show, understandably) and the last week's show airing on the Thursday at 4:00 p.m., Saturday mornings at 10:00 a.m. was the current one that aired the previous Wednesday, or sometimes one from two weeks previously. The point was, I was all over television! Once, while walking through the electronics department of a local department store, I saw my show airing on all of the televisions at once! All the TV's were tuned to CVW at the exact time my show was airing, and when I was walking through! Coincidence? I would sometimes be mistaken for "Ephraim" from the a major Winnipeg group of rockers, who had just gained global fame for their "Superman" song. The video for this song often aired at night, and he and I both looked very similar, even unintentionally dressing similarly, with knee-high boots, tight black jeans, and "poet-shirt", our long black hair framing our thin face, we were also small-framed and shorter in stature. Sometimes people would come up to me and say "Hi, so-and-so!", and they wouldn't believe me if I said that I'm not him. More often than not, with both TV-shows, I was even more easily recognized everywhere, with knowing smiles and glances, and even requests for an autograph for their children.

On a return from one of my regular visits to Montreal, I was standing at the luggage carousel at Winnipeg's airport, angry, sad, ungrateful, and resentful to be back in a city which I judged back then as not being as "cosmopolitan" as Montreal; I used other words to describe it, which I still regret to this day. Suddenly, a woman standing nearby with an infant in her arms and smaller child beside her, said to me, "You're Magic Mike, aren't you?" Suddenly, my whole demeanor and energy transformed, as I beamed in delight at this "angel" which God was moving through at this moment. "Yes, that's me!" I began to tear up, as she said to me, "My son watches your show every day and even made his own "Magic Mike" costume, with boots and a sword! He draws, sings, and performs magic thanks to you!" Suddenly, everything was put into perspective for me, and beaming once again, I signed her requested autographs. Another time, at a caricature job at a community centre in River Heights, as I was drawing, a twenty-something year-old female and her parents approached me, having noticed my "Likey" signature on the drawings. The mum asked me, "Are you the same "Likey" from that recreational park in Toronto?" I confirmed this, and she continued, "My daughter here, had you draw her back then and she still has it framed in her room!" I was filled with gratitude, and emotions of pride and thankfulness, as I proceeded, at her request, to draw her a current one! I could barely see past my own tears to draw her. All of this meant so much to me, not because of fame and being "recognized", but for in the ways that I impacted on people, whether with cartoons or with magic. How many other kids have their caricature framed on the wall? How many other kids are emulating "Magic Mike", inspired to draw, sing, and do magic? I never forgot these further "signs" and reminders from God, Infinite Intelligent/The Universe that all is working the way its supposed to, in the way that its supposed to, and that I'm on-track doing my "Soul's Purpose", or what I'm meant to be doing. How could I have forgotten this, some years later, and left Winnipeg? Everything seemed to be perfectly and smoothly functioning, with an overlapping of all of my careers too: I used my drawing skills to create Magic Mike coloring pages, and for the displays and packaging in my magic-shop; I donated prizes from my magic-shop to special events and causes, and even had a "draw drum" in my shop for people to enter the contests and promotions I had on television; I even had as prizes for my contests items donated from those two chains of family restaurants/bars, as well as a certain kids' festival, I felt that it was a way to give back to my public, which allowed me to eventually buy two homes, as well as the venues that gave so much to me, either socially, or professionally, as I had always, on and off in my years in Winnipeg, done magic for these three sponsors. Yes, all was well, but unfortunately, and as usual,, not with my personal life!

Katarina VS. Adriana

A couple of years had passed, and cracks began to form in the concrete of my relationship with Katarina. I grew weary of her; she was creative and pleasant enough, and even voiced a new puppet on my TV-show when I had temporarily fired Darren. She was always creating new crafty things, and enjoyed her new floral design job with a major U.S. grocery store chain. I suppose I craved more adventurous social outings with her, and we had grown into a bit of a domestic "rut".

For whatever reasons, I developed a close personal relationship with a female, "Adriana", with whom I was now spending most of my free time with. It's thanks to Adriana, whom I knew from one of my dance clubs, that I gained confidence as a medium, frequently conversing with her dead mother, A translating the Italian words which I supposedly heard from her mother in spirit. I suppose I liked Adriana's continental style and attitude, which reminded me a lot of Montreal and my childhood there. We also went out to many bars and clubs to dance, which I had done with all of my other female friends before Katarina. Nonetheless, and in retrospect, I realize that my many nights away from Katarina was probably hurtful for her, but my selfishness at the time blinded me from this. I believe that some people thought that Adriana and I were an "item", but this couldn't be further from the truth, as we were only platonic friends, like Hermiome and I were, and many others. There was something fulfilling about my relationship with Adriana, but I soon realized that it was creating a number of rifts in my relationship with Katarina. Adriana went through a few lovers, and I was there to counsel, advise, and to comfort her; I even made a song out of a poem she had written years before, called "Mystery Friend", which eventually appeared on one of my albums. I also developed a similar friendship with another female that I knew from the blues bar, named "Wilamena". We enjoyed drinking and dancing at local clubs, and eventually she relocated to Victoria, on Vancouver Island in B.C., where (as far as I know) she is still living with her boyfriend.

Certainly all of these extra curricular activities were straining my main relationship with Katarina, to whom in the early part of our relationship, I informed that I would never marry or have children with; when we met, she was already engaged for ten years to someone she wasn't happy with, making it clear to me that she too, didn't want children. In retrospect, I believe that my not wanting to wed her may have been hurtful as well. again, I was very "dense" in those days, and I probably still am.

The Traumas of 1993

At this point, I was at the height of my careers, although business at my magic-shop was declining, due largely to the fact that my customers were now ordering and receiving their tricks quicker from shops advertising in magic magazines; my suppliers took two to six weeks, far too long for magicians, many of whom are spontaneous-shoppers!

Resentment on my part began to build, as I sat alone now for many hours in my home-shop, when I could have been out earning $250.-$350. per magic-show! Unfortunately too, I had informed my agents to put the breaks on giving me shows, as I wanted to concentrate on my shop, which theoretically was going to be my retirement plan, as was the case in those days for most magicians. Where were my regulars now? Where was "Magic Jackie"? Where was "Martin P.", son of famous Winnipeg musician/producer "Ralph P."? Ralph P. had supplied me years earlier with rare, blank 15-minute (each side) cassettes for my 1990 debut album, "Magic Mike"; amiable and efficient, I'm grateful to Ralph for his business acumen. Where was "Steve W."? Actually, both Martin and Steve have honed their skills and today, they separately live and perform regularly in Las Vegas, one as a hypnotist, the other performing large stage illusions! I remember when both of them, then fledgling magicians, purchased several of my larger illusions, including my "substitution trunk" which I had originally ordered from my friend's Florida magic shop! How far we've all come. Nonetheless, I made the decision in 1993 to close my mail-order magic supplies business, as well as my retail location on Grosvenor Avenue in the Fort Rouge area, near Wellington Crescent. I must admit to feeling resentment at having to do this, and even handed attendees to the last day's below-wholesale-price "Stock Clear Out" an article from a magicians' trade journal; the gist of the article was how many brick-and-mortar" magic shops were closing thanks to the "big guys" on the Internet and in magazines who could provide faster (but not personalized) service to the customers. In very recent years, many famous magic shops in North America have gone under for the same reason! Vancouver shops never seem to thrive, and always shut their doors even after a few years. What is it about these B.C.-ers and their "no-fun" reputation? Could the relatively smaller population and scarce funds be the real culprit?

Regardless, my income was rapidly declining now, in 1993, except for, thankfully, the family restaurant/bar, which hired me one-night-a-week to do Tarot readings for the patrons, free for the patrons; this was my boss's idea, "Marsha", in order to hang onto me, and not have me move away to Vancouver, which I told her I was thinking of doing since I was tiring of Winnipeg's winters! Her eyes widened in terror when I told her of my tentative plan, and then she cried out, using expletives and what I was sure was exaggerated rumors about Vancouver. To be honest, there was a rumor I regularly heard about Vancouver, besides it being expensive. Even Darren spoke of this same reputation to me, informing me about an infamous historical character, who used to own a home on Vancouver Island. Nonsense! Superstition for sure!

I remember a fellow magician friend of mine, "Bob", who had relocated to Vancouver, only to return five years later to Winnipeg, looking shaggy and full-bearded; he was none-the-worse-for-wear, and he told me about his difficulty in earning a living there, so he had to drive a cab. Months later after his return to Winnipeg, a clean-shaven Bob walked into a store I was in, happy and smiling with his new girlfriend, back to his old, glowing self again, obviously thriving once again! These incidents, and the owner of my favorite Winnipeg deli informing me back then of all he really didn't know about Vancouver. He denies ever having spoken ill of the city to this day, himself and his wife and grown son having relocated to Vancouver in recent years.

Nevertheless, the family restaurant/bar paid me $200. for two hours to sit at a booth in my favorite dance-club and wait for patrons to approach me for a reading, which, by the way, became very popular, with line-ups of (mostly) women wanting to know if they "were getting laid tonight"! It was a living, and paid my rent, and also paid for my brand new, candy-apple red 4x4 "Sidekick" with white, convertible roof! I checked with Marsha from the restaurant/bar before I invested in the new vehicle, asking her to give me a month's notice before letting me go if she could; she dismissed this with a "You'll be here forever", but something told me otherwise! In return, I "threw in" table-to-table magic for the restaurant on Sundays.

I was informed that year that the nine-year run of my CVW TV-show was winding down, what with the CRTC changing it's public access policy, and all locally-produced kids' shows ending, including "Fred Penner's Place" CBC show, and, yes, even the broadcast-television kids' show I was on! I was losing both long-term "gimmicks" to my fame, and all I could see was "loss" during that time, rather than being flexible and going with the flow. I was shaken to my core, and rather than simply approaching a few businesses for more magic-shows, I felt frozen, shocked, and too scared to approach businesses as I had done previously on "cold calls". My head reeling, I decided that I needed to create a new gimmick, which would be a brand new music album. I busied myself writing a dozen songs, a local producer taking the time and energy, no charge to myself, to start to record one of the songs, which he guaranteed one of his closest friends, a radio station manager, would play! Daily for a month, I went to his home studio, trusting him that all of his meticulous care and fussing, all of those hours, would pay off.

The day came, one cold day in January of 1993, as I headed over to pick up my weekly check from the local family restaurant/bar. It was the only steady and dependable pay-check I had at the time, and I had just, days earlier, made that request of Marsha about giving me a month's notice, which she had dismissed. I found it odd, as I approached the building on Grant Avenue, near the shopping mall, that their parking lot was empty. I could hear the "cracking, cracking" sounds echoing from beneath my boots of the snow as I approached the front doors of the restaurant; the sky was grey, overcast just as it was on that first day I visited Winnipeg in 1979. Then I saw it, as I reached for the handles on the front doors: a thick, black chain, wrapped multiple times around the door-handles, to keep out those who longed to gain entrance into this den of happiness; I shook and shook the doors in disbelief, as I noticed the paper taped on the door's window; it was a notice of "Repossession". Sure, the restaurant had gone through several owners, but these last ten years were the longest it had carried on with one owner. This place, my "home away from home", my source of gainful and joyful employment, this place of music, alcohol, dancing and "acceptance" during my recreational times, would yield its doors to me no more. Never again. All that now existed were the ghosts of happy days and nights passed, spirits flowing and spirits dancing, flirting with one another, engaging in mindless chit-chat, the bar-man smiling, giving me endless beers "on him"; surely this wasn't over, the playground where I met and mixed with my supportive social group; surely it wasn't over, the television in the bar playing the kids' show when I was there, or "Magic Mike & Company" when I was sipping a cold one during the day, reading Marsha's or Adriana's tarot-cards. all of the dancing, all of the music, all of the other local celebrities sitting, conversing, drinking, laughing and smiling, all finished? My head reeled, as I slowly made my way back to my beloved "Sidekick"; how was I to pay for it now? How would I make my rent? How would I tell Katarina, oh, wait; she wasn't around any more. A cold wind blew in and around me, and for the first time in my life, this shivering feeling didn't feel refreshing and cleansing. I tried to control my feelings of anxiety, as I took stock of my life, void of magic, void of employment, void of the television shows, void of "life" or so I thought back then, not realizing that this was actually all a "blessing", a good thing, as God, The Universe, Higher Intelligence was in reality clearing a path for me to take, on the road to Greater Heights, which I wouldn't have been able to see without the clearing away of all of the bracken, and a soon-to-be "re-paving" of my life's path. I was being "coerced" towards something more long-lasting than anything I could ever have imagined, but during this time, all I could see and feel was trauma, loss, and emptiness.

I severed my business relationship, some time after, with my potential producer; one morning, when he finally played back some of the tracks that took us weeks to "perfect", I heard it; it was an infernal "hissing" sound, quite predominant, behind everything: behind my multi-layered vocals, behind the musical tracks of my guitar and synthesizer, and so, something just snapped at that moment. I asked him, "What's that sound?" His reply was simply, "I guess I forgot to use the Dolby." Shaking, restraining my emotions, I put my guitar back in its case, snapping shut the hasps. My only and last words to him were "Thanks, but no thank-you", as I quickly made my way out the door of his home, and onto the cold January, snow-packed streets of Winnipeg, towards my candy-apple 4x4. I drove towards my home on Grosvenor, again pondering my future as I gazed up at the overcast winter's sky. I felt sorry for myself, mistakenly believing that viewers of my television show, or even of my live, in-person shows, didn't really know (and therefore like) the "real me": I believed that people liked only a "mask", a shadow of the real me. Years later, I realize today that that was okay, since my "Magic Mike" persona actually was part of the "real me", one of the many mythic characters/extensions of myself within my subconscious-mind that Jung might call the "magician" or "miracle-maker"! I believe that all of us posses on that "collective unconscious" level of our mind, due to social conditioning, as well as hereditary factors, images of devils, angels, saints, gods, and other archetypes such as the "hero", the "villain", the "whore", the "victim", the "seeker", and the "magician" among many others; I had studied this broadly-accepted belief through my studies of Jung, Freud, and metaphysics years later.

Yes, 1993 was quite the year, with Katarina and I separating several times, her moving out, me moving downstairs to live in the one-bedroom home in an effort to get used to living differently should I move to Vancouver. I didn't like living in this smaller abode, no sir, not one little bit. I gazed out my window, which was partially obscured by the newly-falling snow. It felt at that point that all I had to look forward to was forty-below and snow; that and unemployment; I couldn't see that I had really lost nothing, that my reputation of twelve years was still intact, and that I could acquire gainful employment in an afternoon, as I did when I first arrived in

Winnipeg. All I could see was loss. Gone now was the downtown newspaper, the weeklies, even the Jewish newspaper. Gone was the medieval feast. Also gone was my magic shop. More importantly, gone was my current (and last) place of gainful employment, the restaurant! I heard tongue-in-cheek rumors around that time that the restaurant/bar regulars wandered the streets, looking for a place to dance and drink, this came from Adriana, who also grieved the brass-railing-lined, tiffany-lamped establishment, with its tropical foliage in the atrium by day, and the top-forty music blaring at night, the smell of beer running rampant; I had become a martini-fan near the end of the restaurant's run, which they served in breakfast-bowl-sized martini-glasses for $7. All of the realtors drank martinis there, so I felt acceptance by joining them in this ritual. Before its demise, I drank at the family restaurant/bar seven nights a week, to "escape", more aptly to "avoid" confronting Katarina about my unhappiness with our relationship. Where she went or what she did when I was out, I couldn't care less about. I remember returning earlier one night, with her not being home. Eventually she did return, wreaking of alcohol.

I decided to phone Allen and reconnect with him and his "goings on" in Vancouver! I had to find out if this was the place for me or not, never having visited it before. All I knew of that city were the abundant beaches and semi-clad women in bikinis that I had seen on television, while I watched the always-hip on-air broadcaster, that city's famed ambassador and television personality. Allen answered his phone. "I've never gone a day without making money out here!" he declared. "I'm wearing shorts and flowers are coming up now", he responded during our January conversation about Vancouver's weather. I was intrigued: warm and career-potential for me, but, "Would you and your wife be willing to keep me until I got things together out there?" to which he gave me an affirmative response. I was all set; I could look forward to starting again in a brand-new city that didn't have minus forty winter temperatures! I didn't have to move to Florida or the Bahamas to have a nice climate. I made up my mind then and there, thanking Allen and wishing him well, as I hung up my phone. I would start a brand-new life in Vancouver.

But not just yet. Not that easily, either. The following year would prove to be more than hectic, to say the least!

1994: The Year I Left Winnipeg

Early 1994 was upon me, and I did the occasional magic-show to get by, but I still felt like I had been hit by a truck: nothing was the same! I even had two house-guests: Darren, who had split up with his wife, and Arthur, who had just returned from London, England, having survived a relationship breakup with a younger woman. One slept on my floor, the other on my couch, each taking turns at that. In retrospect, we were three sad bachelors, filled with hope and unrealistic expectations. I had recently begun yet another relationship, this time with a female with the same name as Katarina! She was our server at the now-defunct family restaurant/bar years earlier when I was still with Roxanne; I liked her style, looks, and sense-of-humor. We sort of connected back then, but neither of us followed up on it, as I was married, and she was happily single, having sex on the bar after hours with various partners, she informed me. She was "Banquet Supervisor" at a major, upscale hotel, and I was always invited to be her date at some of her work functions there, which I enjoyed. Her room-mate was well-mannered and intelligent, although I had the feeling that she spied on us during intimate moments in the living room late at night; it might have only been my over-active imagination, however. After several break ups, (I didn't like her bossy manner with me, nor her tendency to dominate and control various situations) I called it quits permanently, but not without trying to iron things out, which she said she liked about me: I was playing the part of our counselor while actually participating in the relationship as well. One morning I returned to my Grosvenor residence from this Katarina's place, when my other Katarina came by at my request. We talked, and we talked, and I liked the maturity that Katarina was showing, especially her newly-acquired independence, after all, she came out of a ten-year relationship to be with me, and that doesn't always bode well. Regardless, we hit it off, since she seemed almost like a completely different person whom I was willing to get to know again. Most importantly, she felt more like my equal now, someone I could depend on, quick-thinking and resourceful in times of a potential crises. This was now my criteria for a viable partner, not just looks, but intelligence, being well-read, creative and quick-thinking; above all else, loyalty. Believing and seeing this in Katarina, we moved forward together.

I left my Grosvenor residence, where Darren and Arthur remained, until the upstairs, larger part of the duplex (my original residence) became available; it was there that Arthur, his sister and brother-in-law from Florida, and Darren moved to.

I moved into Katarina's apartment near Stafford and Corydon, the same building where our mutual friend "Mary Lou" lived for many years. Mary Lou is still a good friend whom I saw at a book-signing I did seven years ago in Winnipeg. A fascinating collector, she had magazines from the 1960's stacked up in her apartment, with newspaper clippings of the Beatles' arrival in Canada taped to her walls. Crafts and materials strewed the living-room, where she built props for theatrical productions, gratis. She lived on welfare, gathering bottles and cans for money between 5:00 a.m. and 9:00 a.m. every day, down neighborhood alleys. Generally happy and fulfilled with her life and aging cats, I once gave her $200. to put together my new

"Magic Mike" castle-set; she did a better job than I did when I painted my original castle set. She constructed realistic-looking torches which she Velcroed to the castle wall! Amazing attention to detail! No wonder she was always in demand by several local theatre companies to construct their props!

Nonetheless, Katarina and I progressed in our relationship again to the point that we decided to buy a home together, with our parents' help. We secured the property, a small house with a basement right on Corydon, again near Stafford, as that area was in development and was expected to be a major trendy, Italian area, with bistros lining the street, so I felt that this would be a great investment in the future. We purchased it in May of 1994, with June being the move-in date. Before then, though, I felt the need to visit my parents in Montreal and have a rest from all the changes. At the last moment, I felt anxious about the flight, (on one previous flight to the Bahamas from Florida, on a prop-plane, turbulence and oxygen-masks dropped down on the final descent, leaving me traumatized, with a permanent unease with flying altogether) so I gave my ticket to Adriana, so that Adriana and Katarina could both go together and have their own vacation; I was hoping for them to bond and to feel comfortable with each other, but more importantly I wanted to get my mum's impression of them as people. Upon informing my mother that Katarina and Adriana were coming to Montreal without me, my mother exclaimed, "Are you crazy?" Still not sure what she meant by this, nonetheless, her opinion of Adriana was: "She's too wild for you!" She liked Katarina, however. Upon their return to Winnipeg, Adriana told me of the night they went to a dance-club in Montreal. A reported to me, "She let guys be all over her!" I wasn't sure how accurate this feedback was, so I simply ignored it, never confronting Katarina about that night in Montreal. At least Katarina didn't "disappear" with anyone for any length of time, according to Adriana, so I was alright with everything, after all, I was no "angel" myself!

A Quick Vacation Alone In Montreal

I overcame (at least temporarily) my fear of flying; or at least, my desire to go back "home" overshadowed the flying anxiety! My parents bought me a ticket, and I was on my way in May or June of 1994 back to Montreal.

I stayed in a hotel recommended by my uncle, saying that if I mentioned his name, I would get a great discount, which I did. It was one of several famous motel-chains or some such, near the airport, and the first thing I did was lock my door and lay on my bed. I turned on the television, and I watched in silence as a white Ford Bronco, not unlike the one Hermiome drove many years before, was being chased by police cruisers in L.A. What was going on? I later learned that it was the beginning of a long criminal trial that would last for at least a year after I relocated to Vancouver; a famous athlete was accused of horrendous crimes. It looked that way, at least, as he fled the law.

It felt so good to just lay there with not a care in the world, for the first time in many years! My anonymity was quite a relief, Montrealers not recognizing me from my local Winnipeg television shows and appearances at just about every major function there. It felt great to simply go to a K.F.C. outlet and take home a chicken dinner and eat it whenever I wanted to! That night, I dropped the empty box into my waste-paper basket, flipping on the television again. I fell asleep watching the first season of "Frasier", recognizing him from the recently-ended "Cheers" show, which my local family restaurant/bar made a night of, airing that final episode the year before, as I sat in the lounge, reading people's tarot-cards!

I was awakened a few hours later (3:00 a.m. to be exact) by my phone's shrill ringing. I had called one of my friends, and a few other Montreal pals the day before, leaving the hotel particulars in the hopes that they'd call me. I was sure this was one of them calling, they being "night owls". "Monsieur, would you like a blow-job?" asked the voice at the other end of the phone. I chuckled, and replied, "Very funny...how are you?" The angry and insistent response was, "Monsieur, this is no joke, would you like a blow-job?" This being a very liberal Montreal, I realized that this potential "booty call" was not out of character in a situation like this. I declined the gracious invitation nonetheless, for many reasons, sharing this (what I considered to be humorous) incident with others over many years.

The visit with my parents was all too brief, as I could only afford to stay in Montreal for a few days. Little did I know that this would be the last time I would see my father alive, and in good health! We all made amiable conversation, my father smoking his trademark cigar, and with my mother (as usual) trying to convince me to permanently relocate back to Montreal, and to also get back together with Roxanne, whom she apparently liked. As usual, I emphasized this would not be. They confirmed that they would help me out financially a little, until I got back on my feet, and they also agreed to contribute $5,000. towards the mortgage's down-payment, Katarina contributing (also with her parents' help) an additional $5,000. Feeling secure with my parents' continued emotional support, and my self-reassurance that I was not a "Winnipegger", or had "Become like them," as my father feared years previously, I was on my way back to a place that today, ironically, I consider to be my true "home", despite Montreal being my place of birth!

We took possession of our new home on Corydon Avenue that month, with Katarina going to work at the American grocery-chain daily, and myself fixing up a room in the house as my new tarot "consultation office", complete with comfy leather office-chair, fax machine, business-looking phone, and two chairs for guests! My filing cabinet added to the cozy, yet professional atmosphere I was trying to create. It felt good, I even added one of my old glass display-cases from my magic-shop, with prop mock-ups of a book that I had "written" on Tarot, a few decks, and a mock-up of an original Tarot deck that I had designed. Little did I realize that I was being premature, having actually "seen" what was to eventually physically come to pass in Vancouver; it all felt very familiar, comfortable, and "right". The next step was to actually gather Tarot clients! I considered an ad in the local papers, or even in one of the famous "scandal" newspapers, but I didn't want it known that "Magic Mike" was "reading Tarot" for some reason; perhaps the public's stigma about matters superstitious? Perhaps it was the stigma of the very skeptical magic community? Regardless, I opted instead to make a fair-sized sign, taping it to the living-room's window of our house, complete with phone-number, in the hopes that it would attract the attention of people passing by on this busy street. Katarina had the desire to transform the front living-room into a tea-room, complete with Persian area-rug, and wall-hangings, Tiffany-lamps, etc., where people might come to savor a hot cup of tea and have their fortunes read. I liked this somewhat old-fashioned, romanticized vision, which I, too, held in my mind! I transformed our semi-finished basement into my graphic-design work-space, and all was coming together. I vowed to myself to not be distracted by Adriana and her personal problems, nor my friend Ray, who was unhappy with his twenty-year-old city-clerk's position, getting embroiled in petty office politics and bullies. He didn't have the psychological-education I was privileged to have obtained thanks to Roxanna, so he didn't know about Transactional Analysis, and how to deflect immature and petty conflicts. One day, after numerous voice-mail messages from both Ray and Adriana, I decided to put an end to all of this, hopefully empowering the two of them in the process. I recommended several books to both Adriana and Ray, even supplying them with these particular books, one of them being the still-popular "I'm O.K., You're O.K"; I asked them to not contact me until they read the books thoroughly, and so, that was the last I heard from them until we moved to Vancouver!

As days passed, and no potential clients called nor knocked on our front door, I began to feel disenchanted again, wondering if things would ever improve business-wise. Perhaps I should design an eye-catching newspaper ad for my fledgling business? Performing magic and drawing cartoons were now the farthest thing from my mind, oddly enough. A famous local psychic and friend gave his boss a referral for me to work at the brand-new, upscale dining-and-Tarot restaurant in the ever-growing warehouse district. I'm still grateful for this potential employment at this place! Having subsequently successfully completed a reading for my friend's boss, (who also owned a legendary restaurant on Portage Avenue) I was immediately hired, and the feeling of elation and hope continued until I learned of the financial arrangements: a 60/40 split, with my receiving the 40% for several dozen readings a day, at $15. a piece! A quick calculation told me that this would not be worth my while, so I gratefully declined, thanking everyone for the offer. At least I now knew that I was "good enough" to do readings professionally, not just because a friend had hired me for their establishment, as Marsha and the deli-owner did, and to whom I am still both indebted!

This still left me with a new mortgage for us both to pay down, plus payments on my relatively new, beloved 4x4, and no foreseeable income per say! For whatever reason, I didn't think to just go to several restaurants to perform magic at, as I had previously done; I couldn't think straight, and so I began my old pattern of descending into unhappiness and resentment again, with low-self esteem as a base!

One day, while watching the last episode of "Star Trek: The Next Generation" on television, it hit me! The episode was about the captain, whom, while laying there dying, stated that he had no regrets about never trying anything new; in other words, although he went for something that resulted in his death, he at least didn't play it safe, as he did in an "alternate-world" scenario in which he chose to remain an underling and not go for the captain's position! Smiling, and with a satisfied and a knowing grin, he passed away. That did it! I felt that if I remained in my "comfort zone", I might never grow, nor ever have the opportunity to become more than I had ever dreamed I could become!

I started to consider selling our home, after two months of ownership, to rid ourselves of the mortgage-debt, so I called my friend Mary Ann who was now a realtor! She was more than happy to oblige, and so after discussing this with Katarina, I also added that perhaps we should move to Montreal, where I could surely obtain gainful employment as an artist and performer, after all, magic was still riding a wave of popularity, and Montreal paid top-dollar for variety performers of all kinds! We got more and more excited about this prospect, and then one day Katarina showed me this self-help book she was reading, offering to buy me my own copy if I wanted to read it too. I couldn't get past the picture of the author on the cover and her smug, smiling face! It was like she knew something I didn't, (which she did) so I immediately rejected the offer, quite literally "judging the book by its cover"! I would eventually come to love this book, devouring its "New Thought" (not "New Age") philosophies and interpretations of "A Course In Miracles", later on in Vancouver, it helping me cope through my father's death. Little did I realize that eventually, I would write and publish globally more than forty books of this same ilk, after having obtained several Ph.D.'s in metaphysics. But at this moment, I rejected most things before they rejected me! I was tired, and had enough; I really wanted a true, "fresh start"!

The Plan

We mutually decided to sell the house and relocate to Montreal. I had a vision of doing caricatures in Old Montreal, as research I did during my last trip there, speaking with the artists on the street confirmed potential for me to make double or triple that I ever made at the Toronto recreational park, with the long season starting in April or May, and finishing in November or even December! The license-fee was extraordinarily reasonable, considering the potential financial return for caricatures! I would "get by" for the remaining three or four months on social assistance if need be, but certainly doing cartooning, and signs as I had done previously, perhaps even acquire a contract or two with a local newspaper again! We never discussed how Katarina would get by with the large French-speaking population, but she liked Montreal now, and I assured her that she could acquire gainful employment through the two-million English-speaking populace that existed there, likely getting a floral design position at one of the numerous floral shops there.

I also decided to "cover our butts" by constructing a small set with a medieval theme, complete with wooden interchangeable signs that read "Magic", "Caricatures", and "Tarot", very big in this medieval-garbed, hippy populace of Old Montreal! I was excited! I was bilingual, and we now had several plans, and could connect with my aging parents in person whenever we wanted. Katarina was very flexible and willing with all of this.

One day it dawned on me; what was the main reason for our relocating? The answer was without doubt, Winnipeg's harsh winter climate! How much more different was Montreal's climate from Winnipeg? Minimal at best. I started to make some phone-calls days before we were set to relocate to Montreal, having packed up everything in my new used van, trading in my beloved Sidekick 4x4, and having given away most of worldly belongings, keeping only that which would fit in this long, deluxe vehicle. Our two cats, "Paisley" and "Tyffin" would also have to endure the cross-country drive with us, as well! I called David, who was the most well-travelled of us all, who described Vancouver as "rainy". Another friend and ex-lover of Mary Ann's described his home-city as "depressing", which is why he left Vancouver. I had in my mind all of the negative feedback I had heard of this west-coast city, and was frantically looking for some positive feedback; I remembered what Allen had said, so I called him again. "Yes", was his response, "You'll never go a day without making money," he reiterated. "We'll also let you stay with us, rent-free until you're on your feet!" That did it! Vancouver, with its temperate but rainy climate and limitless financial opportunities would be our destination, not Montreal as everyone else believed!

Mary Ann informed us that our home had finally sold, with Katarina and I splitting the $350. profit that it accrued after only three months of ownership. An Italian entrepreneur had purchased it, and he and his son would renovate it, making it ready to be zoned as a bistro! Before leaving for Vancouver, we had a look at the amazing renovation job they had done, even making a parking "pad" for four or five vehicles behind the property! On top of that, Mary Ann (as promised) waived her full realtor fee, which would have left us at a financial loss! I'm still grateful to her and her husband, who also stored our remaining belongings in their garage until we were ready to depart.

Removing the majority of our belongings from the house was no small feat, and quickly became an exercise for me in feeling loss and mourning, not so much because we gave away our living-room furniture (including my beloved roll-top desk and Lay-Z-Boy recliner to a needy senior, nor my donating my office furniture to my friend and TV-show peer Ray, but because of the "loss" of my drafting table, art supplies, and magic costumes! In reality, I donated my table and art supplies to Darren's mother, a "mitzvah", or good-deed, but it sure felt like I was throwing away a part of myself, even though intellectually I knew otherwise; it was still all about how I "felt" at the time, and it felt like a "death" as I gave away most of my "Magic Mike" costumes, feeling like that part of my was dying! I gave my big red neon "Magic Mike" sign to Darren, who promised to donate it to the Magic Museum in Clandeboye, Manitoba, which also housed a performance stage and theatre, and an R.C.M.P. museum, as the owner was also a former "Mountie". Nevertheless, and despite knowing that this was all for the good, I had a profound sense of loss and mourning which I never dealt with until years later in Vancouver. Even "leaving" Adriana created a sense of mourning our friendship, she later admitted to me. With our former home cleared out, and remaining belongings loaded into our "Voyageur" van, we were preparing for our departure, occasionally looking at the van, parked on Grosvenor, in disbelief that our entire "life" was sitting out there in such a relatively small and compartmentalized space. As fate would have it, I also ran into Victoria while shopping at the local department store at Grant Park Plaza. She gave me a hug goodbye, and asking me to pass that on to Katarina. I finally felt some degree of closure with this.

We had a month between the evacuation of our home, and the day that we agreed upon with Allen and his wife, that we would arrive. I decided to charge up my credit-cards further to allow us to: A) Rent a motel-room in St. James until our departure, and B) Provide us with enough finances for the actual physical journey. (which included gas, food, and more hotel rooms) I wasn't worried at all about paying down my five credit cards upon our arrival in Vancouver, as long as there was as much work for me as Allen had suggested. The "Voyageur" van, a second-hand, but deluxe, extra-long and roomy vehicle would be our mode of safe transportation across the prairies and over the Rocky Mountains. It had cruise control, air conditioning, and electric "everything's"! We were fortunate to trade in my relatively-new, beloved Sidekick 4x4 for this older vehicle thanks to a bank which organized the re-financing of it. I was greeted with a "It's Magic Mike!" as soon as I entered their premises, my television "fame" preceding me. The loan/re-financing was thus easy to procure, even though I would now be making payments on a vehicle worth considerably less than my 4x4, at four times the cost! No wonder they were so happy to re-finance everything for me! My ex brother-in-law was currently a used car salesman at a St. James car dealership, and was more than gracious and helpful in showing me a number of potential vehicles based on my needs for the move. Recently, he, his three children and his wife (Roxanne's sister) had relocated to Winnipeg from Israel.

To further cover my butt, and with the help of Arthur and his friend Annabelle, we recorded my second album in the twenty-four hours straight, no sleep, before we departed for points west! Arthur played amazing bass-lines on his "Beatle-Bass", his beloved and used "Hofner" guitar, which he purchased at a Winnipeg pawn-shop for only $50., Annabelle and I playing synthesizer and guitar, and myself mixing the tracks at the engineer/producer's home. This album I eventually released as "Mys'try", containing the song that Adriana had penned and which I had set to my music. I released it several times over the years, both as a cassette, and later as a "digitally re-mastered" CD. I re-released it again in 2016, it being the twentieth anniversary of its original release. I had done the same with my self-titled debut album, which I re-released as a digitally re-mastered CD on its twenty-fifth anniversary of its original release!

With our worldly belongings and cats in tow, the day came, and hugging everyone and bidding everyone a fond "adieu", we set off on the adventure of our lives, never again to be the same.

5 VANCOUVER
1994-PRESENT

The journey itself, although taking only two or three days, was a hellish affair, seeming to take much longer, what with the cats cavorting around in the van, and Katarina and I constantly bickering. It was around September 23rd or so of 1994, and thanks to one of Arthur's friends, we were given free room and board overnight at her home on our way westward. There was no doubt at this point, though: I was stressed, second-guessing our decision to leave Winnipeg. All of the things that my friends had said about Vancouver was now swimming around in my mind, creating a vortex of turmoil, fear, and uncertainty. Katarina's attitude began to resurface again, and I began to seriously doubt her ability to hold up her end in a number of areas of our supposed and proposed western life. I felt like a pioneer of sorts, "breaking new ground" with our worldly belongings in the van. Various scenery passed before us, as well as various times of the day, from early morning to early evening; exhausted from continuous driving, (Katarina had no driver's license) we agreed to have me drive only eight hours a day, during the day, with rest-stops and overnight breaks at motels along the way. The cats would be smuggled into our room, their food, water, and litter box neatly set up in a corner of the room, until our early-morning departure. This would mean it would take longer to get there, but I didn't care anymore about that. All that I knew now was the constant feelings of regret, loss, and mourning. I was about to start a new life, in a place I had never seen before! How different could it be from Montreal, Toronto, Winnipeg, or any of the other major cities I knew in North America? At least there was no winter as I have known it previously to be!

Finally, we reached the highway which was about to take us over the Rockies and into British Columbia; I paused and took a breath, or was it a sigh? The appearance of the mountains since we approached them from Alberta were breathtaking, and somewhat imposing. Closer and closer the mountains appeared to approach us, and we were experiencing an anxious anticipation which was now over-shadowing our petty squabbling, the cats being seemingly oblivious to it all, happily playing with each other throughout the journey, except for the times that they slept, which was frequent.

We were "straddling" the mountains now, via the highway, which carried our precious cargo over it. I must admit, that during this time, the view was as if it was straight out of those old, gothic horror movies: a single, tall mountain peak being surrounded by shreds of clouds, the peak thrusting up and out in a frightening mountainous erection of sorts! All that was missing was the thunder and lightening! This intimidating and depressing sight seemed to be a foreshadowing of future impending disastrous events, and it actually turned out to be that way in time! A feeling of anxiety gripped my heart now, yet again, like icy-cold fingers surrounding, and then slowly squeezing my heart until every last drop of life from it was gone. I'm convinced that I was consciously experiencing a shift in energy between Alberta and B.C., the Rocky Mountains being the gateway (or Gate-Keeper?) containing a sign which might have read "Enter At Your Own Risk"! Katarina seemed oblivious to this all, smiling confidently to herself; the cats played on.

Whether the Rockies act like a giant crystal amplifying everyone's negative energy, or whether or not the plentiful ancient native burial grounds located throughout B.C. harbor "evil spirits" which influence one's moods and ill fortune, I do not know, not even to this day. I jest here, of course, attempting to mirror the beliefs and superstitions of a very small segment of the local population. One example was of a female friend that I was sitting with, a year after my arrival, at a local bar in New Westminster, facing the boardwalk; my friend Jackson wheeled by quickly on his specially-made bicycle, he himself being a paraplegic. He was intelligent, well-read, and a leader and advocate for local differently-abled individuals, with several medals and college degrees. He spoke at many colleges, universities, and high schools exactly about responsible behavior and drug-taking. He was also the author of a best-selling book. Immediately, and very matter-of-factly, my female friend snapped, "Oh, he's so irresponsible! Dangerous and impulsive!" I asked her how she knew this, and her reply was, "Oh, you can just tell! Look at him!" I was floored! Was this an isolated incident, or indicative of more?

There was no doubt in my mind, I was "no longer in Kansas". I chalk this "mis-judgment" up to a younger environment that B.C. is, after all, it is the youngest part of the country, being the most recently settled, versus Quebec or Ontario having been populated and settled in the 1400's and

1600's. There was much more time for the people in these two eastern provinces to evolve, eventually adapting to and accepting immigrants from all countries and races.

Through decades of observation, the mentality and priorities are different here from cities to the east; rather than putting their young children in more arts/culture/entertainment activities such as ballet, painting, sculpture, piano, etc., as some of my peers from Montreal, Toronto, and Winnipeg did, some of the parents here put their children in more physically-oriented activities, such as outdoor activities and sports, at a very early age. Generally speaking, people are more oriented towards outdoor activities such as kayaking, mountain-climbing, and careening off the side of mountains, etc. mainly because of the beautiful (and accessible) nature here, (as well as more temperate climate) as opposed to the colder, indoor-activities-oriented eastern cities. This being said, skiing does exist (as well as snow-shoeing, snow-boarding, etc.) to a large extent in the eastern provinces during the winter, as the geography (with mountain ranges and great forests) also exist there; it's just that it can get so darn cold out east! It can discourage a timid heart from braving the winters outdoors! Not that being physically healthy is a bad thing, I'm just saying that a balance between indoor (arts and culture) and outdoor activities (sports) in B.C. would be great; I suppose the high cost of indoor-activities could make them somewhat prohibitive for some. But things are getting better and better here.

I have heard first-hand, people in Vancouver refer to themselves as "laid-back", but many are far from that: many are stressed by the higher gasoline prices and cost of homes. What a pity; such an overwhelmingly beautiful and breath-taking city, financially beyond the reach of many!

The driving here is an entirely different matter as well! When I moved out here in 1994, the traffic was somewhat faster than Winnipeg's pace. Upon returning to Winnipeg a few years ago for some book-signings, I actually found the pace faster in Winnipeg! Recently, a newspaper article revealed that they were going to increase the speed limits here, (Vancouver, B.C.) in an effort to "speed things up"! Apparently others, too, have noticed a slowing down here, so now a potential solution is being offered.

I was confused at the manner of driving out here when I first arrived, and the following is still relevant: Everyone keeps at the same pace, in effect "boxing" everyone else in. Don't get me wrong: I love driving here, where generally drivers are way more cautious than in other cities! (although Vancouverites would disagree with me) Here's the thing: when someone tries to pass, they'll speed up, preventing this from happening. It's as if they're all moving en masse at the same pace, no-one in particular wanting (or allowing) others to "get ahead" or further. This is almost a metaphor for many (but not all, as I have seen a few exceptions here) and their philosophies, and I do have fun playing with the local driving patterns. Often, bored in needless bumper-to-bumper traffic, (there are never that many cars at a time on the road, they merely insist on keeping that steady, boxed-in pace!) I'll signal my intent to pass, or begin to speed up, to get the guy in the next lane to competitively speed up (which they do a lot of here, as well!) That's all; I just like getting the person in the lane beside me to speed up! It works every time. Since rarely will I be let into the next lane to pass the person ahead of me, rather than signal first my intention, (always resulting in that "speeding up"!) I'll do a shoulder-check, and just scoot in! It works every time! They hate it, but I don't care! I do it safely, and quickly! In Montreal, where drivers pick no particular lane, cut you off for no particular reason, and drive at a pace unparalleled anywhere else, except for, I'm told, on Germany's Autobahn, just try to cut over several lanes on a highway in Montreal, with trucks going 200 kilometers an hour behind and beside you! I challenge you! You sort of have to get into the "feel" or pace of traffic there, cross your fingers, and just "do it"! It works every time! Miracles are accomplished daily in Montreal traffic! If this is too much for your delicate constitution, perhaps you should retire to a cave! (or just not drive in Montreal) Perhaps this too is a metaphor for life, ascribed-to by some of us: Just do it, without worry or concern!

Nonetheless, with my so-called "sense-of-humor" and "driving skills" still relatively intact 25 years later in Vancouver, I continue now with tales of trials and tribulations during my early years here.

Early Years

Interestingly enough, from the moment we crossed over via a North Vancouver ("North Shore" as the locals call it) bridge, landing upon those shores, I was positively impressed by this delicate-looking town, framed by the natural beauty of trees, mountains, and such. It still reminds me (geographically) of my Montreal and Quebec in general. Would these pristine, man-made structures survive "the big one"? (an earthquake) Some here do not concern themselves with the impending big earthquake, predicted (and severely over due) for many years. I suppose that if someone commits to living here, they are required to avoid the potential for obsessing over this impending natural disaster. Why worry over something that may not happen in our lifetime?

Nonetheless, I pulled into the parking lot of a nearby storage facility, parking the van. After securing storage-space for our furniture, we proceeded to unload everything, and then locking it up. The person who was attending the counter initially, reassured us, after we shared with him that we literally just arrived from Winnipeg, and stating that the people here were "mostly nice". I felt comforted. We phoned Allen, who gave us directions to his nearby home.

Allen and his wife lived above an alternative school. She had earned her teacher's degree with them, and was one of the educators at this institution. When we pulled up to their home, parked, and got out of the van, Allen rushed to us, hugging us both happily and patting me on the back. He seemed sincerely happy that I was there now! His wife remained at the entrance to their home, quietly observing everything and giving us both the "once-over". She was a tall, dark-haired woman with sharp features and a fit build. Standing there with arms crossed, she sniffed, and then led us into their house. "This will be your room", she stated matter-of-factly, gesturing with a sweeping motion towards the mattress on the floor and the open closet; I found her German accent both familiar and reassuring somehow. I suppose it was because my mother was Jewish, of Austrian/Russian descent. Nonetheless I noticed that the bedroom window was wide open, with no screen; all of the windows were like this! I inquired about bugs, flies, and insects in general making their way in. They both looked at each other, and smiling, Allen said, "We don't have any flies here!" I didn't realize at the time that he was probably kidding me, so I took that to be true. In retrospect, nary a bug nor creepy-crawly thing found its way into our room! His wife had graciously prepared some "natural" vegetarian cuisine that was completely flavorless; this reminded my of the vegetarian cuisine I had enjoyed vegetarian cuisine with Roxanne years earlier, when we were both vegetarians. Nevertheless, the food looked great, consisting of a myriad of colors and textures. Unidentifiable to me as anything familiar, we ate everything, gratuitously complementing her on her fine cooking. It dawned on me that night, that his wife, unlike Allen, was completely involved with all things holistic and natural, a completely foreign concept to me; she seemed healthy and happy, so I immediately embraced and accepted her belief in such a lifestyle. Allen, however, carried on with his own habits and lifestyle under their one roof. That included frequent trips for nachos (as we did years before in Winnipeg) and fast-food, prohibited by his wife to be brought into their home, for fear of "corrupting" their young son, "Little Allen", who was two at the time. He is approaching thirty today! Their arrangement was that his wife would work during the day while Allen watched his son. On weekends, Allen would earn money "busking". I had never heard this term before, but quickly learned that a "busker" was a "street entertainer". In other parts of the world, street entertainers are highly regarded for their skills and the romantic nature of their "career" and lifestyle. I had witnessed these world-renown entertainers in Old Montreal, and was impressed by the fire-torch-juggling, unicycle-riding entertainers, who would perform amazing acrobatics and other feats requiring years of practice and perfection, and who would also earn upwards of several thousand dollars a day in Montreal and New York. Quebec's famous

"Cirque de Soleil" got their start that way. Toronto's street performers were sparse, I suppose because of licensing bureaucracy, which that city was infamous for. Allen's plan for me (unknown to me at that point) was to take me to his favorite busking spots, in the hopes that I would earn money doing "street magic" and/or caricatures.

I slept, it seemed, for hours and hours a day, and I found myself exhausted my first three weeks out in B.C.! Furthermore, I found that simple walks in Allen's Lynn Valley neighborhood simply exhausted me! I was very fit, but I seemed to get "winded" regularly for my first two weeks. I attributed this to the heavier atmosphere/energy out here. Others said it was because Vancouver/"Lower Mainland" is actually below sea-level, causing some sort of atmospheric pressure effect. Regardless, I felt a repressive sort of energy then, and ever since my arrival twenty-five years ago. Things seemed to shift that way at that specific point in time as we were making our way over the mountains, as described earlier. Katarina seemed completely unaffected, even happy and enthusiastic, and therefore quickly acquired a job as a Floral Designer at an upscale West Vancouver mall, serving such luminaries as one of the stars star of the Canadian television series "The Beachcombers, who weekly bought flowers for his wife!

I however, spent the next few weeks going to a nearby "Starbucks" with Allen, discussing our former lives in Winnipeg, and what he loved about B.C. I asked him to show me places where I could work, and to connect me with people he knew who might help me do magic show, caricatures, etc., and so he introduced me to the manager of a little market by the water in a suburb of Vancouver. I was excited to put on my "business outfit" consisting of brown narrow wool neck-tie, blue denim dress-shirt, jeans, and brown tweed blazer. My rimless round glasses topped everything off, and so with resume in hand, we made our way to the market by the water.

The Market: Early Days

Liza, the manager, was certainly an affable woman, with graying hair, and a tall, dignified stance, manner, and attitude. I could feel her compassion as she shook my hand, and invited me to sit down.

She looked over my resume, smiling. Allen, who was sitting beside me at that point, made eye-contact with me. I had the same expectations based on my previous experiences that I had had in Montreal, Toronto, and especially in Winnipeg: the management would read my business and marketing plan for them, which then would usually result in me being hired by them to do magic-shows and/or caricatures, maybe even organize special events for which I would get paid on top of my drawing or magic services; this always resulted in a great influx of business to the particular mall or business involved, leaving me with a hefty paycheck of several thousand dollar for a week's work. Smiling and standing up, Liza then shook my hand again, saying, "Do whatever you want here; I'll take 40% of whatever you make, and I'll require weekly reports of your financial income". That was it. Nothing further was ever spoken between the two of us until a few months down the road. I was in. I could start any business I wanted to do here, and I felt that the sky was the limit. She asked Allen to take me downstairs and to show me around.

The market was a thriving, bright place, with customers and business-owners smiling and bustling about. It felt like one big family to me, and it turned out to be so. It also reminded me very much of "The Forks" market in Winnipeg, down to the wooden signs, fruits and veggies stands, and coffee outlets. Granville Island had a similar area, which I had visited a few days previously with Allen. A huge, garage-style door (really a multi-windowed, whole wall) opened up to the boardwalk, where buskers played tunes on electronic keyboards, and jugglers juggled. Singers strummed and played their guitars, all of them having the proverbial (and quite literal) hat on the boardwalk before them. Customers to the market sat out on the boardwalk, enjoying the sun, the entertainers, and their coffees. I felt excited to be part of all of this, thanks in part to Allen, and to of course, Liza.

"You can set up anywhere around here", stated Allen, gesturing to the small area between some kiosks and a coffee shop. "What do you mean?" I asked of him, somewhat apprehensive. "I'll be over there, doing the "Mechanical Man", and you can make balloon-animals here!" I was stunned and confused. "I'm supposed to busk?" I asked. Images of years of agents calling and faxing me with contracts for thousands of dollars worth of business doing what I loved flooded my head. But I was here now; the expectations were such that I would make balloon animals for pennies. How would I pay down my $35,000. debt incurred while making my way to B.C.? This is all that went through my now-anxious and panicky body.

"You'll make a lot of money, don't worry", Allen continued. "On some summer days I even make $20.!" I almost fainted. His reassurance was well-intended, but his idea of a "good financial day" and my definition was completely different. I had left thousands of dollars a week doing shows, drawing caricatures, and minor fame, to come here and experience relative anonymity and poverty? How would I pay for my van? How would I pay down my credit cards? Allen had never had such responsibilities, generally living here from hand-to-mouth. I looked out at the performers on the boardwalk: their clothing now seemed tattered, to me, and their body odor wreaking! They seemed to be desperately "begging", or, "busking" for their next "meal", and Allen was friends with most of them. A man walked in from the boardwalk, approaching us; he had been playing classical music on his elaborate keyboard. He sported a large top-hat with a feather in it, long tuxedo-jacket, and even longer, greasy, stringy hair. He looked like a horror-movie undertaker to me! As he smiled at me and Allen, I noticed several of his teeth were missing, and others were grey. "This is Magic Mike", he introduced me, "He's from Winnipeg!" I cringed when the performer shook my hand affably, not because we made physical contact so much, but because, yes, I arrived here from Winnipeg, but I wasn't originally from Winnipeg, I am a Montrealer! It was as if Allen was trying to draw me down to a street-level, encouraging (even helping) me to become part of this street-performers fraternity. I was further shaken up, likely over-reacting to all of this, I started to have a sinking feeling. I felt suddenly like I was in a deep, dark hole, with no chance of escape to see the sunshine ever again! Rather than me being grateful to Allen for taking me here, and feeling love and acceptance for my fellow performers, I felt utter horror and repulsion.

Today, I'm embarrassed to admit all of this, this judgment that I had towards other human-beings likely doing the best that they could, under circumstances that I could never fully understand; instead, I reacted with judgment, no compassion, nor a semblance of gratitude. I was completely and consciously unaware of all of this, and so, with fear, judgment and resentment below the surface, I reluctantly set up my caricature easel the following day, sitting for hours and hours on end, customers mirroring my subconscious feelings: people scurrying on past me, glancing down with judgment, derisively sniffing their nose as me! Unbenounced to me, my subconscious biases were likely being mirrored in the faces and body-language of the people around me! Had I been a bit more spiritually aware at that point, (or even self-aware!) I perhaps would have worked on myself and these issues. Instead, I went days on end sitting there to no avail. I became disenchanted after a month of this, not to mention more fearful of the bills that were adding up! Allen had me set up my caricature-stand at several other locations, including on Robson Street, in front of a large chain drug-store; dozens of other buskers and artists lined the streets back then, including several other magicians, fine artists doing portraits in charcoal, and an amazing, long-haired male painting huge, multi-colored galaxies with spray-paint only, on huge paper laid out on the street, several feet back from the curb. I had never seen anything so well done, and so quickly! Little did I realize that this was the height of Vancouver's "golden age" of street performers, and years later in retrospect, I feel honored to have been a little bit a part of this, which eventually vanished from the streets. I did well, earning $80. an hour drawing caricatures for the visiting tourists. Allen advised me previously to put a sign up which read, "By Donation", so that legally I required no license to do caricatures. I noticed all the other buskers did the same thing. People "donated" $10. or $20. at a time for my drawings, but all I could think of was the hundreds of dollars a day I had earned drawing caricatures at Toronto's recreational park! I didn't even notice that I was actually earning more here, and quicker, and for less effort! I continued on with my subconscious negative attitude which probably attracted this next event, at Granville Island.

As part of introducing me to potential busking spots, Allen kindly and enthusiastically took me to his beloved downtown Vancouver market spot. At this point, I was earning a few dollars on Robson Street, but very little at the suburban market; this location could prove to be not only fruitful, but also necessary. "Here", he directed me, "You can set up over here!" As I did on Robson and the other market, I opened up my easel and paper, putting up my "By Donation" sign, opened up my two camping stools, and unfurled and taped to the edges of my easel several samples of cartoons I had had published in newspapers, which would hopefully entice potential customers. I stood there, feeling confident and optimistic on the outside, almost arrogant and challenging, as if to say, "Well, c'mon, I don't have all day! Why aren't you lining up for me like others before you?" despite subconsciously waiting for "the other shoe to drop", which, naturally, it did! As I glanced around, judgmentally observing the other buskers, some of whom appeared brash, yelling at potential customers to watch them do God-knows-what with a rope, it happened! Two middle-aged, white-haired women, well-dressed, rushed at me, each picking up my easel in their hands, lifting it up and quickly carrying it away, stating matter-of-factly, "You can't do that here; you have to go through our judging committee!" Shocked, and feeling violated and humiliated, I ran after them, scooping up my camping stools and knapsack, Allen following quickly behind. I, nor my work, had ever been "judged" before, let alone been before a committee of what, little old, grey-haired women? What could they know about art? Were they educated in Montreal, and ever have any of their works published ongoingly in many world-centers? These judgmental and uncompassionate thoughts flooded my head, all at once. I just wasn't getting it back then, that as soon as I judged someone, the same for myself would almost immediately come to pass, mirroring my attitude! If only I had known then what I know now, I likely wouldn't have panicked either! In fact, had I been the person I am now, all of this probably would not had to have happened! Regardless, they dropped the easel down on the ground some distance away, and without any further explanation or even an apology at their rudeness and judgment, they scurried away, back to their office, I assumed. Shaken up yet once again, I stood there frozen, feeling as if I was going to cry, Allen now at my side. "I'm sorry, Mike, I didn't know!" "What do I do now?" I asked him. "Come with me", was his reply, as he helped me with my easel , and scooting around the corner to a window/ticket-taker sort of booth. The man behind the "cage" seemed sensitive, his smiling face greeting Allen with a, "Hey, Allen, what's up?" Allen's reply was, "This is my friend Mike;

can he set up here?" "Sure, no problem" was the courteous response. I thanked this gentleman, again following Allen around yet another corner, to a more colorful, juvenile-like area. "Set up here", Allen again directed me. "Are you sure?" I asked, since I was still shaken by the events just a few minutes earlier. "Oh yes", Allen replied, "That was the director of the "kids' market"!" I felt relieved, and finally exhaled after several minutes, it seemed. I was filled with relief and gratitude. The afternoon was a "success" both financially and spiritually, my being "in the moment" and feeling grateful for sitting in the sun at this lovely location, but also for the customers who came up to me, politely requesting that their caricature be drawn by myself. That evening we went back to Robson Street, which again proved to be fruitful.

One day, a blessing in disguise happened, when, on my way back to West Vancouver to pick Katarina up from her job, loud, deafening bangs started to emanate from under the hood of my van! The more I drove, the faster and louder these sounds persisted. It sounded like there were several hammers beneath the hood pounding on the inside of the steel hood. Again shaken and horrified, I drove to the nearest gas-station, which also had a service/repair station. After looking under the hood of my van, the mechanic got ready to give me the news: I was out of oil, completely dry! "When was the last time you checked the oil?" he inquired. "Yesterday! It was topped up!" was my response. We both looked at the oil-stick, which appeared to be well at the "full-level"! The mechanic remembered that in these models of van in particular, that the oil pan was installed unusually higher or lower, thus resulting in an inaccurate oil reading. "Great", I thought! "What will repairs cost?" I asked. After some calculations, his response was "Six-hundred dollars." I had charged up my credit-cards to their limit, and didn't have that much cash. "Can I trade it in for something else?" I asked. "He directed me to a nearby dealership, one of the managers greeting me upon my arrival, the great hammering beneath the hood being like trumpets heralding my arrival. "A Manitoba plate, huh?" was his first comment. "That automatically reduces the vehicles' value!" Feeling somewhat skeptical and defensive, I asked him, "Why?" He educated me about all vehicles originating from eastern Canada, and the "rust problem" on the bodies, which immediately devalues the vehicle by at least half. "Hmm", I thought.. Judgmentally I thought to myself, "I can fast-talk this guy into trading my van for a better vehicle!" Naturally, my attitude immediately cancelled any hope of this actually happening! Instead, he presented to me a small, white, not-unattractive Pontiac sports-car, which I actually liked the looks of. "We'll take your van and you can have this!" he said. After clearing this with my bank in Winnipeg, I found myself driving to West Van to retrieve Katarina, who I informed of that day's occurrences, with my "new" sports car. The car drove well for awhile, even seemed to have some "chutzpah", until one fateful day on a North Van bridge: the car coughed and sputtered, eventually coming to a neat spot on this secondary steel bridge. I managed, as it sputtered, to coast it off to the side of the bridge. Walking to a nearby phone-booth, I called the auto club to come and help me, which they did. Looking under the hood of the little vehicle, the mechanic proceeded to tap the engine with a small, steel hammer, successfully re-starting it once again. "Just do that if it ever stalls again", was his advise to me as he drove away into the night. I stood there, relatively satisfied.

The summer season ending, and the rainy-season upon me, thank goodness I had the suburban market by the water to potentially make money at. The downtown market, and Robson Street's summer tourist season had just ended, and the days grew noticeably shorter and cooler. I began to feel somewhat let-down, in anticipation of the "winter" season that I had endured all of my life; but Vancouver did not have feet upon feet of snow, with minus twenty to minus forty sub-degree temperatures, yet my body, due to prior conditioning, was starting to go into "hibernation mode"! That included a general feeling of sluggishness, lethargy, and sadness. Imagine my surprise when those symptoms suddenly ended, as we entered into November without a trace of snow, nor a hint of sub-degree temperatures! Feeling overly-optimistic, I sat for eight hours-a-day, five-days-a-week, enduring nary a trace of caricature business. I was beginning to lose my confidence and hope that I would ever earn as much money as I had previously, rather than actually enjoying this quaint and friendly environment! Several merchants made efforts to approach me, saying hello and making idle chit-chat with me! I loved this to no end! One of the maintenance/security men even approached me for a caricature! His name was Jayden, and he set himself down on my folding camping-stool to be drawn! I learned from him that he was from Saskatchewan, and had won the lottery many years before. Like myself, his finances had dwindled down to nothing, but like myself as well, the suburban market and its merchants and management were his "family". He had a nice son whom I met on several occasions as well! Occasionally I would accept a meal given to me from the coffee-shop, with gratitude and appreciation; I saw this gesture as kind and compassionate, not like "charity". I suppose that everyone was watching me, unbenounced to me, as I sat there, day in and day out earning on average of $50. for the week, 40% of that going to the management. After a while, they had me file monthly income reports and percentage-splits, as opposed to weekly.

Pressure from the credit-card companies and the bank caused me to consider bankruptcy that autumn, which I discussed first with Katarina, and feeling like there was no other recourse, on a damp, grey, and rainy Vancouver day, sporting my genuine wool sweater purchased from a consignment store, I declared bankruptcy, which not only wiped all debt clean, but also gave me a fresh new start! Well worth it, I thought, but I would soon have to adapt to not having or using credit-cards for seven years. Since I had already been doing this, my cards having been charged up to their limit, this wasn't difficult! I also enjoyed organizing my cash income into various envelopes: one for rent, one for utilities, the other for just living, which included food. The most difficult part was adapting to living without a vehicle, at that point in my life for the first time in almost twenty years! I felt paralyzed and trapped, like I couldn't go anywhere I wanted to, when I wanted to! Plus the inconvenience of having to have change for public-transit was off-putting, let alone sitting closely with all sorts of strangers, many of them with body odor. People's general manner, voices, and verbal expressions appeared to me to be rougher than in the other cities I was familiar with. This was inaccurate, of course, and a reflection of my own sadness and poor self-esteem!

A Chinese woman swore at me when I fell on the floor of the bus one day, right in front of her with my easel! I was on my way, this rainy day, once again to the market to earn some money, when the bus jerked, causing me to fall. Waiving her fist at me, (I had made a small tear in her stocking with my easel) she yelled, "I sue you!" Picking myself up, and as I was getting off the bus I turned to her, and shrugging my shoulders, I simply said, "So sue me."

Likely due to the stress of my bankruptcy, Katarina and I had developed great rifts in our relationship again, especially after moving out of Allen's and his wife's place: we were "encouraged" out, as apparently one month there was "long enough". After enduring the same "New-Agey" smiling faces in his wife's books and literature as that same smug, mocking, and all-knowing face on the book that Katarina tried to get me to read a few years before, plus the incessant "singing of orders" by the teachers to the children downstairs, we were both ready to leave and get our own place, which after some trial-and-error, we did.

Through the help of a Jewish Community Centre, who suggested we look on Oak street for an apartment, we did it! We secured our first Vancouver "real" residence at Oak street near 10th avenue, a small and beautiful heritage building which still exists at that very spot. A nearby pizza-joint and convenient store provided us with cheap sustenance, which we enjoyed. It was also stressful trying to hide our two cats, since we got in on the pretext that we had no pets. This "No Pets" law further irked me about Vancouver: what kind of a place doesn't encourage pets? Years later, I realize that that law is only used as leverage to evict unwanted tenants. We lived a few steps from Broadway, which seemed run-down and depressed to me, but has since been re-energized and revitalized twenty-five years later. And so, on a cold, grey fall day, myself, Katarina, Allen, "Little Allen",

Allen's wife, and her daughter all celebrated at a small family restaurant in North Vancouver, our newly-found (or imposed) "freedom"!

After my bankruptcy, life seemed more and more drab to me. Katarina continued to thrive, having gotten a new floral design position at a downtown Vancouver floral-shop on Hornby Street.

One Sunday morning, after she had left for work, I rose from the mattress on the floor of our new apartment, with a vision! I decided that I would not try doing caricatures at the suburban market anymore, it wasn't serving anybody! I was only getting more and more depressed. The visual I was "given" was that of a small sign, painted on a faux-marble-green background in "Old English" lettering that read simply "Tarot"! It was sitting on my folding magic-table, surrounded by my two folding camping stools. On top of the table, and next to the sign, was my beloved Tarot-deck, in particular, the colorful but dated "Rider-Waite" deck. This felt like one of my previous inspirational and creative "ah-hah" moments which came in a "flash", and made me feel excited and hurried! The way one might feel when inspired to sing, write a song, act, or play a musical instrument, create, etc., a sort of euphoria combined with an obsessive compulsion. I had no choice now but to follow this "guidance", which I would come in time to recognize as my "soul" speaking to me! Another way to look at it might be "God-guidance", intuition, etc. Nevertheless, I had to follow up on this "divinely-inspired" message/visual! This was a "sign" or signal to me that something bigger than myself was still (and always) at work, as I had lost some faith in myself and life in general.. What "Perfect" timing! This would repeatedly be shown to me throughout my six years at the Quay! More on those later.

I tried calling the administrative office of the market, to no avail: it was Sunday, and they would not likely be in today. No matter, I faxed a note to them, informing them of my change of plan, or strategy. From now on, I would be doing Tarot-card readings, with their permission of course, for patrons at the market, and on this cool but sunny October day, with portfolio in hand, and for the first time in months feeling free, I took the bus and the "Sky Train" (above-ground subway) to the little suburban market by the water!

No sooner had I unfolded my table and "chairs", placing my newly-drawn (and still-wet) "Tarot" sign upon this minimalistic set-up, that I turned to face several people who were already lined up for a reading! I knew in my heart this was "right"! I had to think quickly when the first person asked me the cost; since no license was required at the market, I could charge whatever I wanted; I didn't want to scare them away, nor lose business, so I simply said "$10. for 30-minutes". It was as if people from near and far were listening, as no sooner did I say this, that several more appeared, lining up as well. I was blown away, reading one person after the other, and finally, after the last customer left, I looked down and counted $50. cash in my hands, for a relatively short period of time! I was moved emotionally, for after what seemed to be an eternity, (really three) I believed that I found what I was meant to do, at least for now, and at least at the market!

I was back on track, alright, earning $1,000. during the month of December, while now situated at a kiosk, which administration okayed at the same 15% fee! I felt even more elation, and things really seemed to start to escalate! I raised my fee from $10. per reading to $15., and finally to $20. for a 30-minute session which included a cassette-recording of the session, free for the client to walk away with, my business-card tucked neatly into the front of the case. I got the idea to record the sessions with a hand-held recorder, from a Tarot-reader who busked on Robson street at the time: my friends "Denise" and her girlfriend "Rorie" schlepped me down there one night in an effort to "sell" their city to me, when they felt I was getting too negative about it. They showed me the closed stores and boutiques, (it was, after all 8:00 p.m.!) all of them being common throughout North American cities, except for being even less plentiful here, apparently unbenounced to those two! They pointed out the "hussle-bussle" of several people hurriedly scurrying away, lest a street-person asks of them, "Spare change?" To Denise and Rorie, there was an apparent "night-life" in Vancouver! Perhaps I shouldn't compare all of this to world leaders like Montreal, New York, or even Toronto, but Vancouverites openly call themselves "World-Class". I no longer debate this, leaving it instead to their travelling a little more to truly "big cities" and see for themselves how accurate or not this moniker is. Rorie and Denise were honestly well-intentioned, and were also trying to "cheer me up" after the break-up of Katarina and myself, which wasn't as traumatic as they believed!

Regardless, the administration at the market soon "promoted me" to my new Tarot set-up: a long table with two folding metal chairs across from a cheese concession. For this, I made up a larger, square sign which rested on a green-velour, gold-lined fabric. Two clear, plastic holders (one housing my business cards, the other presenting my 8x10 promo-sheets) completing my set-up, which I carried in my portfolio to the market; "easy-breezy", with no cumbersome wooden art easel and materials to schlep with no good results! Because I no longer had a vehicle at that point, I found it necessary to cancel the magic-show bookings that my brand-new agent had passed along to me, thanks to "Rob", a professional magician and former cruise-ship entertainer, himself back home from 13 years at sea, so to speak! We had much in common, as we were both used to receiving "professional fees" for our shows, during the same amount of years that I was in Winnipeg! Allen was/is our mutual friend, who introduced us when I was still boarding at his home. Rob would rather do shows gratis than receive a few dollars for his shows. I agree with that nowadays. $50. (the average local fee for a show) is more like a "tip" to us, $350. -$450. being the accepted fee everywhere else in North America per show.

It was now January of 1995, and for the first time in my life in the middle of winter, I was standing on a dry surface (no snow or ice) holding a coffee and sporting a heavy sweater, as opposed to the wearing the recommended winter parka, mitts and snow-boots, with the occasional balaclava to protect one's face from instantly freezing. We were standing on the boardwalk at False Creek on New Year's Day, (just a block or two from our apartment) and I was in wonder, like a child! The bright, cloudless sky was highlighted by a full ball of sunshine, beaming down on us like a blessing confirming Existence itself. I was very much now in the present moment, as I had begun to do since my "success" at the market. Allen was no longer doing his thing at the market, and I heard rumor that he was trying his hand at reading Tarot cards at the downtown market. I don't think he believed I really had a "gift", but that I had stumbled on to a new "gimmick" for making a buck, which was entirely untrue. Unfortunately, most of the magic community (in Winnipeg and Vancouver) comprised mainly of skeptics who "pooh-pooh" psychic phenomena of any kind, providing their own explanations for various phenomena of a metaphysical nature. I couldn't care less about this, as I know and knew who I am, which is many things, without internal conflict of any kind. I would in time learn mine, as well as everyone and everything's "True" nature! More on that later as well!

February of 1995, and "Valentine's Day" (what would prove to be our last one) was upon us, so we jumped over the trenches of newly-fallen snow, unusual for the city, but not unheard of, as we made our way to the neighborhood Indian Restaurant on Broadway near Oak. It was bittersweet, as I already knew that I didn't want to continue a relationship with her; I felt, again, that we were "out of synch" and nothing could change this as we were both the people that we are, and I couldn't (nor shouldn't) expect her to change, nor should she expect that of me. By that point, I was meeting many more people that I had a lot more in common with, feeling "let down" at the end of each day when we would reunite at our apartment. I even tried to teach her meditation, to no avail. All that we seemed to have in common with back in 1990 in Winnipeg was gone, as we had both grown, and had outgrown those things. What was left? I had no clue at that point anymore. One night, I did it, I "pulled the bandage quickly off" and severed things; she cried, and the next night she gathered up her belongings, both our cats, and calling for a cab, made her way out into the night. Five months later I would hear from her again, as she left a note of condolence for me at my father's passing, in addition to the self-help book she tried to get me to read a few years back in Winnipeg; with the trauma of my dad's passing, I was finally ready to read the book. We remained "just friends" for a while, both of us enjoying our single life, and occasionally meeting for dinner or dancing. She boarded first with a girlfriend from work, and then eventually shared an apartment in west-end Vancouver with a supposed gay-male. After a while, I no longer felt comfortable with our friendship, so expressing this to her, severed ties for what I believed at the time was for good.

A New Life And My Father's Passing

After Katarina moved out of our apartment, I was left with several options, and I had a month to figure things out. Meeting with Denise at a Kitsilano coffee-shop, (Katarina and my apartment, located near Oak and Broadway, was considered to be located in "Kits" area.) Denise offered no solutions at that point, other than to declare me that evening to be her "Healing Work"!

Of course, I had no clue that that was actually "Infinite Intelligence" at work, taking care of me, helping me to evolve and to be all I can be. It was another "blessing", in effect! "Fate" had obviously brought Denise and I together for many reasons, unbenounced to myself, on that fateful day at the suburban market when she approached me for a reading. I learned during that session that Denise was a "self-made person", who, after leaving her abusive husband years before, started to earn a living by doing accounting and organizing peoples' "books" and taxes, thus raising and supporting her two young children, and eventually buying her own townhouse in Port Moody! She was truly someone who forged ahead and past her former circumstances, and now, learning about my previous life in Winnipeg, decided that she would "coach me", teaching me everything she knew! I was of course resistant to this new proposed growth and evolution, but it would prove to be necessary and crucial for my emotional coping and survival in the months to come. I would have to trust her implicitly, and so eventually I finally did give into her supposed knowledge of things metaphysical, as well as to her caring, compassionate and half-Jewish nature, becoming her "student", in effect.

We met for coffee for several months, her sharing with me her mystical methodologies which included burning sage and sweet-grass to energetically purify the immediate environment. "Purify from what?" I inquired. "There's all kind of things out there, both physical and non-physical, some of them nice, some of them not-so-nice!" was her response. Previous to this, I had only positive experiences with the "non-physical" world of ghosts and spirits, mainly doing mediumship for Adriana's deceased mum in Winnipeg, and for several people at the market, but I had not as of yet encountered any "malicious" entities, other than some locals. Nevertheless, I trusted her, and decided to learn as much as I can, whether I believed in it or not; I would file some of this away for future retrieval, if necessary, in the back of my memory. The other things I learned from Denise, was the supposed value of stones and crystals, but not in the ways that a mystic named "Amos" had taught me in Winnipeg! Showing me a myriad of New Age books on the subject, I began to realize that there was no "standards" of meanings anymore; definitions, and uses for rocks and crystals were now almost completely different from what I either had researched from decades-old tomes, and/or what Amos had shared with me. Previously I knew mainly of "Tiger's Eye" for "banishing" things, and a few other rocks and stones' uses, but what was being presented to me at this point was very overwhelming! There were literally thousands upon thousands of stones and crystals I had never heard of, let alone their uses and significance; to add to this, archeologists were daily discovering hundreds more "new" ones, safely housed and wedged beneath the immediate surface of the world, shielded until their use would be required! A daunting task sat before me, but I voraciously now absorbed Denise's "wisdom" and knowledge. She shared some of her books with me, which included fictional tales written as a pretext to teach Mexican "magic", cards which taught First Nations spiritual animal-guide (or "Totem") belief-systems, and much more. One book that I quickly "absorbed" was a book called "The Celestine Prophecy", from which I learned to see my own and other peoples' energy-field, via specific exercises outlined in this book. Other books such as "Conversations With God" intrigued me for the clever way that it was written. This book was lent to me by another friend, Marcie. I began to realize more and more, that whatever book was necessary for me to read and/or acquire, despite my lack of funds, would either just "turn up" at my kiosk at work, or would be "gifted" to me by strangers and friends! It was as if a seamless string of knowledge and information on subjects spiritual and metaphysical was being "gifted" to me by some sort of Higher Power! "Infinite Intelligence" at work again? It was as if I was being prepared for something, and that turned out to be true.

By April of 1995 I was temporarily boarding with a friend, (along with several other people) at her townhouse in Surrey. Little did I know that my future wife was at that time only across the street, visiting her sister who resided nearby! Again, the "Universe" had "bought me more time" to decide whether I wanted to lease a room in Denise's townhouse or not, she recently having made me that offer, as "the extra rent-money of $350. would help pay the mortgage"; her daughter's "dance-studio" would be converted to my room if I gave her the okay. This meant a lot to me, as, although I was generally happy with my "single life" and work/business at the market, I still was blinding myself to the beauty that existed in B.C., mourning my long-gone life of fame and debauchery in Winnipeg. Fortunately for me, and unbenounced to me, Denise, reading between the lines of my verbiage, was monitoring my progress here during our coffees, dinners, and even our phone-conversations. She knew more about what was really going on in my life than I even was aware of at that time. I cringed at the blunt "truths" she hurled at me, which at the time I wasn't ready to hear, such as: "You had your time in Winnipeg! Your TV-show, and performing magic is done! You're meant to help others spiritually now!" How could she know what was in my heart? Little did I realize at the time, too, that often what is in one's heart, is not always the same as one's destiny, or "soul's purpose", and that these things can change throughout one's lifetime, as the soul opens and expands more and more! As Denise said to me, "We don't always get what we want!" which although pushed my buttons, actually meant that we always get what we need, not always what we want! I have long-since accepted this with gratitude and appreciation. What a gift from the Universe Denise was for me, although at times she seemed to be more of an irritant; I chalk this up (today) to semantics, and our differing communication-skills.

I had also befriended a client at the market that I had great admiration and compassion for, "Suzanne", who after recently overcoming alcohol addiction, earned her credentials as a nurse, subsequently acquiring a position as Triage Nurse at a Surrey hospital, and leaving her group/recovery home to make a new life for herself and her thirteen-year-old daughter, whose wealthy father helped her out financially from Calgary. I remained close friends with Suzanne for several years, going for walks along the market's boardwalk, discussing matters spiritual, of which she was no stranger. During that time, I was also befriended by an intelligent, former engineer from South America named "Jackie". She was, at the tender age of thirty (maybe forty?)-something writing her memoirs, and about how different her life had become since her relocation to Vancouver! It all sounded very familiar, but I couldn't see at the time, that her lack of gratitude, and her resentment and bias (like my own) manifested, or at least attracted ongoing difficulties and hardship! I must have been having a particularly positive outlook during the time of my early friendship with Denise, that or the Universe was consciously and obviously stepping in to eventually give me strength and tools to cope with the events that would shortly follow. Nevertheless, Jackie and I are friends to the present day, despite getting together for our annual coffee, and discussions of our mutual knowledge of New Thought Metaphysics, which we both acquired separately, and unbenounced to each other until years later, when she lent me a book on "Mind Treatments" and its inventor, Phineas Parkhurst Quimby, whom I had studied about through the University of Metaphysics, and she, through a related school of thought, "The Science of Mind"! We finally, after 15 years, had something in common! With friendships, a social life, work and options now in place, it happened.

My Father's Passing

During the month of April, I had received a phone-call from my father's social worker in Montreal.. Apparently due to several minor strokes which had left my father paralyzed, bed-ridden, and on oxygen and life-support, I was asked if I wished to have my father taken off life-support or not. Somehow, some sort of "power" "kicked in" and kept me strong, focused and detached; I asked, "Is he suffering? How is his quality of life?" The response was, "He communicates through his eyes, and he doesn't appear to be suffering." "Let me know when his quality of life declines, and then we'll talk about it then", was my decision, as we both then hung up the phone. My mother, according to this social worker, wasn't coping well with all of this, having become emotionally depressed and distressed and unable to make this decision; as a result, I was called to make a decision either way. During this month of April of 1995, parallel to all that appeared to be going well with my life was also the ongoing knowing that my dad was unwell.

It was now early June of 1995, and with me happily boarding with Denise and her two teenaged kids at her Port Moody townhouse, (across from Eagle Ridge Hospital) I received a visit from Rorie at the market. Approaching me, Rorie simply said, "I see you're wearing all black, that's good: your dad is going to die in two weeks!" Shocked and my head reeling, I didn't feel at all like this information from Rorie was an intrusion, but rather a gift for me. She and Denise never minced words, nor were they subtle, exactly what I needed! "Start preparing! Release him, he's only sticking around for you and your mother; tell him its okay for him to go." she said. "How?" I inquired. She replied, "Denise can help you with this; prepare a list of all of the things you loved and admired about him, and burn that list along with all of his pictures during your ritual." With that, she hurried on her way, not saying another word. This left me somewhat uneasy, both the foretelling of my dad's demise, of course, as well as this "ritual", of which I had no clue how to construct; I would have to trust my instincts and just do it; I would do it that night! I trusted implicitly Denise and Rorie, my best friends.

It was early evening, the sun was still up, streaming brightly through my room's window, and I had recently returned from a successful day at the market. I felt happy and strong, so I decided to just "go with the flow" for this ritual, and so, gathering all photos I had of my father, except those taken with my mum, I began to write a letter to my father, thanking him for all of the good he provided me, as well as all of the bad. It flowed, and it wasn't as difficult as I thought it would be. The time came for me to burn everything, and all I had handy was a heavy, three-legged, cast-iron cauldron which Katarina had bought me years before. I placed it in the middle of my room, along with a fat white candle (to symbolize God) beside it. Remembering some Wiccan rituals that I had read about years ago in Winnipeg, I set up improvised symbols of the four directions/four elements around the cauldron, starting towards the east, and making my way southward around the cauldron, and culminating eventually to the north. I used a bowl of water for the west, rice, symbolizing earth at the north, a prop-sword from my medieval feasts symbolizing air to the east, and incense, symbolizing fire to the south. Reading my letter to my dad one more time silently to myself, I then set all ablaze with the help of the fat white candle, placing the lit letter and photos atop some pre-lit charcoal in the cauldron. Smoke filled my room, along with the scent of amber and frankincense, which I had also placed upon the charcoal disk. The idea being that the frankincense would create a "pure" atmosphere, cleansing the energy in my immediate vicinity in the process. I sat, meditating very deeply, eyes closed. I focused upon my breath, which was becoming more and more relaxed.

I leave the reality and validity of the following events to you and your own experiences and belief-systems.

An image of my father filled my "mind's eye", or imagination. I spoke to him mentally, saying, "It's okay for you to go, dad!" His eyebrows meeting upward towards each other in the anxious way that he would do this; his lips seemed to be moving as he began to apparently speak to me, but I could hear nothing. I took another breath, relaxing myself some more, and then I heard him speak the words, "What will become of your mother?" I replied, "She'll be okay, she has her brother and sister. I'll be okay too!" I could sense his reluctance as he appeared to turn slightly away from me, pondering all of this. This was occurring so smoothly and effortlessly. He turned towards me again, smiling. My heart was filled with joy; a joy and feeling of freedom that I had not ever felt at this depth before; so strong, that it moved me and I began to cry. I couldn't stop crying, and with my eyes still closed, he seemed to diminish in size with a smile still on his face. Finally, this image dissolved into a light so bright, ironically I had to actually open my eyes to try to make it subside! The light and feelings persisted, as did my tears. I was sobbing at this point, just knowing that we had just said good-bye to each other. I stopped crying, and felt that same cleansed, cold, "cried out" feeling that I had experienced with David's father's passing some years before. I looked around me at the now-dark room, the sun having set. I saw only the hint of smoke now, floating lightly around myself and the cauldron. It reminded me of the wisps of clouds that had surrounded the towering mountain as I was driving into B.C. almost nine months previously. I felt at ease, calm and relaxed. It felt like yet another brand-new beginning, and as it turned out to be, it was.

Upon my arrival home from the market one sunny early evening, I was greeted by Denise. She asked, "Did you have a good day today?" I responded in the affirmative. She continued, "Well your night isn't going to be very good!" I braced myself, though still completely unprepared for the news. "I just got a phone-call from the hospital: your dad passed away around 6:30 tonight, our time. My legs gave out, as my head reeled and I collapsed onto the arm of her couch. This was the first time I had experienced the loss of a close family member. It didn't feel like it, but the pain would lessen, but never completely vanish, over time My eyes welled up with the tears I was trying to hold back, embarrassed to show Denise my emotions. All she sais was, "Forest or water?" upon which time I instinctively said, "Both."

She drove us to what I now believe was Port Moody's "Ioco" area, a sort of campground with richly-forested trees and a small body of water. There were some children and their families playing near the water, as we approached. She lay down on her back, head upon a rock, and facing the water, inviting me to do the same, which I did. She guided me to observe the rocks and the flora's details, coaxing me to imagine worlds within worlds. It was almost as if her own words were not her own, but were being "guided" by some unseen force. I could still barely see through my tears, which continued throughout the evening. Suddenly, seven Canada Geese glided into view upon the water from towards my left. They stopped in mid-swim, and in unison, turned their heads, looking directly at me! Maintaining their gaze with mine, they slowly made their way up onto shore, approaching me, all the while maintaining their fixed gaze with mine. Denise looked on in awe, silently. The families seemed to disappear at this point. It was only me and the geese. At that point, I experienced a feeling of re-assurance, as if my dad was patting me on my leg, saying, "All is well!" All at once, the geese turned their heads, slowly making their way in unison back into the water, and continuing on their way. I was left with the same feelings of awe and wonder that I had experienced previously during my wedding ceremony: there was more, much more at work, than the human senses can perceive, or the human brain for that matter can comprehend. I knew this for sure now, doubtlessly remembering other "miracles" like this in the past.

Denise said, "Do you want to go for a drink at the "Frog and Nightgown"? There's a magician there!" She drove us there, and still unable to control my tears, I managed to enjoy the drinks, as well as the magic performed that night at our table by a local close-up magician. I would meet him years later at a "Science World" magic-show that I was doing with the other members of the local "Society of American Magicians". I thought it ironic that he was dressed in my original namesakes' costume, a "Merlin"/wizard's outfit.

The next morning, I decided, in my grief, to phone my maternal aunt and her husband in Toronto to inform them of my dad's passing. My cousin, surprisingly, answered the phone. I could hear the sound of many voices in the background. "Hey", I started to say, "How are you?" "Not very good", was his reply, "My mum passed away this morning from Emphysema. She was in the hospital for a long time." Shocked and feeling even more grief, I said to him, "I'm so sorry. I loved her. My dad passed away last night." He replied, "I know, our uncle is here and he told us. He's going to take care of all the arrangements." I said, "Tell him "thank-you" for me; is he there? Can I speak to him?" My cousin's reply was, "He's not really in any shape to talk to anyone right now, sorry." I understood completely, after all, he just lost his sister and brother-in-law, all at the same time. I thanked my cousin, asking him to keep in touch. I hung up the phone, saddened even more and still in shock over my dad's passing. The following year, my aunt's husband would pass from the grief of having lost his wife, and my mum's brother would pass as well some time after the passing of his other sister, my mother, who passed five years after my father, having given up all hope in life. She had starved herself to death, I was informed by her social worker at the seniors' home where she resided. Despite Denise's offering to lend me the fare to fly in for my dad's funeral, I declined, not wanting to owe her something I might not be able to repay. I went to nobody's funeral, and I have no regrets about that, as the grief from others was something I didn't need to add to my own hurt and sense of loss. I managed to continue on doing readings that same day, and everyday since, getting by on alcohol at night, and through tears during the day while doing my readings. No-one knew why, except my kiosk-neighbor "Ralph", who was trying to cope with his beloved father's recent brain-surgery, (we supported each other, somewhat) and one of the women at the nearby "Crepe" business, who sent me flowers of condolences. Twenty years later, I still feel sadness and loss, a pain in my heart at having lost my parents; Denise referred to me as being an orphan, which didn't help at all. I have "Father's Day" as a yearly reminder of around the time that my father passed, and autumn being a reminder of the afternoon that my current wife and I were visiting the suburban market, and I received the phone call informing me of my mum's passing. It was little consolation, but at least I was surrounded by "family" at the market, (the merchants) where I had my business for six years, seven-days-a-week, nine hours-a-day.

After my dad's passing, and much philosophical introspection, I asked myself, "Why do people die?" I was walking around the market, completely relaxed, and actually curious, while mentally asking this question. Again, I leave the following to your own religious/spiritual/philosophical perspective: I received an almost immediate and audible answer, which said in a male voice, "So that they can do even greater things." The voice actually said "more", not "greater" things, but I understood the words to mean "greater". This floored me! A simple, quick, yet profound and multi-tiered answer came to me so easily, with me just mentally asking! Now, one may analyze this, concluding that it was my own way of coping with my dad's passing, that it was actually my unconscious mind assisting. I was so moved emotionally by the answer, though, that I'm going to continue with a more metaphysical perspective. I mentally asked again, but this time, I asked for an elaboration on the answer. The non-verbal, and partially visual response subsequently provided this elaboration: "The soul, while in it's temporary human body, has limitations on a physical as well as emotional level, taking on the self-imposed emotional as well as (naturally) the physical limitations that the flawed human mind has extended over the personal (human) will and physical body. This is due in part to karma, and the conscious evolution of the soul, as well as what is actually pre-determined to occur as the person's "soul's purpose" (God's will) in this lifetime". I understood this to mean that as humans, we are subject to the frailties of our limiting emotions and physical bodies. Our flawed human mind (and sometimes flawed human body, with all of its physical limitations) can only accomplish what it believes it can accomplish, based on all of the positive and negative experiences, the environment, as well as hereditary factors in this lifetime; if we believe that we are at some sort of disadvantage, then we'll limit what we believe that we can achieve. "If our mind can overcome (while still in our physical bodies) this self-defeating attitude, (regardless of "realities" that we think exist) then we can achieve almost limitless goals, the mind, our will, and our human/personal attitude being the key!" I understood. "Even then, once we leave our limiting physical body", the non-verbal response continued, "Our mind carries on within the bodiless soul, (sometimes called the "astral body") and this limited, human mind which formerly occupied a limiting body, now takes on a whole new limitless, Universal perspective. With this new perspective after death, the astral body (or soul) can begin to influence people and events, although, obviously, somewhat subtly, and more on an energetic level". Keep in mind that these answers/understandings came in an instant, quicker than it took for me to write them! I began to realize that the souls of the dearly-departed (sometimes referred-to by mediums as "spirit") can theoretically accomplish more than when it inhabited the living physical body! I asked for specifics, "Exactly how can the soul influence physical events, decisions and attitudes of others, etc.?" The answer came: "These limitless souls can influence by "whispering" thoughts, ideas, notions, and attitudes into human-beings' ears, which then "come to them" as inspiring and motivating ideas." I responded with, "I always believed that inspiration and intuition was God/Higher Intelligence at work, when we relax enough to receive it!" The response: "There is nothing in your illusionary, physically-individualized existence that is not comprised of the life-force called "creation", "creativity", "inspiration", "Higher Intelligence", "love", etc. How then, can "spirit" not also be yet another form of Source?" I completely understood, and this information would be revisited by me years later in my metaphysical studies with The University of Metaphysics, and The University of Sedona, confirming and validating this information, and a lot more which I had either figured out for myself, through trial-and-error in the "field". I was filled with gratitude and re-assurance that everything was exactly the way it was supposed to be, and that in some way, I might be influenced by the guidance and wisdom of my deceased father. As time went on and I was grieving, it was probably the spirit of my dad who gave me this "ah-hah" revelation: "Would your father want you to be paralyzed by grief over his passing, or would he rather you use it as a "spring-board" onto greater things?" Still sad but inspired after a year, I slowly moved on, never forgetting those answers to my questions I received shortly after my dad's passing. The market and my fellow merchants were indeed a support, almost family for me during those challenging times.

The suburban market was significant as well, for Sue, my current wife, being informed while sitting with me in my kiosk, by our friend, that a phone-call to administration from Sue's mum's social worker of her heart attack, eventually resulting as well in her passing. The market seemed to be a place that the Universe provided us for some comfort and shelter, apparently. It provided for me a dependable room-mate, (two different ones, in reality) as well! One of them, "Lance", took me for drinks the day my mother passed.

The Room-Mates

After a year or so, it was time for me to "leave the nest" that Denise had provided for me during my grieving and spiritual-learning period. I felt I had a social life, and my work was going well, with my income at the Quay having significantly increased, so I desired something more than a room in a townhouse to live in. I was hoping to acquire a two-bedroom apartment which I could share with a room-mate. No sooner was my enthusiasm and faith in attracting this scenario into physical reality ignite my passion even more, than one of the sales-persons who was originally from Winnipeg approached me about this very thing! "Beth" and I had developed a mutual respect, speaking frequently about the things we mutually loved about Winnipeg, when one day our conversation led to us both mentioning our desire for different living accommodations from what we currently had. There was that "ah-hah" moment for us both, as a "flash" of inspiration!

By that time, I had "mastered" the books "A Return To Love", "The Celestine Prophesy", among many other spiritual tomes, which I studied both at home and at work, making notes and putting into practice their various techniques and philosophies. Being befriended by the owner of a coffee-shop at the market, herself on a spiritual quest, who expressed great support, admiration, and faith in me and my work, also helped to "bump me up" vibrationally, meaning I was consistently feeling happy and driven! She even utilized my graphic design skills to have me design the new logo for her promotional plastic mugs. Thanks to her, I developed a new perspective on my work, re-designing my own logo and business-name to "Readings From The Heart", a butterfly being the logo, as opposed to the sign just stating "Tarot Readings By Michael". The butterfly represented the potential freedom one could gain from my sessions, although many would stop by, unknowingly believing that I was going to give them a poetry reading! Nonetheless, this was quickly straightened out, but I must at this point share with you several "incidences" which I encountered during my tenure at market near a river, before proceeding with my room-mate adventures.

Besides being bombarded daily by well-meaning religious extremists, hoping to "save me" by "encouraging me" to halt my "work of the devil", I remember a visiting senior, who proudly displayed her amateurish oil paintings of still-life lavishly framed for sale. The market annually allowed her to set up her work as an "exhibition" of sorts, and annually she would let me know how much she despised me, and my work. One time, she said to me, "I'd rather be on welfare than do what you do!" I felt sad for this Octogenarian and her judgment, after all, she knew nothing of my past, my education, nor my work experience. She, like the other religious extremists, made pre-judgments and conclusions about myself. Was this truly being compassionate and loving? I of course, not wanting to hurt or insult her, and knowing that her education and life-experiences were obviously limited, (despite being another "easterner" from Ottawa she proudly once declared to me!) I decided to say to her, "I don't care!"

If I couldn't educate these folks, I would at least have some fun! I would put into play all of my knowledge of Transactional Analysis, making this a study for myself of human behavior; unfair I know, but so was my being abused by strangers. I felt I had nothing to lose, and really couldn't care less anymore, likely the stress of constantly dealing with the public was getting to me. All of the questions, despite my clearly marked signage, of "How much", and "What do you do here?" was quickly getting to me! I even stepped out of my kiosk once, to answer these questions: "Well, let's see," I said sarcastically to a potential client, "Hmmmm; it says here, "$25. for 30-minutes! Let's see what else the sign says", I continued, stepping back, and underlining the words on my sign with a finger as I read, "Tarot/Psychic Readings", Hmmmm..." I couldn't even imagine that some of these folks might be illiterate, which I had not previously encountered, but was later told by confidants that this might be the case!

To this day I regret my own sarcasm and rudeness to the one or two I acted in this way to, and I was even given the chance later to apologize for this, which I did; but there's still no excuse for a merchant to potentially ruin a visitor's experience, ever. As a consumer, I know that I wouldn't appreciate that, and might even report it to administration, which I'm lucky never happened!

Nonetheless, I continued to have "fun" at my abusers' expense, even deciding to play up the "psychic" aspect, when a female with large, bookish glasses, already shaking her head with that familiar "I'm going to save you, you poor soul" facial expression, approached me. She was wearing a name-tag, and I immediately called her by name which surprised her. Nervously, she asked me, "How did you..." upon which time I immediately replied, "It's what I do!" Then I pointed to her name-badge, and we both laughed. She continued with her potential crusade, reading my sign, which by now included "Rune-Stones", "Palmistry", and "Astrological Services" in addition to the "Tarot"; she looked up at me asking me, "Isn't it against Christianity to do astrology?" Fed up, I turned away from her, saying dismissively, "I don't know, I'm Jewish!" Confused, she staggered away, not having expected this response. On another occasion, several extremists started shouting at me to cease and desist, fearfully making the sign of the cross at me! They appeared well dressed, which encouraged me for some reason to threaten to call security if they didn't leave. "Why are you so angry?" they persisted. Frustrated, past my five-year limit of having endured all of this, and ignoring the fact that mental illness might be playing a part in all of this, I answered, "Look, I'm not interested in having a theological discussion with you!" They looked confused, cocking their heads to one side simultaneously, obviously unfamiliar with the word "theological". "I'm Jewish; I'm not interested in being converted", I continued, "and college-educated. I choose not to get into this with you, go away or I'll call security!" I pulled out my cellular phone to do this, as they rushed away, and looking back at me yelled out, You're going to hell, "college-educated Jew"!" This hurt somewhat, but the empowerment I was finally feeling for doing this trumped the feelings of hurt. Don't get me wrong: I don't believe in fighting fire with fire, plus, this really wasn't a fair fight. I just had to say something, after staying mostly silent for five years and enduring objects and threatening words being tossed at me. I felt I was worth more than that. "I was finally healed", I thought, "from all of the losses and abuse I suffered here, and now I have the strength to stand up for myself!" On some days when I didn't feel so strong, I would put up a sign which read, "Back at..." which had a clock with arms that I would set for two hours away, this when I would see potential "missionaries" approaching me for a conversion! I learned to "cope", I learned how to stand up for myself again, and I learned when to avoid confrontation. This place was certainly my "life class-room"!

On another occasion, a potential client without money offered to exchange sexual favors for a reading! Nearby fellow-merchants had a laugh at both the offer, as well as my surprise and discomfort! Good times! On yet another occasion, a woman, child in one of her arms, snapped down on my glass display-case with a sound that echoed throughout the market, a quarter. She looked at me, then she looked at her baby, which she proudly and confidently placed on this glass, the diaper making a "squishy" sound upon impact. Looking at me again and nodding, she asked, "It's twenty-five cents for you to read her, right?" Not wanting to embarrass her, I stated, "No, it's twenty-five dollars, sorry!" Confused, she waddled away, child scooped up again into her arms. Then there was the eight-year-old boy, who, while peering up over my table once said to me in my early years at the market, "You're a fraud! My mum said you're a fraud!" There was the woman who approached me, insisting that I wasn't "Michael"; even showing her my I.D. didn't help to convince her! One of my favorite stories, which I share often when reminiscing to others about the market, is about little "Jimmy"! Another bespectacled female with the familiar head-shaking approached me one day, this time with her eight-year-old boy "Jimmy" by her side. She asked me about what I do, and why I do it. I replied honestly with, "I do this to lead people to God! If they're troubled or have questions and have not first approached their bible, I send them on their way to try to get answers from the Bible!" I honestly did this for people whom I had assessed initially in a brief intake, and deemed them as needing something more than just a "reading", in other words psychiatric care, and at the very least, "faith". Her child then piped up, "But mom, I thought you said he harnesses his power from Satan!" upon which time she briskly grabbed him, pushing him behind her and saying, "Now we don't know this for sure yet, Jimmy!" Exhausted, shocked, and amused by this, I excused myself, not to return to my kiosk until I was sure they were gone for good, observing them covertly from one of the market's vantage-points that some merchants had shared with me.

I had a brief "leave of absence" from the market for a year, around 1997, when I was asked to do readings for a merchant at her store at yet another suburban market north of Vancouver. I loved doing this, the money was great, but due to some personal issues, (a girlfriend, "Shyrene", at the time demanded that I not keep Katarina as a friend, as well as being jealous of my friendship with my boss) and so, I felt it necessary (and easier) to return to my old kiosk in the original suburban market, with a brand-new perspective, and leaving the so-called, on-again-off-again "relationship" with Shyrene, whom I encouraged to go on meds to stabilize her mood-swings; she insisted she had no mood-swings. The former mayor of this particular suburb owned a confectionary business at the market; my friendship with her daughter who worked at that business was probably the impetus for him wanting to train me to eventually work at the confectionary's main office. Trying to train at that business while also attending my own kiosk created too much stress for me, so I gratefully declined his offer. Generously, he eventually offered to supply candy for my future wedding with Sue in 2000. The market went through several administrations during my tenure there, Liza being the first one that I had worked with. After several others, eventually my favorite one was a senior named "Brenda", who was fair, and had a healthy perspective on most things. When she left in 2000, after six years there, I gave my notice, wanting to branch out to other retail locations, which I eventually did. Besides, I had come full-circle by then, grossing only $50. for the week, (like I had done upon my arrival in 1994) despite having set up a magic-shop and caricature-stand, in addition to the readings. None of that helped, my time was evidently up there!

But I digressed! Back to my story of the room-mates!

I already mentioned how and why Beth and I became room-mates; she owned two birds at the time, a twenty-one-year-old finch, who peered over its own beak as if the beak were eye-glasses, the bird's myopic eyes straining to see where the sound it heard emanated from. It's scrawny body supported by weak, spindly legs, I wasn't at all sure if its sparsely-covered body was alive, or in actuality an automaton, or an A.I. ("Artificial Intelligence", simulating a life-form) She loved that little bird, whose breathing appeared forced and difficult, but nonetheless, it was still living, very unusual for a bird of that species. Her other pet was a small love-bird: colorful, expressive, and cute, it "rode" its toy fire-truck, as Beth moved the truck back and forth. This was a lovely household, or so I thought, until one day Beth invited me to inspect one of the curios on the head-board of her bed. On this head-board, besides some books, was a full-color, framed picture of her beloved, deceased dog, a German Shepherd, if my memory serves me. Beside this picture was an attractive brass vase. Picking this up, she asked, "Do you know what's in here?" I jokingly responded, "Don't you know?" I suspected the truth. She smiled sarcastically at my comment. "It's my dog's ashes", she responded, as she proceeded to unscrew the lid to show me the contents. I peered in at what appeared to be sand. I thought to myself, "Those animal crematoriums are quite the business!" I said out loud to her, "Thanks for sharing this with me, I've never seen anything like this before." That was the truth. Later on, her twin-sister from Winnipeg came to visit us, and I enjoyed sharing memories of that city with them; they remembered me from my television-show. Eventually I moved out, when Shyrene and I decided to take our relationship to the "next level", and you know how that turned out!

Now in a bit of a jam, my friend "Sandy" decided to share an apartment with me, until he moved to Bowen Island. I asked an acquaintance of mine, "Bobby", another alternative-wellness practitioner, (he was a massage-therapist, having developed his own techniques which he was much in demand for in Las Angeles) although I had not acquired my Reiki (energy-healing) education and degrees yet, nor did I ever think that would happen; more on that later. We both had "channeling" in common, in that I did psychic-readings and mediumship for a living, being the go-between between a dearly-departed and the client, and he channeled various "cosmic" entities, who entered his body, using it to provide bits of useless but fascinating information for anyone who would listen. I believe he really believed he was doing this, but I seriously question to this day what earthly good (pardon the pun) that this process does for a client, unless the "entities" have a specific agenda of teaching things we don't have knowledge of yet, (as in the case of Esther Hicks and "Abraham") information about the origins of the universe, or short-term answers that a client might have about love, health, and/or finances. Nevertheless, Bobby would often become drunk and loud, and subsequently we were evicted from our apartment. In a jam again, I boarded with yet another psychic, a female, "Elayne", an ex-girlfriend of Sandy's, divorced, and who had a little boy in a wheelchair, and a little girl who was not differently-abled. This bought me some time until New Year's of that approaching year. It was at the suburban market where I met my future room-mate: "Lance" was a security-guard posted at that market, who would frequently stop by my kiosk to chat about life, love, and many matters intellectual. He was a law-enforcement student at the nearby college. One day, Elayne informed me that I would have to leave, as a male that she had developed an online relationship with was coming to stay with her shortly. She also added that an astrologer had suggested that the best thing for everybody was that I left immediately, as Elayne and her male friend had some past-life issues that needed immediate attention! Needless to say, part of me resented and/or questioned "New Age" things; not "New Thought", whose information has been clinically proven over a millennia, but "New Age". Nonetheless, I had two weeks to find a new home and/or room-mate; this was between Christmas and New Year's, I had only a few hundred dollars to my name (hardly enough for first month's rent and a damage-deposit on an apartment, which would average roughly $1,200.!) and Bobby refused to keep me for a month, (until I could at least secure a new apartment) as he was now residing with a female in White Rock, whom I had introduced him to. This hurt, since we were evicted because of him, and he wouldn't have met this woman without me.

One rainy day at the market, as I once-again pondered my situation, I decided to go for a walk along the boardwalk, and meditate. I grabbed my umbrella, and after putting up my cardboard sign indicating when I would be returning, I headed out into the cold, damp, dark early-evening. I walked and walked, enjoying the fresh air. I walked some more, and then stopped walking. Standing and looking out at the beautiful darkness, and the river which underlined it, I closed my eyes, turning inward. I focused upon my breath and the interior-region of my third-eye area. I saw, as I had since age twenty-nine, a bright, golden light, doughnut-shaped, with a dark, pin-point in the center of it. My breathing became more and more relaxed, as I began to feel a calmness, a peace, overtake my entire body. It was a re-assuring feeling, like many times I had felt before, doing this practice. Then, focused with exactly what I wanted, I "put in my order" for an apartment: this apartment had to be a walk-away from the market, cost me no more than $350. a month, and be a nice, safe dwelling; this suburb had some "rough" areas and apartments housing drug-addicts and prostitutes; there were however plenty of the opposite types there as well. I also asked that I earn the means to easily acquire this as soon as possible. Slowly and re-assuredly, I returned to the market and my kiosk, as closing time was nearly upon us. People were already lined up for their readings on this previously-quiet day, and when all was said and done, I had exactly $350. in my pocket, in cash! I was pleasantly shocked! My head reeled as I realized that the universe immediately answered my request, or at least part of it.

As I began to close up shop for the day, Lance approached me with a look of concern on his face. His room-mate had apparently left abruptly and without notice, leaving Lance in a bind for his rent and a room-mate for next week! Not believing this almost surreal series of events, I asked Lance how much his former roommate was paying a month. "Three-hundred and fifty-dollars", was his reply. I thought to myself, "What a dump it must be!" I asked, where is your building?" Lance responded, "Just down the street, about a block away on Carnarvon Street. It's the concrete high-rise with the white lions in front!" It dawned on my that this was probably a good building; (with two elevators and a swimming pool and sauna, as it turned out!) God/The Universe/Intelligent-Universal Mind had answered my prayers! "I might be interested! Can I confirm it on Monday?" I asked. "Sure", he responded. Those few days were to insure that I made a few more dollars, and to secure some physical help for the move, after all, I had a sofa-bed, dresser, and other living-room/bedroom items that would require several pairs of hands to assist me. A fellow merchants' brother assisted me in this task early the following week, as I moved into the eleventh floor of Carnarvon Street at fourth avenue, down the street from the market..

Life With Lance

After moving in, I spent my days working at the market, and my evenings trying to wrap my head around "life", studying numerous self-help books, including one called "Are You The One For Me?" by Dr. Barbara De Angelis. This book would eventually help me to understand why, and what sort of relationships I had allowed into my life, how to avoid future ones like the ones I had previously welcomed in, as well as how to attract healthier, long-term ones, providing tools to able to identify the signs and symptoms of ones doomed from the start, as well as how to maintain the "good" ones. That was my favorite self-help/personal-growth book for many years, and I continually recommended it to the clients of mine who conveniently required it! Come to think of it, just as in the past, whichever book I was reading would almost always directly apply to my newer clients, providing me with tools and knowledge for assisting them on their life's journey. Of course, many didn't want to do this hard "work" of self-evaluation in order to understand and avoid future pitfalls; they merely wanted a "psychic reading"! This would eventually prove to be an irritant for me as my education and life-experiences grew and evolved.

One night, while watching "Touched By An Angel" on T.V. in my room, it dawned on me that the theme of that particular episode was forgiveness. This was approximately one month after my perceived betrayal by my supposed friend, John. In the show, someone had betrayed someone else's friendship, the "victim" maintaining a sad, victimized attitude, with events starting to downward-spiral for them. The Irish actress who portrayed one of the angels said to this "victim", "Once you forgive, the healing begins!" This immediately moved me to tears, as I pictured John in my mind, and then forgiving him! It was as if a weight was lifted off of my heart, and I began to cry and cry some more, light appearing to fill me from within and around me, my room taking on a glow of sorts. Grabbing a tissue, I wiped away my tears, feeling cold, empty, but renewed as I had on a number of occasions before! New beginnings, I felt, once again; truly, brand-new beginnings, as I was now cleansed and healed of any resentment and "victim-hood". I wrote down this quote, "Once you forgive, the healing begins", sharing it with as many people as I could at the market! There was a sudden knock at my bedroom door; it was Lance. "I don't mean to darken your door-step", he started, "But why don't you get your head out of your butt and join me in the living room with my girlfriend? We're watching T.V.", he said. "Sure", I said confidently, now feeling more healed and ready to face part of what was Lance's social-life.

Lance fancied himself an intellectual, certainly well-read in many areas, and carrying himself with a sort-of "bookish" manner, his rimless glasses perched above his nose, his gait well-measured. He was tall, slightly over-weight, with his frame supporting many lofty ideas that ruminated in his head. He sported a short, light-brown military haircut. He also fancied himself, at his tender age of twenty-something, something of a "ladies'-

Man".

Unbenounced to me, Lance was seeing three different females, scheduled over consecutive evenings, then repeating this three-night schedule over and over. Unfortunately at the time, I couldn't tell the difference between young Japanese and Korean women, of which he favored both. One evening, while joining him and one of his girlfriends on the sofa, I mistakenly called this woman by the same name as his previous night's date! He whispered diplomatically to me, "Don't try to call them by name; this isn't the same girl as last night." Embarrassed nonetheless, I made efforts to distinguish one girl from the other for future reference. Lance went through a few heartaches, usually discovering that they were unfaithful to him; I found this to be ironic, and perhaps evidence of karma. Lance's fondness and compassion for me was evident, as he often gave me valid marketing tips and ideas for my Tarot business, even typesetting and printing out from his beloved computer and printer, promo-material, far superior to the hand-typed, sometimes hand-calligraphied material at my kiosk. I was grateful to him for this. He saw me as his intellectual equal, and I still don't know if this was a compliment or not. He also gave me advise on how to dress and present myself at the market; he, as a twenty-something male dressed somewhat "older" than his years, stating that being from Toronto, (in actuality, "Kitchener", a small Ontario town near Toronto) he disliked how the locals (both men and women) dressed here. He suggested that I sport pants and shirts of a different quality fabric, himself preferring "Dockers" brand of pants and collarless shirts. Being into my early forties at this point, I resented his suggestions, somewhat, but nonetheless kept that all in the back of my mind. I still had my black hair and ponytail, attempting to emulate the look of the television character from the "Highlander" show, while Lance, also a fan of the series, related more to the actor who portrayed the movie-character "Highlander", looking somewhat like him, while some told me I resembled Adrian Paul, from the television series. I was flattered, of course! I suggested to Lance, jokingly, that for Halloween we should go to a party dressed as both Highlander characters!

Lance, for some reason, perhaps having come from a broken home, began to see me as his "family", both of us being "only children", and himself having only his dad, who still lived in Kitchener. All I had was my mum, unwell at this point, residing in a seniors' care-facility in Ville St.-Laurent, a Montreal suburb. Lance spoke of us one day renting a house, where we and our future wives could live. My unspoken thought was, "If I ever get married, it'll be just me and my wife living together, of course!"

After a year of living with Lance, and my Tarot-business still doing well at the suburban market, I met my future wife in 1999, for the second time, unbenounced to me, as apparently she insists even to this day, that I did a reading for her the previous year, and then she subsequently returned the following year for another reading. How was I to know, that one of my favorite senior-couples, almost daily visitors to the market for coffee, and who would almost always stop by my kiosk to say "hello", were my future wife's parents! This white-haired couple carried themselves differently than the other seniors at the market, with a kind of a quiet dignity. Their manner, and manner of dress was a "cut above" the manner and dress of their other contemporaries at the market. I liked these two, and how surprised I was one day when they said hello to me, telling me that they were there to meet their daughter for coffee. They gestured towards Sue, whom I had already done a reading for awhile back. My mouth agape, (according to Sue) I apparently said to them, "You're her parents?"

Sue

Let's backtrack to my memories of my doing a reading for Sue at the market. I was still recording the sessions with my hand-held tape-recorder, but now inserted my newer, Celtic-inspired business-card/covers into the cassette cases, the labels on the cassettes matching all. Apparently Sue held onto the recording for awhile, playing it over and over again in her car afterwards as she drove. I was glad to know that people did keep and listen to the recordings of their readings, and as I still say, "What didn't make sense will, and what did make sense won't anymore over time."

I recall looking at Sue's face during her reading, and feeling great compassion for her, as I felt that she herself had great compassion for others, perhaps to her detriment. Her face seemed to glow, her bright, shining green eyes reflecting a certain spiritual depth. Unbenounced to her, I could "see" during the reading her then-husband, who, not appreciating her or their kids, "hid out" a lot upstairs. This was all very unusual for me, the manner in which I was seeing this client: there was (and is) usually total detachment, I rarely even see "details" of their physical bodies, it usually only appearing as a bright light. Many times I can't even tell the sex of the person I'm reading. I suppose this means that I see their "soul" only, and with objectivity, a necessity for this kind of thing. One must be as detached and neutral as possible, seeing things diplomatically and from a "higher" perspective. But this reading was different. Bear in mind that I had done hundreds of readings, probably closer to a thousand or more at this point, all in the same way, only seeing the subjects as "light". I had to consciously ignore seeing Sue as a living, breathing, human female, and managed to, mostly. She never admitted to me during the session that she was about to leave her husband of twenty-five years for the third and last time. Like I've said before, "It never takes the first two times!"

Sue visited me from time to time afterwards, chatting with me a bit as she was walking through the market. Her parents lived in the same suburb as the market, and she lived in Surrey. Her sister was also planning on leaving her husband shortly, and those two resided in Surrey as well. She tells me of the time she was sitting at a table across from my kiosk, and apparently we both looked up at the same time, making eye-contact. She tells me that she knew then that we would one day be married to each other! Being a man, of course, I was completely oblivious to this all, apparently later mentioning to her that I felt I had met the woman I was going to marry one day, I just didn't know who it was! This was true, as I had a few platonic female-friends who hung around my kiosk a lot, and regularly, sometimes on a daily basis! Apparently I had developed quite a reputation for myself of being a "ladies' man"; if they only new that these women were "just friends" of mine! I suppose magicians and musicians aren't the only ones who accumulate "groupies"! Nonetheless, I avoided the temptations of dating Sue, or even just going out for coffee with her, flat out saying to her, "When you leave your husband and some time has passed, then I'll think about it!" I was tired of past relationships that didn't work out; I had spent the last year working out (thanks to my book "Are You The One For Me") certain issues which resulted previously had resulted in me subconsciously attracting certain types of women into my life, and I wasn't about to date a newly-separated woman. In fact, Sue told me years later that she respected me even more for telling her this, even though she apparently wanted to develop something with me sooner, she felt that confident and sure of us. According to my professional as well as personal experience, allowing at least a year after separating until you seriously date again is a relatively safe period of time, as often people reunite with their "ex" within that time-frame. Imagine Sue's disappointment when I kept changing the boundary-line from a month to six-months! By observing and speaking to her on occasion about her separation, I was confident that she was well "over" her ex-husband years ago! She had moved into her parents' home in New West until she found her own place. She was on a waiting-list to be accepted into a housing co-op, and she had been working for two years as a "Teaching Assistant" in a suburban School-Division, so this suggested to me that she was focused and that she knew exactly was she was doing.

After six months, I finally asked her out to dinner. We went to the fine-dining restaurant upstairs of the market, co-owned and operated by two friends of mine. During our date, I got suspicious, as she excused herself in order to supposedly call her parents. She left her cellular on our table, which I found odd, using a pay-phone to make the calls. I thought it also odd for a forty-something-year-old-woman to call her parents while on a date, so I became skeptical that she had actually left her ex-husband, and I began to believe that she was actually calling her kids at her ex's, or even chatting with her ex for some reason. In actuality, her 17-year-old son was still living with his dad, and her 19-year-old daughter had been on her own for a few years. Sue was really calling to re-assure her parents that she was still "alive," since she had left their home early in the day, and it was now early evening. She hadn't called them all day. I had to learn to trust again, I realized.

Sue relates this story from time-to-time when I bring it up. I was speaking with my friend "Barrie", whom I knew from the market, over the phone about my new relationship with Sue, who was standing within ear-shot. He asked me what she looked like, and my response was, "Well, she has blonde hair and big blue eyes!" Sue yelled out, "They're green, not blue, green!" Embarrassed, I corrected myself to Barrie, whom I'm sure understood that it wasn't necessarily Sue's eyes that I was preoccupied with lately.

Our relationship evolved, and after a year, Sue was also voraciously reading the book, "Are You The One For Me?" at my suggestion, a book I believed would insure us of maintaining a healthy, long-term relationship. I invited her to move in with myself and Lance. Lance saw this as an opportunity for us to share the rent in thirds; he appeared to be somewhat accepting of Sue as a person, and as my partner, he was even initially impressed by her ability to bake some apple pies for us! Then one day, he left a voicemail on my cellular. It was, "I know that as you're listening to this, Sue is probably right there. Take a minute and look into her eyes, and see if you can find anything but a void." I was standing with Sue at his work-station at home, as he was hunched over his computer. I shut my phone off, saying to him, "That wasn't very nice!" He turned to me, saying, "It may not be nice, but it's true, isn't it?" I refused to continue the conversation, as Sue was right there and oblivious to what was really going on. It was obvious now what he truly thought of her. I understood that his mother deserted his father and himself when he was a child, leaving him with his own void, and subsequent distrust of women. His general condescending manner with females in general started to become more and more obvious to me, using them and discarding them before they discarded him; his comments about his mother being "white trash" still rang in my ears. I realized what was going on now, on a few levels, and I didn't much care for it. I saw potential for his resentment towards Sue and I to build, and I felt he didn't have the maturity to deal with his feelings, after all, he was on medication for depression, and he also had a history of violence, which ultimately hindered him from further pursuing a career in law enforcement. Our days with him as our room-mate were numbered; Sue and I would look for another apartment, our own apartment, perhaps somewhere within this fine building. Speaking with the building's managers, and having dealt with Vance before, they completely understood. Besides, they liked Sue. These managers, "Jerry" and "Cathy", were quite understanding, and their tenure as managers would be coming to a close within a few short years, as they approached retirement age. They told us of a vacant apartment on the sixth floor; sure, it didn't have the same view as our eleventh floor apartment did, but this one-bedroom was affordable for us, as long as both of our jobs remained intact. Speaking with Lance a few months later about our decision to move out, he reluctantly agreed, as we had also given him ample notice to find another room-mate. Sue and I stayed in contact with him for a few more years, until he "snapped" one day when we visited him to retrieve the magic-books I asked him to hold onto for me until we found more room for them. I allowed myself to try to counsel him about some issues, and apparently he wasn't ready to listen. He condescendingly called me a "girl", stating that I can't even afford my own rent or to support myself, and then in a fit of rage, started throwing large and heavy boxes of books at me, as Sue and I ran towards the elevator; he managed to throw a whole box into the elevator as the doors closed, and as the elevator began to make its descent, I pressed the button to send it back up to his floor, where I hurled the box back towards his door, causing a loud "thud"; we quickly left. Fortunately, we were all not living in the same building anymore at that point, so no-one there knew us. I wouldn't contact Lance for several years after that.

Several changes did occur for Sue and myself during our time on the sixth floor of the Carnarvon apartment in 2000, and rumor had it that administration at the market was about to change. It was the end of May of that year, and the new administration, whom I had previously met, would begin June 1st. I gave my notice, since my income there was so low regardless, and six years was enough; I moved the contents of my kiosk out on the last day of May, 2000. Saying a slightly tearful good-bye to my fellow merchants, Sue and I both took stock of my time there: I had grown technically, spiritually, professionally, and personally there. It was at the market that Sue and I first met; it was at the market where I had met Lance; it was at the market that Sue learned of her mum's heart attack, which eventually resulted in her passing; it was at the market that I met Sue's children, (my step-kids) and it was next door to the market that we spent our overnight honeymoon at, while a fellow-merchant watched my kiosk for me; it was at the market that I would have regular coffee-breaks with my sister-in-law, and father-in-law "Gord"; I felt that there were more good memories of that place than bad ones, as I was forgetting the many quiet days with no business there! I forgot at that point the verbal abuse that I had endured as well as the threat of physical violence twice by two different merchants, both of them drunk at the time. I forgot the anti-Semitic slurs hurled at me by a few other customers, and to be honest, it all didn't matter to me anymore; this place didn't serve me anymore, I was somewhat burnt out from dealing for so long with the broad public, and so, with a heartfelt "so long", and with Sue in tow, I made my way out of the "protective" and somewhat familial arms of the market, and "into the real world" to seek my fame and fortune once again! It was time to move on, perhaps either to another retail location? Time would soon show me.

The Wedding

Sue and I married on March 19th of that year, after being together for almost two years. I had no doubt in my mind that this was the right thing to do, and it was one of the few things I was ever so sure about! I felt that many of my relationship issues were resolved, and that we would both be good for each other, making us a strong team, which we appeared to be thus far.

We decided that March 19th of that year would be the wedding day for several reasons, one of them being that it would be during Sue's spring-break off from school, and secondly, it would be around the time that Sue's sister was planning on visiting with her then-boyfriend from Montreal; that way they could be present for the event.

After much deliberation, we realized that we would have to have something fairly small and intimate, with only family and a few friends attending. My father-in-law graciously invited us to have the ceremony and reception/dinner at his tiny suburban home. I was thankful for that. Since I was still at the market, (I would leave June of that year) I had a number of resources for food which the merchants generously supplied: the coffee-shop at the market supplied the actual dinner, which they personally delivered to Gord's home; the market's confectionary supplied the candies and dainties. With those two contributing, it really felt to me like a family affair. We invited Sue's childhood girlfriend, and her husband. Sue's sister and her boyfriend were in attendance, with him providing photographic services; my childhood friend David bussed it all the way in from Ottawa, with Allen also there; one of Sue's workmates insisted on coming, as she said she would have felt "left out". After a half-day of Sue at the beauty-parlor, and myself and David picking up her kids to drive them to their grandfather's home for the wedding after my haircut, it began.

I sang a few songs for the guests sitting in the parlor, guitar in my hands, which were "our" songs: one was "Beautiful In My Eyes" by Joshua Kadison, and Richard Marx's "Now And Forever". Though a pro for years, I found it somehow difficult to hold back my tears as I sang, getting caught up in the personal sentiments.

The Unity minister, a client of mine, presided over the ceremony, with the kids worked into the actual ceremony for a symbolic "blending" of families, and a big white candle was lit during the ritual representing Sue's deceased mum's presence and spiritual/symbolic participation. I wrote the words with Sue one night over dinner at one of the market's second-floor restaurants, which we now spoke; they seemed to take on, now, a deeper, more emotional meaning.

It was a moving and joyous experience for all, and upon the exchange of our rings, a heartfelt "I now pronounce you man and wife" was declared! I never felt so sure of anything in my life, as I peered into Sue's big green eyes, which seemed to radiate God's Light and Love. She looked beautiful in her new, off-white wedding-dress, which she still has kept to this day. I wore a heavy, black-wool tuxedo given to me a year ago by Sue's mother. We all felt that the suit, actually an heirloom from Sue's deceased grandfather, would symbolically bring me luck in my magic-show endeavors, and life in general. I felt proud and privileged every time I wore it, especially during this occasion. Our kiss capped off the event, and we eventually retired to the kitchen for dinner.

During all of this, my friend David, a former professional photographer himself, took pictures, while my sister-in-law "Reesa's" boyfriend "Francois" did as well; we got the exciting news from Reesa and Francois later that night, that they had re-located back to this suburb from Montreal, all of their "worldly-belongings" sitting in my father-in-law Gord's basement! We felt that their return was our wedding gift from them! Reesa was like the sister I never had, and Francois was my "Montreal compeer", bringing to me a little bit of my childhood and Montreal identity and love of French culture. Francois would also be instrumental in my learning how to navigate the technologies of the Internet, and graphic design programs, which he and another friend, "George", (an ex-patriot from Toronto) generously gave me. They also provided plentiful tutelage until I could "run" with all of the knowledge and tools.

Off to a great start, Sue continued her career for the next twenty years as a Teaching Assistant, or "Education Assistant" as they are now referred-to as, switching schools a couple of times, and loving every moment of it all. The students were blessed to have Sue supporting them, and Sue was blessed to be doing her "soul's purpose", initially "forced" into it as a means of escape from her unhappy first marriage. Sometimes the road to our destiny is not always a smooth one. After I left the market in late May/Early June of 2000, I drifted somewhat for a year, allowed by Sue to tighten my computer and graphic design/animations skills, so that I could do promotions for myself. During that year, I also tried to re-launch my cartooning career, drawing a proposed "Magic Mike's Castle" comic-strip, to no avail. My magic career did flourish as much as it could at the market from 1994-2000: I did regular, paid shows for special events at the market as well, and I also m.c.'d and performed larger "Family Day" shows for a mall in that same suburb, where I received more than generous payment for five years in a row, once-a-year, for the event. The newspaper photos and publicity didn't hurt either!

9-11

It was the morning of September 11th, 2001, and Sue was already up getting herself ready for work. I turned on the television in our bedroom to watch Canada A.M. as was my habit before exercising. What I saw at that moment I mistook for a commercial for one of those "disaster" movies, like "Independence Day", but it was not!

I watched the live television feed from New York City with a chill as one of the towers of the World Trade Center stood erect, but was smoking from what appeared to be a plane sticking out of it! My mind still couldn't comprehend this. Another airplane circled the other tower, quickly careening into it as well! I watched in complete disbelief as the towers began to cave-in on themselves after a few moments, as a result of the weakened structures from the planes' impacts. The world was apparently watching all of this as well, in complete and utter horror. I started to cry, as everyone on my dad's side of the family lived in some of New York's boroughs, including Manhattan, where this was happening. I immediately felt a sense of loss and devastation, as the former World Trade Center Towers, the same building that I had peered up at during a visit to New York years earlier, now lay in crumpled heaps of ash, glass, and steel, smoke rising up from all of this, as if to signal "the end" of something. It actually was the end of what the world perceived as "security" from middle-eastern terrorists, who took credit for this event. The world as we knew it up to then would never seem the same again. All television programs originating from New York, ceased production, except, eventually for a few late-night comedy-shows that decided to defiantly and bravely go back on-air to provide a healing distraction from these recent events. Slowly and surely, New York "came back to life again", "rising up from the ashes", so-to-speak, to become an even stronger, more loving place. The U.S. government at the time felt the necessity to retaliate, which is now legendary, so I'll spare you the details of those subsequent events, stepping back to allow you at this point to ponder the consequences of those actions. What of the thousands of people who were at work in these two towers that day? What of them? What of the police, the firemen, the "first-responders" to this tragedy of biblical proportions?" Fortunately not as many perished as was first expected, and due respect and condolences were eventually dolled out towards all of them. Still shocked and in mourning to this day, the world carries on as best it can, still feeling a sense of loss and fear in anticipation of more potential enemy attacks. All of this because of religious differences.

Feeling a sense of compassion, pain, and identification with my New York family (none of whom were injured) and the U.S. in general at the time, I chose to wear a memorial U.S. flag-pin on my jacket-lapel for a year, despite and in spite of negative comments by the locals, finding this offensive. I approached my new boss of a metaphysical bookstore in a different suburb, a mature woman, who like her husband, are both long-time British immigrants to this country, both of whom also share the same perspectives; I asked her why she felt this way, this anti-U.S. sentiment, and so she began to spew much anti-U.S. rhetoric. My cohorts in Eastern Canada, being somewhat more close in proximity to New York, never shared such anti-U.S. sentiments that I recall while growing up there. How I longed now for the "sensibilities" of eastern Canada.

I didn't immediately begin working at the bookstore after leaving the market. In fact, it was quite the journey! After a year of "perfecting" my computer-skills, and a failed potential comic-strip, I decided to focus on what worked previously in this province, and not what I really enjoyed doing to make a living again. I decided I would work for others, in other words, to try to do readings at metaphysical stores locally. After all, this was the longest period of not working I had ever experienced in my life, and I was starting to feel insecure. I began to miss all that I used to have, including the fame, the fortune, my roll-top desk and other objects that I had earned and identified with. Rather than looking around me and realizing the beauty and relative security that I had, and the skills I had developed over the last several years, I became sad and resentful towards the locals who I started to blame for my not having those objects and fame. I tried doing readings for awhile at a nearby metaphysical shop, ironically, located in the same suburb as the market! It never provided me with enough money to pay half the rent. Restless and longing for a career again, I somehow got my old job back in Toronto, at the recreational park doing caricatures, and a short-term townhouse for Sue and I to stay in for that summer of potential "fortune". Sue just wanted me to be happy and provide some more income over and above what she was bringing in; since she didn't work in the summer at her school position, we left for points east via plane. I would torture you, the reader, or myself with memories of those challenging two weeks, but suffice it to say that Sue hated this "non-vacation", as a result of mistakenly believing that we weren't going to return to B.C.; I blurted out with enthusiasm upon the plane's landing, "Ah, back home, finally! I'm never going back to Vancouver, ever!" She didn't confront me with this misunderstanding, and so she felt sad and anxious the entire time; stating one day that she was returning to B.C. and that I could remain here, I took that to mean that she was leaving me, as opposed to leaving me to work the duration of the summer and then return to B.C. Meanwhile, her kids were eager to help us to relocate to Toronto if we gave the word! My friend who owned the confectionary store at the market said that if we wanted, he would give us the equipment to set up a location at the mall of our choosing, with no worries of paying him back for several years, once the business was on-track. I was so excited about this potential for new beginnings in a city that I truly did love, and which, as in the past, likely held endless possibilities for my various gifts and talents to bring me a "living"; I honestly dreaded returning to a place that I still couldn't identify with. No, I really didn't want to return, but under a misunderstood threat of divorce, I reluctantly and resentfully gave my notice before the season even had a chance to start. Sue didn't let me forget for a long time the money this little venture "cost her", as she had chosen to charge up her credit-card for some of the trip. We returned on a Greyhound bus, which served as somewhat of a relaxing time.

After a few months, I received an invitation to do some magic-shows just outside of Montreal, in Hemingford Quebec. The invite came form a former high school chum of mine, who was now director of a theatre group in Hemingford where he lived. "Gerard" was a bachelor, and enjoyed it! He had a small cottage that he and his father had built together, and he was in semi-retirement, as he had earned his fortune in the business world after college and years of toil. I felt honored, and accepted his invitation, arriving by Greyhound. He let me stay at his home for a few days located in the woods, but close enough to the town. I was excited to perform magic again, this time near my home city, in my home province. The small theatre was part of a zoo located minutes from Montreal, in Hemingford. I was to do a show on Saturday night, and one on Sunday during the day, with my friend paying me any profits over his own costs, which, although the space was filled for each show, only amounted to $50. I was a little nervous, and not completely present, really just imagining myself still in Winnipeg the way I used to be back then, as opposed to who I was now. I even dressed the way I used to; if I was fully present, happy with whom I had become, I probably would have dressed a little differently reflecting the image I had of myself now, and my show would probably have had more passion. Nonetheless, the polite audience clapped and laughed where it should have, and my friend made me a proposal of booking me throughout the province with me receiving $50, per show. He was very excited and earnest in his proposal, but I reminded him that I had worked my way up for many years, and now command $350. or more for a show. He said he'd think about it. I questioned myself whether I ever really wanted to go "pro" again with my magic. I had so enjoyed doing impromptu psychic-readings the night before at the pizza-joint my friend had taken me to. While sitting and eating, I "picked up" an image, a feeling, an "impression" of a recent death, and sadness emanating from a woman seated at a nearby table. Not shy a all, in fact driven, I said "hello" in French, and then proceeded to share with her what I was sensing in English. She started to cry, and I continued on doing some mediumship for her recently-departed sister, whom I identified through some things said that only she would know. Feeling happier and reassured that her sister was "around", she smiled, offering me money. I thanked her but refused it, instead giving her my business-card and inviting her and her family to tomorrow-night's show. They were going anyway!

Something more life-changing happened on that trip, which is probably why the Universe under the guise, or pretext of me doing shows in Montreal, motivated me to go there in the first place. In retrospect, had I not gone to do those shows, I would never have met my future Reiki Teacher, "Helen".

Reiki

While I was in the middle of my act, I noticed a small, round-faced, dark-haired woman, casually dressed, staring at me from the audience. She stood out from the other audience members, who wore dresses, suits and ties, while Helen wore a purple, long-sleeved sweat-shirt with an animal emblazed on it. Dangling from a leather thong around her neck was a small, single, amethyst crystal, attached via a hook on a small copper-wire "cage" housing it. Her energy felt peaceful and reassured, which I could feel from the stage. During the three illusions which I, still to this day, perform to pre-recorded music, I usually meditate, so that my movements become more relaxed and graceful. I utilize the third and fourth techniques of the mediation techniques known as Knowledge to accomplish this.

After my first show, my friend and his girlfriend introduced me to the same woman that I had noticed during my performance, whom they were friends with. "Mike, this is Helen", Gerard said. "Hi", she said. "You meditate during your performance, don't you?" she inquired. Shocked and impressed, I said, "Yes, for parts of it." I was fascinated how she might know this! It was my experience that only other meditators recognize, or "feel" each other, and so it dawned on me that she too meditates. I had to talk more with her! She attended my second show the following day, and it was then that we arranged for me to meet her at her home on Monday-morning. Gerard's girlfriend dropped me over to Helen's house at 8:00 a.m., and we sat at her kitchen table talking. We spoke of our separate lives, and our personal perspectives of them. I shared with her my general gratitude, yet dissatisfaction with the apparent turn of events in my life since relocating to Vancouver. She asked me if I wished to see her "healing room", which I did; slowly we made our way towards it, however I remained at the entrance to it, hesitantly making my way in, following her. I stood there transfixed. I could feel a kind of a coolness, but could not physically detect where this cooler air was originating from, as this room had no windows, only huge amethysts geodes in every corner of the room, and a few scattered throughout the space. Each stood a few feet high, the largest crystals I had ever seen up to that point. I put my hand on one of them: there! That was where the cool air was emanating from! Cool air (or energy) seemed to almost blow out from this geode, much like the cool air emanating out from an electric fan. This fascinated me. The entire room also felt unnaturally "happy", an almost "high" energy which tried to grab my heart and pull it up past my head! I pondered if this was reflecting my heavy heart, of if I felt "normal" and the environment was feeling unusually "high" or "up"! It didn't matter at that point to me. I noticed a massage table, covered with a white cotton-fabric. "Do you want to lay on my table?" Helen beckoned. It didn't feel right; I felt somewhat vulnerable at that point, almost as if it wasn't "right" to lay down in front of her on her table, so I politely refused the offer. "No worries", she responded. "Let's go back to the kitchen", she said, while I followed her there. We sat down again. I looked at my watch: had seven hours passed already? Had we spoken in her kitchen for so long? "My daughter will be coming home soon from school", she said. Gesturing for me to take a different seat at the kitchen table, she invited me, then, to close my eyes and relax. I complied, as it felt alright to do so in the kitchen. I could feel her hands moving about my head, then around my body. I could feel the same cool air on my head, neck and body that I had felt in the "healing-room". My entire body then began to relax, as I allowed it to more and more. I was meditating as she continued doing whatever it was that she was doing. It was as if she was going from drawing symbols in the air, to placing her palms just above various areas of my body, and then back to the symbols again. I could hear "whooshing" sounds as she did this, although I was probably only imagining those sounds. I became aware of her hands just over my heart-area, and I began to cry. I realize now that it was some sort of emotional release. A cleansing, or clearing out of negativity. I sat there with tears running down my cheeks, as I could tell she was finishing up. I felt cold and empty, like the way I felt after hearing of David's dad's death; like the way I felt in the past after "letting go" of "stuff" and accepting brand-new beginnings again. She placed a hand on my shoulder, signifying that the process, whatever it was, was done. Slowly I opened my eyes, and put my glasses on. I sat there for a moment until her daughter and their dog stormed in, joyfully and excited. I looked at my watch again: did only ten minutes pass? It seemed like an hour, at least! The daughter and I exchanged pleasantries, and then Gerard's girlfriend arrived to take me back to his property. Apparently I had received an "initiation", or what I refer-to as an "attunement" into Level 1 Reiki by Helen. I didn't know what that meant at the time, neither the implications nor the responsibilities involved. Nevertheless I thanked Helen for everything, and she suggested that when I get back to Vancouver, that I buy a book by Diane Steine on Reiki called "Essential Reiki". Little did I know what new "doors" were opened up for me now, spiritually as well as professionally thanks to my Reiki teacher, Helen. As we embraced "good-bye", she told me that I "wouldn't be alone" on my flight back to B.C.

The Journey

In retrospect, this initiation into Level 1 Reiki was yet another flag in the road of my spiritual journey, which began long ago, first with my mother, then my Buddhism research as a teen, then discovering my own "mediumistic" abilities, my mystical experiences with the rabbi, my search for God and then receiving "Knowledge", (the meditation techniques) doing Tarot-readings, and now Reiki. I returned to B.C. confident that something "else" was "happening" with my life's journey, which, unbenounced to me, was also my spiritual journey!

Sue met me at the airport, and as always, was very encouraging about anything and everything that I approached, including this "Reiki", which I suggested might mean a whole new, extra career, and thus, a whole new, extra income! She loved this idea.

I continued on with my studies of Reiki, having bought the book "Essential Reiki" from a suburban bookstore. I mixed this with phone-calls of explanations from Helen, as I voraciously completed my Level 1, offering Reiki sessions out of the suburban bookstore for a modest fee. These clients, impressed with the Reiki-energy, wanted to become my students, but I explained that only once I complete Level 3, or "Master" level, would I be allowed to do so. These three students stayed with me over the next year or so, and I gathered more Reiki clients and potential students thanks to Randolph from the bookstore; he recognized that this was good for everyone, including himself. I continued to do the odd psychic/Tarot/mediumistic reading, not yet meeting my half of our rent, nor the bills, which began to both annoy and concern Sue, understandably. "Just get any job", she said. For some reason, this hurt, but I carried on, completing Level 2 Reiki and doing readings.

A quick primer on Reiki for you at this point. Once attuned, or initiated into Level 1 Reiki, (which supposedly clears up any physical concerns the student may have accumulated due to emotional issues) the student gives themselves and others treatments, which consist of hovering one's palms over theirs, or other's body. There are specific hand-placements for various ailments, and a specific symbol must be visualized while doing a treatment. This symbol is to clear physical ailments. Level 2 is for emotionally-related ailments, and so an extra symbol is added in at this point, which heals issues on an emotional level.

Helen gave me a "distant initiation" into Level 2, which I actually felt during the pre-determined mutually-agreed-upon time. I truly felt that I had "bumped up" to Level 2, (more energized than previously) and was therefore ready to practice on clients as well as myself using the additional hand-placements and the two symbols now. I was fascinated now, with the history and origins of Reiki, which are thousands of years old, and as previously stated, are Japanese in origin. "Ling Chi" is the Chinese equivalent to "Rei Ki", the words roughly meaning "God-Energy", or "God-Breath" in both languages. The Ayurvedic, or East Indian-based system is known as "Prana", also meaning "God Energy", but having completely different hand-gestures and techniques, using the breath and specific breathing techniques. Reiki and Ling Chi are less "taxing" on the practitioner, as one merely hovers there palms over the body, visualizing the symbols. Over time, I began to "see" the specific areas of concern for my patients, which I confirmed by asking them, "Do you have pain here?" etc. Whether my "extra" senses were evolving, or were no longer dormant and I was now aware of something that I already had, thanks to the Reiki, I don't know; I just know that I started to, and now can usually "see" upon command, similar to an x-ray or an ultra-sound, even down to the bones if I place that intention there, the condition/state that the patient has. I couldn't care less how far-fetched this may sound, since I have helped so many over many years to cure themselves. I say this, because like anything, a person will only allow themselves to progress, or "heal" as much as they want to, or allow themselves to. Another way to look at this is that the Reiki acts as a catalyst for the body's natural healing to "wake up" and occur, activating God's healing power if you will from within. If a patient really doesn't feel worthy of getting better (due to emotional issues) then the body's healing will be stifled or limited. Another point, is that the actual sensation of the Reiki is so subtle, many novice practitioners are told by patients that nothing happened, because they felt nothing! In actuality, the effects go on for days after a treatment, sometimes resulting in a headache or some such for the patient, (as the physical clearing occurs) crying or laughing during or after a treatment, (emotional release) and finally "revelations" (of a mental/cerebral nature) potentially leading to a greater spiritual understanding, as Level 3 has to do with the spiritual, just as Level 1 is physical and Level 2 is emotional.

Very briefly about the attunements, or initiations: only a Level 3 Reiki Master/Teacher is allowed (or energetically strong enough and capable) to perform the ancient, traditional, and ritualistic blowing of breath and gestures required to move the person's energy-rating upward to the next level. I have performed both traditional as well as western, or non-traditional attunements/initiations hundreds of times, and the students over all prefer the traditional methods, which seem to be more obvious and powerful for them. Again, skeptic or not, don't knock it if you haven't tried it! I'm probably one of the greatest skeptics, and I only share that which has been physically proven to me, so I apparently "know of what I speak"! Nonetheless, at the very least, most people will find a Reiki session "relaxing", which doesn't necessarily mean that it wasn't therapeutic. Just as mystical, or contact meditation may seem only relaxing, but it is also in actuality therapeutic, clinical studies have proven.

Nonetheless, I eventually earned my Level 3 Reiki-Master certification certificate in May of 2002 thanks to Helen and her long-distance attunements and tutelage, and my hands-on practice and clinics!

I was chomping at the bit to teach Reiki now, and my potential students and patients were chomping at the bit to be my students! I started teaching Reiki now, as well as doing Reiki sessions, and Tarot/mediumship sessions in the basement of the suburban New Age bookstore in New Westminster. It apparently still was not making ends meet, so I decided to explore, thanks to Sue's encouragement, additional professions.

New Careers

At forty-six years of age, I started exploring potential new careers for myself that I had wanted to look at, but as of that point, I never did. One was law-enforcement, the others being driving instructor, and cab-driver. All my life these careers fascinated me, and at this point in my life, I was willing to try them as a means of financial security, and to keep up my end of our marital bargain, after all Sue was financially stressed, and she didn't deserve to be!

In order to drive a taxi in Vancouver, one needed a great deal of initial capital, which I did not have, so that eliminated that immediately. Next, I attended a police recruitment seminar, my sort-of brother-in-law Francois in tow, as Reesa and he were still living with her dad, my father-in-law, and this was over a year; Francois as of that point wasn't able to duplicate the same financial success here that he had in Quebec with his career, which was "I.T." work, or computer-systems related work. We each took a seat in the auditorium, and listened intensely as the police officer spoke. He asked, "Who here wants to catch the bad guys?" Some of the two hundred people in attendance raised their hands. "Who here wants to help re-habilitate criminal offenders?" he further asked. Still more raised their hands. His final question was, "Who here wants to help the bad guys?" Myself and many others raised their hands; I don't remember to which question Francois responded, but it must have been the "wrong" one, because the officer continued, "We train you to catch the bad guys. If you want to help them, become a social worker; if you want to rehabilitate them, become a psychiatrist, nurse, doctor, or therapist". I realized at that point, that was that. We sat through the first half of the presentation, which included a video to educate us about the physical and mental requirements of the job. The mental part was fine, and with six months of practice, I could build my body up to the physical requirements. Still, we had answered the initial questions in a way that would not likely make us good officers; not bad officers, but not good enough for this often life-and-death career, and so we felt it was time to leave.

The remaining career for myself was "driving instructor", and I was excited to pursue it! To make this already-long story just a little bit shorter and hopefully more tolerable, I cut to the chase, so to speak: after weeks of education and training and earning my Drivers Educator's license, after two weeks on the job, more than ten-hours a day, six days a week, my paycheck barely amounted to $150.! I was both devastated and disappointed, since I was good at my job, and furthermore, I enjoyed it! Another financial failure! The good thing was, I can say that after much toil, I earned my license; showing Sue my pay-check, something made me blurt out, "Now can I continue to read cards and do Reiki?!" She realized that something was going on, and so did I: perhaps at this point in my life and our life, I was meant to earn a modest income at something I was good at and enjoyed, and which also helped people? Perhaps a different perspective was needed, after all, I never seemed to fully regain my financial income in Vancouver while doing the things I was used to doing (and loved) previously in Montreal, Toronto, and Winnipeg; perhaps we should just try to "go with the flow", doing our best, but also accepting the not-so-good with the good, choosing to focus with gratitude on what was great? This new-found attitude helped us both to move forward with faith, confidence, and passion!

I decided to add another metaphysical location to where I could do readings and healings, and with that in mind, I pursued a psychic-reading studio in the Vancouver-area market, which soon successfully provided for me a far greater income than I had known previously in B.C., including the job reading Tarot in West End Vancouver, or the job at the retail store in North Vancouver. This part-time job, along with my work at the New Age suburban bookstore, provided some much-needed financial relief for Sue and I, and I started more and more to feel "at home" here. During that time, I added another New Age suburban bookstore to all of this, beginning to read Tarot cards on Sundays, the only day of the week now available for me! The previous reader left due to health issues, and I had apparently "proven myself" at their "Psychic Fairs" which they held upstairs of the store, also leased by the bookstore's owner. "What a brilliant business-person she was", I thought. Writing off the rent of the wellness center against her income from the bookstore, and vice-versa, both the wellness center and bookstore providing profits for her. The owner gave me Wednesdays to read at the store as well, immediately providing me with more income than readings at the other New Age suburban bookstore or the place at the Vancouver-area market was, so I kept only the one suburban New Age bookstore for my Reiki sessions and classes, which I continued to thrive with at the wellness center as well, adding as many as ten students per Levels 1, 2, and 3 Sunday afternoons after reading at the other New Age suburban bookstore! Everyone benefitted from all of this, on all levels, and I never enjoyed doing anything as much since relocating to Vancouver, until the next phase! Until reaching that next phase, I earned a few dollars by doing caricatures outside of a store in a major suburban mall, and then moving on to receiving a small but regular check for drawing caricatures free to the public out of another nearby store at the same gigantic suburban mall.

I let that all go to work at the New Age bookstore that had the wellness center above it; that year we also moved from New Westminster to a low-rise apartment building a block away from that same bookstore, where we still reside fifteen years later. During that time, we moved three times within the building, always remaining on the third-floor; we moved into a lovely, bright, south-facing one-bedroom corner suite initially, then relocating to a two-bedroom suite in order for me to see hypnotherapy, metaphysical, and Reiki clients to replace the office I kept at the wellness center for a year, the wellness center's office proved to be not worth it financially. Seven years ago we moved next door to our initial suite, as it had more privacy, and was brighter. During our twelve years in Coquitlam, we rescued a cat which became our beloved pet, "Bella", and Sue and I were asked to organize that nearby bookstore's Psychic Fairs, which we took over when the previous organizers suddenly quit. Never making a large profit, we gave up organizing our beloved fair after five years. The readers from the fair saw us as family, and it was quite mutual. I still stay in touch with a few of them to this day. Eventually, several of the other bookstore readers and the wellness center's yoga teacher consequently moved into our building, not only becoming my work-mates, but effectively also our neighbors! Sadly, the yoga instructor, passed a couple of years ago after twenty-five years of teaching. She lived right across the hall from us.

The Next Phase: Hypnosis Doctorates, Authorship, and Channeling

In 2002 I started working at the suburban New Age bookstore and wellness center, commuting using public transit between New Westminster and Coquitlam. When Sue and I relocated to Coquitlam a year later, I was able to walk a block away to work, and even go home for mid-afternoon breaks! When I initially started to work there, a lot of the terminology and New Age lingo was foreign to me, almost pushing my buttons!

I felt uncomfortable with the almost taking-for-granted attitude there of extraterrestrial life, which I had always believed in all of my life, including from early childhood and my fascination with U.F.O.'s; at the store, everyone seemed to know about the "greys", and areas of adjacent galaxies where we originated from, and from where alien-life-forms were apparently "influencing our thoughts and beliefs"! Most people, including the visitors to this store declared that "this was my last lifetime", as if there was a choice! The many popular misconceptions, herbal remedies, and what many take as fact, have long been disproved years ago by science and technology out east and in other larger cities. Nonetheless many here swear by some of these natural remedies, herbs and vitamins and their "results", but I suspect that some of the positive results are because of "mind-over-matter"! Science has long proven that one would require massive doses of some of these herbal remedies, nutrients and vitamins to see even minute results, if any.

Many locals were excited about "Reiki" (and other culturally-diverse forms of energy-healing, including "Prana" healing) back then, so I was at an advantage, renting the wellness center for my numerous classes, workshops, and clinics. I even taught Qi Gong and Tai Chi for a year there, with many devoted and passionate students. Thanks to that bookstore and my notoriety there, we held thrice-weekly meditation nights at our home, which I eventually used as clinical studies for my dissertations and thesis. I evolved from doing card-readings there to merely "listening to my guides" for the information and advise sought by clients. I dropped using cards altogether, at Sue's inspiration and questioning if I really need to use objects to do what I do, after all, "A world-famous, now-deceased psychic and television personality didn't need cards, she listens to her guides!" Sue pointed this out one day to me. In an effort to "evolve", I set the intention/"put out to the universe" the desire to "meet my spirit guides", and 'lo and behold, one day I did! Whether this was my vivid imagination or subconscious passionately desiring to drop Tarot-card usage, or me "opening myself" to the "next phase" of my life, I honestly don't know, but believe it or not, these three "guides" came to me one morning upon my awakening, so to speak, and seemed as plain as life!

"Chamman" (pronounced with a hard, Jewish "Ch" , and said like "Ha-mahn") looked to me like a middle-aged, middle-eastern male with a round face, and very short, black-curly hair. He would sarcastically, accurately, and good-naturedly "give" me information for my clients, (auditorally, visually, emotionally, and kinesthetically, all at once) as did "Lana", a 1960's-looking 35-year-old-looking female with a brown-haired "bob" hairstyle; she gave me a female's perspective, helping me to relate to my female clientele. A tall, hooded-figure named "Jesus", pronounced "Hay-Zoos" stood behind me, "protecting" me, (who knows from what!) and finally "Dr. Tanaka", a be-spectacled, dark-haired, (parted in the middle) pin-stripe three-piece-suit-wearing guide gave me pseudo-medical/health and wellness information, everything from what vitamins to take, to what foods to not eat. Sometimes all combined with my Reiki sessions, it worked well for everyone! It was a living, allowing us to first long-term lease a vehicle, and then eventually to buy one. We were feeling "comfortable" financially for the first time in a long time. Feeling like I needed something "more" to give my clients and myself, I decided to earn my Clinical Hypnotherapy degree, again, like Susan's Reiki teachings, long-distance, from a Hypnotherapy college in England. It was one of the most difficult things I ever approached, between passing the history and theory, to finally hypnotizing Sue after more than a year's worth of continuous practice, I barely passed the 70% passing grade by 3%! I added "Fear Elimination Therapy" certification to my arsenal, also from the college, all of which I've ever since put to constant and practical use!

I loved the balance I now had between the metaphysical/psychic sessions and Reiki healings, and the more cerebral and intellectual healing-modality of hypnotherapy. I was truly grateful for all of this, and my life such as it became. I performed magic shows very occasionally for special events, including a major, world-wide book-release about a magical boy and his exploits in a magical school at the New Age bookstore! What a great "cross-over" that was!

Doctorates, Authorship, and Channeling

Early in 2005 or so, I set some goals for myself for that upcoming year. I wanted to write and publish a book on metaphysics, and earn some sort of letters after my name that would lend more credence to the metaphysical field I was in. After all, I was turning forty-nine that year, and I felt mature; I was embarrassed to tell my peers across Canada (most of them professionals) that I did psychic readings for a living. I wanted to combine my current skills into something that sounded more professional, in addition to my notoriety out east as a cartoonist, graphic designer, and magician.

There was a "secret" DVD and book released that year, and it was immensely popular. It was (and still is) essentially a great primer, or introduction, for civilians, skeptics, lay-people, and the broad, general public alike to the field of metaphysics and "New Thought" in particular. I'd like to elaborate somewhat at this point on metaphysics and New Thought. New Thought is often confused with "New Age", that broad, crystals-and-incense movement combining health and wellness with psychic phenomena and alternative wellness modalities. Although the New Age movement contains very over-simplified (and sometimes distorted) versions of genuine (not necessarily valid) culturally-diversified ancient traditions, it nonetheless has a place in our society (in my humble opinion) as an introduction to matters metaphysical, spiritual, and even New Thought. Those "secret" DVD's and books fit into the New Age movement, although its roots are in New Thought metaphysics.

"New Thought"/metaphysics, although organized in the late 1800's thanks to great thinkers and philosophers such as Emerson, Plato, the Buddha, and texts which include the New Testament, and Bhagavad-Gita, came to worldwide recognition thanks to the clinical studies, practices of the aforementioned P.P. Quimby, who would initiate self-healing of his patients through affirmative or scientific-prayer, as it was later called by Ernest Holmes, among others. Utilizing mesmerism, or self-hypnosis initially, and later meditation, (brought to North America thanks to The Beatles and their teacher the Maharishi Mahesh Yogi) this form of self-healing and self-development has as an "after-effect" if you will, the "materialization"/manifesting/"demonstration" of prosperity, greater health, and other things which might appear as "miracles", because their coming to fruition seem unlikely under the various circumstances of the practitioner. This has been clinically documented and demonstrated by thousands, and is more and more starting to be accepted, although not completely understood yet. Some mistakenly liken it to "faith healing", (as is sometimes the case with Reiki and Prana Healing) when health improves as a result of the practice. Because the manifestation of wealth is sometimes a result, (I say "sometimes" because the psychological well-being of the person, their attitude, plus other spiritual factors such as karma and soul's purpose, or "God's Will") Those "secret" DVD's and books quickly gained global notoriety, professing to enable people, if they simply follow the steps, to manifest wealth, health, and romance. This is like trying to tell God, or the universe what you want, and then waiting for it to come, which is of course nonsense; however, the chief philosophy of this DVD/book is just that! Those "secret" DVD's and books are a distortion of the ancient, spiritual truths reflected in New Thought/metaphysics, and in fact, has it backwards, according to thousands of years of Buddhist and Sanskrit traditions: one must regularly practice sensing and becoming one with the love, peace, and joy of God first (a.k.a. "Oneness") through contact/mystical meditation for many years, thus eventually (and supposedly) resulting in a healing of the mental, physical, and spiritual conditions of the practitioner, and if combined with affirmative mind-treatments, (self-hypnotic positive reinforcement/reprogramming of one's personal ego mind) a.k.a. "affirmative"/"scientific-prayer", (which is not a "pleading" to God, but rather a "knowing", with faith, that God has already healed the situation, since God knows before the practitioner knows what they have need of, and trusting that God is guiding them towards knowing what they really have need of, therefore God is guiding the prayer through one's Intuition) change, or "materializations" occur. You can see that many years of regular discipline and practice is required to even develop enough faith to be able to even begin to experience any results, and yet those "secret" DVD's and books profess to, if followed correctly, change people's lives!

The other side of the coin is, that I have actually managed to manifest, before knowing, studying, and practicing first the ancient ways, let alone those "secret" methodologies, scores of things in my life, as already outlined! Things like my syndicated cartoon-strip, things like my caricature job at the Toronto recreational park; things like becoming a professional magician and my television-show; things like the finances to support myself and my expensive magic habit; things like my job at the local New Age bookstore/wellness center, new furniture and cars, and the other things I am about to share with you; things like the great support-systems that the universe brought to me (and still is to this day) as friends, family, co-workers, circumstances, etc.

I'll admit that I've had an advantage from birth, that being an almost "Polly Anna"-ish attitude about life, a childlike faith that mostly is still there, which ultimately determines the level of manifesting that I have previously achieved. I have learned that not everyone is born with this kind of faith in others and in circumstances, let alone in themselves, which is the key ingredient to all of us being happy and "succeeding" in this life; many start off with it, then lose it through difficult situations; others manage to gain it because of extraordinarily positive circumstances; still others "count their blessings", maintaining faith through gratitude and appreciation. For me, it is that, but as stated before, its about relaxing enough, not worrying or being anxious, and therefore "getting out of my own way" to allow things to just happen, or for me to "stumble upon" the right person or persons, or situations, or to have them appear to me, that I'm passionate about! It's as simple as that, plus the all-important gratitude for what was received, an optimism about what is yet to come, and almost looking forward to life, sometimes blindly, especially in the face of opposition or "difficult" times! I have found that being grateful even for the challenges helps one to sail through and above difficulties, and that those "troubles" are an absolute opportunity to explore what fears and issues created them in the first place! It was all of this, which is "me", (some would say that I'm one with God) that has enabled me to achieve, through inspiration, hard work, and believing in myself and others! I recently heard a quote by a globally-famous comedian/television/movie-star whom I had met and partied with in the early 1980's, (as previously outlined) "Hope goes through the flames, and faith leaps over them." This reflects much of my philosophy and experiences in life, which is also my goal/mandate for my metaphysical career and the clients that see me now. But this is all leading up to that, and my renewed magic career!

I have just gone on at length about those "secret" DVD/books, and matters metaphysical because I have spent the last thirteen years researching it all, documenting it all in my self-help books available everywhere, as well as living it all, and sharing it all with my clients, thanks to my initial "Doctor of Divinity" degree, and the other two subsequent doctoral titles.

Doctorates and More Books

Thanks to those "secret" DVD/books, a certain globally-famous New Thought minister came to my attention; he's the New Thought minister from that film, who is one of many speaking about the manifesting techniques. For whatever reason, he resonated for me, or "felt right"; ironically a few years later Sue and I would see him and his wife in person at a Vancouver Unity event. Regardless, I noticed the "D.D." after his name, and the "Dr." before his name; "What does "D.D." mean", I wondered and wondered in 2005. Can I earn those letters? I "Googled" "D.D." to no avail; nothing really came up, except the definition, "Doctor of Divinity" which felt lofty (pardon the pun) but also it felt "right". I decided to take my proverbial foot of the gas, and continue with my career-activities, but I really wanted to write a book; it was like it not only "felt right" to do so, but I almost "had to"; I have since learned that I've always had this creative "drive" (obsession?) but never as much as from that point on! It was as if something wanted to be birthed through me, but perhaps I wasn't ready yet; as this famous New Thought minister teaches, ask "Who do I need to become, and what must I know" in order to move forward. I was asking this without even knowing that this is one of his therapeutic techniques; I've always been somewhat curious, asking why, what, etc. And so, as I sat down at my computer to start to write something, anything, I felt a "presence", similar to an umbrella over my head. It wasn't heavy or oppressive, simply "there". I began to write and to write, almost as if the book was being written through me, something using my body to create and express itself. It was as if I was seeing through gelatin, everything was fuzzy, and I couldn't make out the words that I was typing, but I couldn't stop; I was aware of the occasional word being underlined in red, indicating a potential error. I typed and typed, and at the end of each day, I asked Sue to read that day's work, nervous that it all might be "gibberish"! To my relief, it all made sense, and, not believing this, I looked at my work for myself; it was a treatise on health, wellness, and matters spiritual and metaphysical! I was citing my case-load of clients (not using their real names, of course, for their own anonymity) and putting it all together in an organized and orderly fashion! I was what's know in New Age circles as "channeling" my book! But who, or what was I channeling? What was I allowing through my body to create this book? It was almost half-finished, when I decided, before continuing, to find out exactly what was going on? Was it my guides doing this? Previously I had never "let them in" me, they appeared to be outside of me; no, something was using my body to do this metaphysical work. I sat down at my computer, and taking a breath to relax myself and go into an altered-state of meditation, I asked myself mentally, "Who are you? Have I met you before? Are you this "umbrella"/"group"/presence over my head that I've been feeling?"

The answer came all at once, as a "knowing": "they" called themselves "Elijah" (pronounced "Ell-lee-yah") and they were individual guides, who were included in this group, also containing the guides I was already consciously working with; they were "non-physical higher-resonating entities", similar to another, more famous group of "higher-resonating entities" that someone else channels.

From what I understand today thanks to my doctoral studies, because of where I was in my spiritual evolution, this was how it made sense to me at the time; in actuality, it was really my Higher Mind/subconscious appearing in this way to me.

Now I understand that this creative process may be likened to "God", or "Universal Mind"/"Higher Intelligence"/"Higher Mind", etc. coming through us as our individualized bodies in this lifetime. We apparently must have the illusion of separateness/individualization so that "God" in It's many limitless and Infinite forms may materialize/express Itself. I believe that everyone can allow this creative process to occur, either as writing, drawing, magic, comedy, whatever creative "medium" or outlet, or "talent" if you will. Many do not allow it, in other words, they think that they can't sing, or draw, or write, etc. Really, it is one of the Highest forms of inspiration that we can allow in this lifetime! If only we wouldn't judge ourselves, if only we didn't allow our personal ego-mind to get in the way of creation! Just remember how a particular singer, song, work of art, etc. moved you to tears: this was "God" from the creative work touching God in you!

Regardless, I accepted "Elijah" as being the creative-force behind my very first book, "Magic Happens!" which is still in print to this day and is available globally. I was so excited to be able to "channel" this information, that Sue and I began to hold regular meetings at our apartment for me to channel Elijah, free audio-recordings of the info given, and any questions answered that night. This was all by donation, if memory serves me, and I garnered the potential attendees through our local New Age bookstore/wellness center, where I was still working at the time. We would often have up to a dozen people seated in our living room, enjoying my guided meditation, and then the channelings. We served coffee afterwards, and this also became over several years a social gathering for us as well!

I'm so grateful to those who attended and supported me! Around that time, I suppose God, or the Universe felt I was open enough, or ready: something told me to "Google" "D.D." again, and that's when I learned of the oldest and largest metaphysical university in the world, located in Sedona. The parent, ministerial-branch of the university (actually two of them!) offers non-secular university-level degrees, from a Bachelor in metaphysics, to a Masters, and eventually various kinds of Doctorates, including a "D.D.", or Doctor of Divinity. All of their degrees are legal, and the equivalent to seminary-school degrees, being of a "religious" nature. Needless to say, the universe provided the means for me to enroll in this distant-learning degree-program. The six textbooks were shipped to me, along with books of exams: 48 open-book exams from the first four text-books to earn the Bachelors degree, and then 18 open-book exams from the other two text-books plus a strict Thesis to write to earn the Masters in metaphysics! Should one pass all of the first 48 exams successfully, one earns their Bachelors diploma, a (Spiritual-Healing) Practitioner's diploma, (which is how I studied and qualify in Prana Healing and Affirmative Prayer) and also the title of Metaphysical Minister, being able to legally preside over wedding, funerals, and baptisms in the U.S.

It took me several years to complete in my spare time all of the necessary scholastic requirements, including a difficult Dissertation to earn my Doctor of Divinity, but I did manage to, and just in time! My first book, "Magic Happens!" would now have the credit, "By Rev. Dr. Michael Likey, D.D." I was over the moon!

I had earned my first doctorate-title and had written a book on self-help/metaphysics, which was globally published! This was as a result of the aforementioned inspiration, faith, passion, and hard work. Was I manifesting as a result of watching those "secret" DVD's, or was I just being my usual creative and passionate self? I leave that up to you, the reader to decide, as I also manifested during that time a brand-new car for Sue and I, and the means to keep it!

My passion for doing psychic readings at the local New Age bookstore was beginning to wane, what with "meditation nights" being held thrice weekly at our home as well! Guided by the information gleaned in my metaphysical studies, attendees to these nights were beginning to break free from their self-made hindrances and achieve beyond their wildest dreams! One night was "Guided Meditation" night, for beginners, really a mystical, or contact meditation evening designed and inspired to help participants to heal their unconscious mind of negativity. "Past Lives" was actually a combination of the past-life regressions, and soul regressions I did in my hypnotherapy practice, combined with the mystical meditations, so attendees to these experienced what they believed were their previous incarnations, giving their current life meaning and understanding. The third evening was an "Angel-Guides" meditation, designed to have participants meet their guides while in meditative-state; this worked for most of the attendees, the rest experienced various multi-layered, "multi-dimensional" "journeys" which they described in detail afterwards. It's impossible for someone in meditative or hypnotic-state to make things up, according to several doctors whose work I had researched, so knowing this gave us all the confidence that the experiences weren't all the result of an overly-creative mind, so-to-speak. This was all very enriching for everyone, and because I was charging a minimal fee for the evenings, I was starting to earn as much as doing a dozen readings in a day at the bookstore! Plus, I was able to "control" who attended; I was quickly tiring of the years of unwell people from six years at the market, and seven years in total at the bookstore. In time I developed the drive to earn a Ph.D. in metaphysics from the Sedona metaphysical university. Again, the universe provided me the means to earn this Ph.D. in "Mystical Research", while also guiding me to write my second book, "Journey of the Mind, Journey of the Soul", for which I used the research from the three meditation nights to discuss meditation and the clinical as well as spiritual value of it for one's growth. This book is also available globally, and coincided with my completion of my second Doctoral studies.

Feeling really excited and grateful for everything in my life, and confident that I would be alright financially if I left the bookstore, after seven years of doing readings there on Fridays and Sundays, I gave my notice. "Why?" asked the owner. "I'm tired of listening to other peoples' problems", was my response. That was absolutely true! The nature of doing readings is to provide hope and comfort for those troubled clients. They didn't (generally) want to take responsibility for their life or their troubles, they mostly wanted someone to tell them that everything will turn out fine. But that wasn't where I was at anymore in my life; I had many tools to help them break free of any negative cycles; I could hypnotize them, I could give them Reiki or Prana; I could do a spiritual mind-treatment (hypnosis) with them to heal issues of low self-esteem, for example, which was hindering their success and progress, limiting themselves as to all that they could be! No, I was armed with many tools which were proving their worth in private sessions, and our meditation nights. I didn't want to feel the anxiety of having to "prove myself" to new clients anymore either: "Show me that you're the real thing", some would demand. I felt that at fifty-two, (at that time) and all that I was doing and had already accomplished, I had nothing to prove to anybody; I preferred seeing the clients that knew my work, appreciated me, and were growing and more importantly willing to keep on growing with my guidance. To this day I am so grateful to the handful of clients who have stayed with me over the years.

Confident in my decision to leave the bookstore, and with Sue's support,

I did that. Sue had just switched being an Education Assistant at her former high school, to do that at her former elementary school! She still enjoys that to this day, and at the time of this writing, is looking forward to retiring in two years. I always had faith in Sue's God-given abilities, her love of children, and the way she has with them. My incredible step-kids are an example of her raising them! At thirty-eight and almost forty, they are strong and independent, one working at a social-housing position and making a difference for the homeless in Vancouver, the other using his God-given talent for creating new food-dishes, served at a creative, privately-owned restaurant. Both of them have defied social norms in order to maintain their creativity and to make a difference; I love them so and are so proud of them!

After "retiring" from the bookstore/wellness center, I decided to earn yet one more Doctoral-degree. It came to my attention through an e-mail from the university in Sedona. The CEO had put together something entirely new, yet something that I felt I would find useful personally, as well as professionally. It was (and still is) a PsyThD., or Doctor of Theocentric Psychology. Again, the universe provided me the means to enroll in this program, and again, my passion for writing was ignited!

I began writing what would become my most comprehensive metaphysical tome to date, "The Science of the Soul" in 2011. At well over 300 pages, it contained my first two books, plus entirely new and updated material. I added in "The Spiritual Laws of the Universe", a chapter in itself, to help others to see how everything is interconnected with an intelligent design. I'm very proud of this book, which is still available globally.

The Theocentric Psychology degree-course was the most difficult diploma I had ever attempted. The five books of study-material each contain 25 chapters, of which exam-questions were required to be answered successfully, again, open-book style, but nonetheless arduous and daunting to approach. Because each chapter had meditations required to do, this started to make the journey a lot more pleasurable. I absorbed the information within these five books, living them and sharing them to this day! I find them crucial for myself and my clients and students. I learned, thanks to this course amongst many other things, why scientific-prayer doesn't always work, which I've already explained previously, and how to correct it. I learned in clinical terms why and how it does work; in fact, for my dissertation towards partial completion of this degree, (besides answering correctly the 125 or so exam-questions) my topic was "Scientific-Prayer"! Exploring and citing quotes and examples from a dozen or so metaphysical books, including Ernest Holmes' works, and my newly-acquired Napoleon Hill classic, "Think And Grow Rich", I managed to complete the paper, after a year or so, only to learn that I had to correct the specified structure, and do a re-write! Finally, after learning that I had passed the exams, and that my dissertation was accepted for review, I carried on with my metaphysical consultation practice, trying not to think about whether I had earned my third doctorate or not. I kept as busy as I could, but it felt like something was missing, now that I had completed several years of academic work. I had also finished reading three different versions of that Napoleon Hill book, which gave me some new-found inspiration and passion, yet again.

I was busy with my "Blog Talk Radio" podcasts. The original title of these internet-based "podcasts" (or broadcasts) was the same as my book, "The Science of the Soul". It eventually evolved into being called "Dr. Likey's Soul Dialogue", and finally "Dr. Michael Likey: Higher Thought" (the title of my full-color meme-book) which is what I call them to this day. Essentially, I invite guests who are involved with metaphysics, and/or matters of the soul/self-help to share their knowledge and inspiration. I do a meditation or two, as well as play a pre-recorded song from one of my CD's. I developed a large following, as all of the shows are archived for the public to review and re-play. I once again "stumbled" on the idea of podcasts thanks to a health and wellness shop I visited in another suburb of B.C. one day. Originally, I approached them and a nearby metaphysical bookstore to either do readings and/or healings at; I required space for my lectures and workshops since we had outgrown our apartment for this.

Although neither location worked out, one of them had a podcast, I noticed, after checking out their website. "What's a podcast?" I wondered, as I clicked on a website logo. Suddenly I found myself mechanically and without thinking, putting together my own! "On Air in 15 minutes", said the warning on their web-page; "I guess I'm doing a podcast!" I thought. This was how my now six-year-old podcast came to be, with potential guests e-mailing me wanting to come onto the show, from all over the world! Listeners with questions call in from all over North America, and I've noticed more than 3,000 listeners are either present during the live broadcasts, or listening later to an archived show! It dawned on me that I could reach way more people this way, than organizing live in-person events! I even added an Internet "live" (in actuality, pre-video-recorded) "web-cast" to these metaphysical shows! I gave up several years ago on working in retail locations, when a fruitful job doing healings and readings at a retail store in yet another suburb ended suddenly, despite my loyalty and efforts in accumulating a large clientele there. Content with my Internet-shows, clients, and writing self-help books, I learned in 2013 that I had earned my third doctoral title, Doctor of Theocentric Psychology, PsyThD., and that I was now also qualified to teach it and write books about it!

2013 also marked the year I got inspired to do magic again, after more than ten years of focusing on my metaphysical career, studies, webcasts, and books.

The vision of seeing my new "Magic Mike" websites plus a brand-new "Merry Minstrel Majick" magicians online-supplies store (now since re-named "Magic Mike Likey's Magic-shop") ignited my passion for performing and earning a living from magic again!

It felt as if I had come full-circle from 1993: The "Magic Mike" of Winnipeg fame, was no longer the same "Magic Mike" of Vancouver fame! How could I be that same person? Everyone evolves, even within the course of an hour or a day, let alone over the course of twenty-one years! For one thing, I love myself more now; I recognize "God-within-me", and all of the sacredness and responsibility that that entails for myself and my relationship to others and humanity. I recognize that I'm not just my careers, or the things that I am accomplishing, but rather, I am Source manifesting through me as my outer-shell, Source doing the actual creating and using my body to do so. Had I realized this back then, I never would have polluted the only physical body that I will ever have in this lifetime, with alcohol; I never would have taken some things for granted, believing that I will always have the things that I had; I would never have disappointed some people with my carelessness and indifference! Yet, I harbor no regrets about the past, nor any decisions that I've made. If, as my New Thought convictions believe, everything is Source, including thoughts, actions, things animate and inanimate at their core, then there really is no such things as mistakes! Every thought, every action, every consequence is God-guided, (or is "Higher Intelligence) and has a reason, although in the short-term it may not appear so! If we come out the other end of it all loving ourselves and others even more, appreciating "even the dust", then we know why all of the good, and the apparent not-so-good occurred! No, I am certainly not the same person that I was back then; I have learned much about myself, others, and the universe in general; I have shared all of this and more, as I believe it to be; I am "Magic Mike" now, just better, different, and I love it! In 2013, I was determined to bring back the "magic" in myself and others, not only through my metaphysical knowledge, but through performance-art! I used to believe that my shows only gave superficial relief, but now I know that was only my perspective based on what I knew back then; today I recognize that everything that we do in this life, even the littlest smile, simplest of kind gestures, makes an amazing difference universally. I'm important, and so are you; so is everything that you can imagine. "Magic Mike Likey" came back in 2013, although he never really went away: he just stepped back for awhile to allow more to occur without distractions.

A few years ago, when I was consciously trying to "meld" or combine "Magic Mike" with metaphysics for my metaphysical lectures and presentations, I kept feeling frustrated! "How can a guy doing tricks also share Scientific Prayer in the same concert?" I asked myself this over and over again, slipping into the metaphysical presentations a magic segment, asking for volunteers to help out with an illusion or two, then going back to the "regularly-scheduled presentation". I've even had respected colleagues suggest to me that I combine the "magic" of life into my metaphysical workshops and presentations, but it still doesn't feel "right" for me at this point in my life. I prefer to simply accept those feelings, and do magic-shows (as "Magic Mike Likey") which bring joy, mystery, and wonder to kids and families, but also be "Dr. Michael" the metaphysician, author, and Blog Talk Radio host/producer who provides tools for personal-growth and spiritual evolution. I'm alright with the two distinct entities! No problem at all!

Recognizing that I wasn't the same "Magic Mike" as in Winnipeg, I became passionate about allowing the "Magic Mike of today" to come forth in my manner of presenting my tricks, my choice of tricks, and in my costumes! Even my recorded-music, when utilized in the show, is different, in that I use commercial songs with a magic-theme from the '60's, '70's, '80's, and '90's! Everyone recognizes those songs, and it adds to the enjoyment of the shows. My costumes are "hybrids" of my past costumes, including variations of the medieval ones I still love, but with w new hood and redesigned boots, for example. still recognizable for Winnipeggers who remember me, but true to the "Magic Mike" of today! Even my summer, predominantly-red, gold, and white costume will look familiar to Winnipeggers (my main market) but will work fine locally; rather than the red "running-shoes" of yesteryear, I wear red "gym-shoes" which feel right, and are more contemporary, also matching the red-motif of the summer costume and feeling like "me" now. Ironically, before my "Magic Mike" days when I was still living in Montreal and then in Toronto, I had two pairs of "tennis/gym-shoes" that I would alternately wear, blue with white stripes, and white with blue stripes: just bringing the "old me" up-to-date", I suppose! Even my animated-adventures and color comic-books, "The Adventures Of Young Magic Mike" (available globally as a paperback-comic and/or DVD) brings "me" as a youngster (sporting aviator sunglasses and my 'fro) up-to-date with the castle, and "Desmond Dagon" and "Forgetful Lion" from the old TV-show, a sort of a prequel to it! To further bridge the gap, combining the past with the present, I produced four seasons of my webcast "The New Magic Mike's Castle" for the old fans, and for new audiences! I painted a brand-new castle-set for this, built some new props, and drew and animated some new characters/inhabitants of the castle, including creating animated versions of Desmond and Forgetful, utilizing the original puppeteer's voice for those characters; I'm really proud of that project which you can stream or own as a DVD from Internet sites. It provided a bit of "closure" for me as well.

Only recently did I realize that I hadn't really ever done "closure" with the "Magic Mike" of Winnipeg days! In some way, while performing in the last two years, it was as if I wasn't truly present, but "re-living" if you will, the past! This created a kind of "stress" for me, and I didn't realize why; so I went about exploring all of this, recognizing a distinct point in time when Winnipeg's "Magic Mike" "died"; (when my TV-show, the family restaurant/bar-gig, and magic-shop went under) this wasn't something for me to be traumatized by at the time, (although I was) but merely a "gift" from the Universe, letting me know that it was time to move onto another career, in this case metaphysics! I even recall back then when it all ended in '93 and '94, I didn't even try to get more magic-gigs, instead I automatically pursued "Tarot"-gigs! This was obviously my Higher Mind trying to ease me into the next phase of my life even before re-locating to Vancouver! It was almost as if I was getting ahead of myself, doing a mock-up of my own deck and book, displayed in a show-case which I would eventually emulate doing years later in New Westminster, at my kiosk! I didn't realize that I was trying to Live the future, but I just wasn't ready yet, I had to experience all that I did at the suburban market to make me the author and metaphysician that I am today, all for me to assist others! And isn't that really why we have all reincarnated into this lifetime? To assist others, giving and sharing of our particular gifts and talents; even if we're not aware of those talents, we can still do our best at whatever we're doing, with gratitude, joy, and appreciation.

The French Community Center

As soon as I acquired the passion for magic again in 2013, I "feverishly" began to design my four "Magic Mike" websites: a generic one with nostalgia in mind, containing photos, newspaper-clippings, and videos of my magic-doings in Winnipeg and early on in Vancouver/New Westminster.

Believe it or not, it didn't take me long to build these sites, but of course, I "had" to also put it all out there on all social-media sites! I even created a social-media account for one of the fictional cartoon-characters in my webcasts, "Winnie The Bat"! I worked hard to design all of the new "Magic Mike Likey" the logos and graphics, plus animations. I suddenly got inspired to write an album of children's songs, the title being one of the songs from the CD, "The Ballad Of Young Magic Mike's Castle" available globally! I sing three songs from the album to this day, including "The Bat", which also has a music-video (as they all do) for it. The inspiration for "The Bat" came from a 1950's and '60's comedian's hit song about a mouse, except mine was about a "flying-mouse"! In fact, the first three seasons of my webcasts and podcasts had a "haunted castle" theme, to sort-of differentiate the Winnipeg "Magic Mike" show from the "now" "Magic Mike Likey" show; I even included some vintage movie-serials and radio-series into my podcasts, while for my webcasts, I found ancient, silent-movies, and even what is considered to be the very first horror-movie, which employed magic-illusions/special photographic effects in this 1800's black-and-white silent film! This movie was filmed at a famous Parisian theatre, named for a famous French conjuror.

I love all of this trivia-stuff, and I combined all of my passions for these first three seasons of "Magic Mike Likey's Castle Mysteries" on the Internet video web-site. Another source of inspiration for these three seasons was an American television horror-movie host, who "lives" in a castle, (or dungeon) and loaded with puns, will sing a song and/or draw a picture related to that week's monster movie!

One Saturday night, while enjoying him on television, Sue turned to me and said, "He's just like you!" I thought about it later on, realizing that he started his show back in the '70's, taking over from another television horror-movie host, a hippy-character who rises out of his coffin to sing songs with his guitar, and introduce that week's celebrity and movie. Yes, today's character is my current inspiration, but not my original inspiration for my original "Magic Mike's Castle" television-show of the '80's and '90's, as we didn't get his show in Canada in the '70's, '80's, or '90's! My costume was (and is still is, medieval; lately I've been toying with a more "western", 1800's look) while his is a "grave-digger-meets-Dracula" style, complete with top-hat and gruesome make-up. The other similarities, such as the format and puns of my original show are uncanny, though! A tip-of-my-top-hat-to-you: do you see what I did there?

Regardless, I was relentless now, in 2013, in my determination to perform regular magic-show again, preferably for money! I was aware (and still am) of the great differences in magicians' salaries between east and west: in Vancouver, the average fee received for a children's magic-show is $175.-$250., depending on the venue. In Winnipeg, Toronto, and Montreal, it is now what I was getting when I left Winnipeg in 1994, which is $350.-$450. for the same kind of show. My expectations locally, therefore, for a salary/fee wasn't much to begin with, but nonetheless, I proceeded to e-mail all of the local community centers my brand-new promo-material. Within a half-hour, "Felicity", the program director of a local French community center, (five-minutes down the hill from where we live) e-mailed me back. She was interested! "Let's get together for a meeting", she requested. As it turned out, we were both "in-synch" and she was also originally from Montreal! She grew up in a suburb called Pointe Claire, where one of my beloved dance-club of the '70's, was located inside of a hotel there. Like myself, she shares a passion for providing to the less-fortunate arts and culture, and I still work with her to this day, accepting the occasional free magic-show from her for the birthday-parties they hold there. Apparently adding my shows into their birthday-party itinerary/package has resulted in their having 900% more parties there, (Felicity tells me) the fees paid by the clients going towards the centre. I am proud and grateful to bring what I do to the centre, both for the service, but also as an outlet for my shows, which are well-received by the parents and children alike.

Getting My Shows Together

It was no simple task to organize myself and my tricks into a show for my first performance in over ten years, which was not at the French community center, but at Sue's school, in a classroom where she works! This would be my debut and "rehearsal" if you will, for the upcoming shows at the community center that year, which was 2014 by then! The idea was that I would put together "kits" of simple magic-tricks that the kids could learn, and which I would teach, and then do a small show for them. I had done this for a fee hundreds of times in Winnipeg, using a world-famous television magician's "project" of tricks, designed to increase a child's confidence and manual dexterity. Sue helped me put the kits together, each one consisting of simple props such as clothes-line, rubber bands, cards, mini-sponge-ball, etc. housed in a small sandwich bag, that each child would receive, thirty in all! As well, I prepared attractive notes and a certificate that each child would also receive. Everything worked out well, including answering any questions that the kids had; I was back in my "element", confidently performing, and teaching! I felt ready for my first of many birthday-party shows at the community center!

I had assembled several tricks that I had performed thousands of times over the years in eastern Canada, as well as on its west coast and throughout North America. This consisted of a sponge-ball routine, a cut-and-restored rope-trick, clowning around while making a balloon-animal for the birthday-child, plus other tricks, as well as singing "Happy Birthday" using my "cittern", a lute-shaped guitar that was my trade-mark, and built for me in the late 1980's by my previously-mentioned Winnipeg instrument-builder.

To my great relief, after weeks of practice, I successfully completed my first "real" performance, to resounding applause by adults and children alike. I asked Sue to video-record the event, which she did, and I later posted it on a famous video web-site, where you can find it to this day!

I started to get wonderful testimonials from the center, as well as from the parents, which I've posted on my websites. I am so grateful for all of that: the opportunity to give of myself and my talents, plus the appreciation I receive for it all, not that I expect nor look for recognition, notoriety, or acknowledgement anymore, but it sure helps! One of the community center's employees, "Jesse", who works at some of the parties, bought me a wireless/cordless lapel-microphone "just because"! This moved me, and I am so grateful to him for this as well! I used it a lot for the community center's events.

I no longer (at almost age 62!) perform 4-6 shows each Saturday and Sunday like in the "old days", (I refuse to burn myself out, ever again) and not just because I didn't charge for the community center's shows; I accepted a couple of shows a month, exclusively for the center; it was enough. It fulfilled my desire to perform, and it was a way to give back. It was also a balance with my metaphysical career, and I don't foresee at this point ever "retiring". Sue feels the same way, and has encouraged me, having faith in me, every step of the way.

I have seen a lot of growth in Sue as well, in the twenty or so years that we've been together, through the good, as well as the challenging times; She is a lot more knowledgeable about matters metaphysical, and is more aware of how much one's feelings and outlook about life determines one's situation; she is even more optimistic and has even more faith now than when we first got together. She tells me she was always like that, and I've seen her "persevere" throughout our time together. My love for her has matured and deepened, as has her love for me. I feel that she accepts every part of me now, as I do of her. As I look forward, I can see the frailties and strengths of my extended-family, with every bit of faith in our future (perhaps more) than ever before.

One day Felicity got her walking papers from the community center and that was the beginning of the end for me and my relationship with the centre. I don't know if it's an east/west thing, but Felicity was the only member of the administrative team that actually "got" me and my attitude, sensibilities, and my humor. She aggressively pursued money-making projects for that community center, which began to thrive under her direction.

A year after Felicity was "retired" from the center and moved back to our beloved Montreal, I quit the center. Over the ensuing year I was beginning to feel less and less appreciated by the center, almost taken for granted; furthermore, at the larger events which included myself as entertainer, the "main-stage" acts were promoted and given professional acknowledgement, and I remained as an "after-thought", so-to-speak: although children and families would clammier for my shows, gathering a huge crowd, I resented being placed as a sort of a "side-show" show. Where once I performed on main stages with tens of thousands of people in the audience, I was lucky that they fit me into their little events, and somewhat condescendingly as well. I think they saw themselves as doling out some pittance to the now-forgotten senior dressed in funny garb; how I longed for the decent, respectful people of Winnipeg, who truly valued everything!

I began to write more and more, until (to this day) I have more than forty paperback books available globally, along with many also available as "e-books". My metaphysical client base has dwindled as well: as part and parcel of "curing" my patients, my case-load naturally decreases, but I'm fine with that. I'm looking forward to starting up my podcasts and webcasts (I do them seasonally) this September, as I am passionate not only about being in front of the camera or microphone and interviewing my guests, but also the subsequent "post-production" of editing everything as well.

As far as magic is concerned, I practice sleight-of-hand (close-up magic) daily, and I've added many more tricks to my close-up routines. In regards to stage magic, I recently purchased a brand-new carpet-bag and refurbished some old tricks of mine, as I have a hunch I will be doing more stage shows (if not locally) then in Winnipeg for sure!

6 AN EMPHASIS ON "MAGIC MIKE"

It is at this point that I would like to focus on my magic career as "Magic Mike", or because of the proliference of other "Magic Mike's", (including the stripper!) "Magic Mike Likey". Hopefully you've seen the progression of my life up until now, so please indulge me as I dream a little bit and look out towards the future. Following is the contents of another book of mine, *I AM Magic Mike Likey!* Enjoy!

7 BEHIND THE SCENE OF THE TELEVISION SHOWS

I'm always getting asked (usually by Winnipeggers) to "give them the dirt" so-to-speak on what really went on behind the scenes of my various TV-shows, even 23 years after the very last episode aired! People speculate, completely incorrectly, about drugs, alcohol, and sex in-between takes of the show! Imagine a stoned or drunk Magic Mike attempting to do a magic-trick on the air, or handling his audience...how ridiculous! First, I could never perform drunk or stoned because magic is a learned skill, requiring timing, dexterity, and a general "being present", let alone my being able to add my now-trademark (may I say "legendary?) quips and corny humor! That would all be impossible if I were inebriated and under the influence of anything other than my silly self!

This being said, there were numerous incidents and accidents that occurred both on and off the air!

I may never have been drunk or stoned during any of my performances on television or in person, but I must admit to occasionally being under-prepared for the TV-show! After all, something had to give, between my (on average) 10 live corporate shows a week, (sometimes they were birthday parties, mall shows, or rural fair shows) the medieval feasts, my full time graphic design and cartooning career with their unrealistic deadlines, last minute bookings that I accepted either personally and/or through my agents, and my magic-shop and global mail-order magicians' supplies business! That's not counting the occasional "steady" or regular gigs/appearances at restaurants/bars. Needless to say, my schedule was over-filled, and I've burnt out at least 3 or 4 times in the 13 years I lived in Winnipeg keeping to this ongoing schedule, but maintaining it was always a joy; I also subscribed to the philosophy (as did most of my cohorts) that you have to "make hay while the sun shines", that is to take advantage of the potentially temporary good fortune and work as hard as you can until the luck runs out. And so I did; and so there were the resulting and now-infamous fails and fumblings of tricks live on-air which also added to the richness of what Winnipeggers call "the golden age of television" in Winnipeg! This attribution refers not only to my on-air fumbling of my tricks, but as well to the numerous other on-air personalities of the now-infamous public-access TV-station CVW, originally "CVW 13", later "CVW 11". From two female seniors playing cover-tunes on drums and accordion, to an overweight gentleman physically dragging across the floor his small, female partner while attempting to teach ballroom dancing, to a semi-clad, middle-aged woman writhing suggestively on the floor while pop-music played and her leering brother sideways glanced at her. This and much more was the "golden age of television" in 1970's, '80's, and early '90's in Winnipeg, and I was blessed enough to be a part of it all! Apparently, according to a curator of these shows, one of the creators of a famous animated television-show about a "southern park" was involved with Winnipeg's Public Access television programming!

Regardless, I recall attempting the magic-trick, during a taping of one of my "Magic Mike's Castle" TV-shows (likely season 3 or 4) "The Rising Card" wherein three selected playing-cards each mysteriously rise from the pack; remember this was a stock item in my close-up magic routine which I performed hundreds of times (successfully) up to this point in time. When the first card was supposed to rise, it did...only about halfway up, coming to a painful and unexpected stop! I immediately and manually pulled the card up and out of the pack, continuing the trick successfully; and although this was a brief second or two in time, people still recall the incident, years later, calling to me from the streets of Winnipeg when I visit, "Hey, the rising card!" Another fun incident occurred during season 1 of my original TV-show "Kiddie Cabaret". One of the producers decided to, off-camera and just to my side, blow "sneezing powder" in my direction while I was on-air, introducing one of the upcoming show's segments! Honestly, at that moment, it only seemed like pepper, (probably one of the main ingredients) but in seconds I found myself sneezing continually, unable to stop! It was hilarious for all of us, including the viewers and staff of CVW. Another potentially disastrous incident occurred during the taping of my "Magic Mike & Company" television program, probably 8th season. During the first segment, I was to promote one of our sponsors by holding up a t-shirt they provided for a promotion I was having; on one side was their logo, and I don't know what made me initially hold it up with the logo towards my body and away from the camera, but I did; as I held it up, and just before turning it around towards the camera, I noticed that somebody had switched the regular one (which was black) for another black t, this one having a huge, white stick-figure who had an immense erection! The caption read, "Shwing!" I laughed, and did not turn the t around after all, merely displaying the back of it! I know that we could have edited out this potentially disastrous display of a phallus, but nonetheless my quick-thinking (or desperate actions) saved the day again! During season 1 of my "Kiddie Cabaret" television show, one of the clowns farted. I myself did not hear this momentous occurrence, however the smell was unmistakable, even from a distance of several feet, where I stood. Several of them were kneeling down and behind a blue-screen partition, readying themselves to perform puppetry for the upcoming segment. One of them yelled, "Somebody farted!" upon which time you've never seen such a quick "parting of the clowns", leaving the offender alone and sitting by herself! With seconds to spare, they all re-assembled in time for the live-to-tape successful presentation of the segment.

I was a "silly willy" when I was younger; I recall one Sunday-night while setting up the set for my show, a brand-new stage-hand was adjusting the lights, microphones, and sound. His name was simply two initials, and I immediately like his relaxed and natural style; a country-boy (really a man!) replete with plaid shirt and jeans, and a "Cat" hat, straight out of Mayberry, from the Andy Griffith show. He uttered a few words, and sounded exactly like Darren's puppet "Forgetful Lion", so I decided to mimic his voice and diction, thinking he was mimicking "Forgetful"! It was his real voice, and immediately recognizing this and greatly embarrassed, I halted my actions, quickly changing the subject. I sincerely hoped this didn't hurt him. Nonetheless, he and several others stayed with the show for a total of 7 years, their loyalty I still appreciate and am grateful for to this day.

These aforementioned incidents were probably only just a few of many more, which escape my memory right now, but which I intend to share with you as they come to mind.

8 MERVIN THE MAGICIAN & OTHER TALES

There are endless stories Darren (the voice talent behind my TV-show's puppets "Desmond Dragon", "Forgetful Lion" and many more) will share with anyone who'll listen. The truth is, I don't remember most of them, and the ones that I do remember seemed a little different than what actually transpired. Nonetheless, to the best of my knowledge, and to the best of my knowledge of Darren's stories, I present to you, "Magic Mike Likey Stories"; oh yes, plus one about "Mervin the Magician" I'm throwing in for good measure!

The one most often shared by Darren is the time we went to a local fast-food chain in a suburb of Winnipeg. Seems on this day, as we were enjoying our meals, some teens gathered 'round us, shouting "Look, it's Magic Mike!" or words to those effect. Before long, more kids gathered around us, while others peered in through an adjacent window, and because of this rowdiness that we caused, we were asked to leave, by the manager. I remember a few kids passing by and commenting, but that's about it.

Another tale involves us doing a show at a children's party place on Donald Street in Winnipeg, an establishment that parents leased for birthday parties; the establishment provided the games and entertainment. On this occasion, I chose to have a "mobile" from the television station that my show aired on come out there to tape my show for later insertion as a segment into the T.V.-show. Unfortunately the T.V.-crew forgot a couple of essential cables, so they stepped out, back to the station's building to retrieve them. I must emphasize at this point that I never drank alcohol before performing a show at any time in my career; I took pride in being "cool, calm, and collected" enough to not need drugs or alcohol to face an audience; besides, how could I possibly perform the sleight-of-hand necessary to accomplish some of my tricks if I were inebriated? No way! This time, however, would be different! It was the late 1980's/early 1990's, and I felt SO confident in myself, that I decided to take the owner/manager of the establishment up on his offer to have a quick drink until the television crew returned, and the kids arrived. I ordered a martini, my drink of choice at the time. According to Darren, shortly I was so "looped", that I had to go out into the fresh air (minus 40!) for a walk to sober up; I remember for sure ordering black coffee, as my head reeled slightly. By the start of my show and its taping, I was just fine, and no-one else was the wiser!

Another incredible incident occurred shortly before we started performing a show for a school. I had many school shows under my belt both in and around Winnipeg, Canada, and for this one, I invited Darren to perform his puppets for the school, who knew me from my T.V.-show. We were asked to set up and perform in the audio-visual room, which had carpeting and was warm and cozy. The kids (who were already lined up outside that room) were to sit on tiered seating, which was precarious for a magician who preferred not having his audience looking down at the stage; I had to be careful of my angles. Darren was ready, a puppet on each hand, as he crouched behind a well-placed piano; he preferred not using a formal puppet-stage, but rather the impromptu challenge (and surprise for the kids) of the puppets popping up from unexpected locations. We did this at every location that he joined me at. Sometimes the puppets would pop up from the most unexpected places, which made it seem impossible that a puppeteer could hide there! Behind Styrofoam tombstones, and up from behind a mad scientist's table with very little squirming room were but a few places Darren utilized at one of my agent's "haunted house" locations for another series of taped mobiles for my T.V.-show. Regardless, we were all set to go at this point, and just as they were about to let the kids in, a maintenance man walked in, and wheeled the piano away, leaving Darren exposed and still crouching, puppet on each hand! He and I just looked at each other and started to laugh! "Um, we need the piano..." I stated almost with a tone that said, "Uh, hellooo...?" The teacher in charge didn't seem to understand initially, why Darren was behind the piano, so I added, "We can't start the show without the piano!" That seemed to make more sense, so the piano was wheeled back in and set in place again. Needless to say, they let the audience in, and the show went well.

Here's another one I just remembered today. It was the mid-to-late 1980's, and I was booked by one of my agents to do table-to-table/close-up magic for a few hours. I remember still having my Afro (or "fro") and aviation glasses, which was a common look, at least in eastern Canada back then. I wore a black tux, with red bow-tie and red cummerbund. I was still into "traditional" looking magician's garb, even though multi-colored-attired magicians were popular. Back then, I performed an orange sponge-ball routine called "Clones", I did an effect involving colored gems on a small clear Lucite stick whose colors changed, the "Invisible Deck", the "Nudist Deck", (in which the cards turn completely blank, fronts and backs, and then turn "normal" again!) among other effects. Back then too, I carried my tricks in a cutlery box painted gloss black with large white stars, and a red-velvet surface (called a "Close-up Mat") Velcroed to the top of the box. I would go table-to-table, plopping this box (likely intrusively) on top of the guests' tables, introduced myself, and then did my feats of prestidigitation. Nowadays I practice "pocket management", stuffing my tricks carefully into my suit-jacket's pockets, as well as my waist-coat and slacks. I seldom carry a close-up mat. Regardless, I was done, and as I headed out into the cold, minus 40 Winnipeg winter air and walking towards my vehicle, I looked back and upward at the hotel's marquee which proudly proclaimed, "Tonight, Mervin the Magician!" At the time, I was known as, and booked by my agents as "Merlin"; I suppose the sponsor didn't hear my name correctly. It also explains why everyone that night kept calling me "Mervin", which I laughed off as a term of endearment, or a joke. The guests were genuinely thanking me repeatedly as "Mervin"! Thankfully my check was made out to my real name.

9 THE ANXIETY FACTOR

"The Anxiety Factor" is a professional magician's term used to describe the feeling that a magician feels just prior to executing a secret move or a sleight. Sometimes this feeling causes said magician to execute the move in a manner that's not invisible nor smooth, thus telegraphing something "not right" to the audience. Maybe the rhythm of the trick feels off; a sudden hesitation, be it ever so subtle; something that suggests to the audience that the ebb and flow is off. Sometimes a magician will try to cover this moment by using some clever line of patter, or worse, a bad pun or a joke. Often times, a way to compensate at this potentially awkward point is utilizing a "larger move" to cover the smaller one. An example would be the classic "pass", wherein the magician secretly transfers the person's selected card to the top of the deck, unbenounced to anyone; this should happen faster than the blink of an eye, and quite invisibly. However, this being one of the most challenging moves in a magician's repertoire, often times a magician will execute any one of a dozen or more alternatives to this move, most of them just as effective, although seldom as subtle. During the classic pass, the magician might (in an effort to cover up his/her lack of smoothness) turn away slightly at the crucial moment, asking the person or their friends a question, for example; this is an example covering a smaller move with a larger one. Nothing wrong with this, as long as it makes sense in the context of the performance of the trick, and is entertaining, funny, or at the very least, logical. This could provide the perfect cover for a difficult, or uncomfortable sleight-of-hand move. As long as everything flows from beginning of the trick right through until the end of the routine.

My intention here was not to discuss the magician's "anxiety factor", but rather his/her anxiety in general.

I've been performing magic professionally (for money) since 1981, after a member of Toronto's magic club (a very supportive and professional hobbyist's organization) passed along to me a magic show just north of Toronto shortly before I relocated to Winnipeg. I'll probably break down the structure and many magicians' faux pas that I made during that show in a future story, but for now suffice it to say that in the eyes of regular people/the sponsor it went well. I'm still grateful for the club's passing along this gig to me after watching me perform bar-magic (another specialty) previously for the club, and excusing my many other "faux pas", my having covered them up with my so-called personality, essentially covering up nerves (smaller things) with larger things, my personality. I segued to Winnipeg with this performance style of trying to deal with nerves by using witticisms and puns, apparently right in line with Winnipeg's sense-of-humor. Over the years I've adapted this style to the particular humor and sensibilities of the particular audiences of whichever city I was performing in. When in doubt, use a conservative sense-of-humor, jokes, and puns, as opposed to a wilder, more clownish and pratfall-ish style, if you use humor at all in your show. I find in general it gets the audience on your side and relaxes them as well. One day, right in the middle of my first year of shows in Winnipeg, I suddenly felt myself relax and be completely "present" or in the moment! This is a very liberating feeling (if you've experienced it once, then there's no looking back) and actually resulted in me being able to improvise jokes and puns, thus enjoying my audiences more; remember, if the audience senses you like them, they'll almost automatically start to like you as well. The opposite is true as well: if you're nervous or uneasy, then your audience becomes suspicious of you, even when they don't have to be! They might even begin to dislike you, because they'll think that you dislike them, even though you just might be nervous! Some quick tricks to settle nerves, taught to me by my father, who himself was a professional "show drummer" all of his life: imagine your audience dressed really foolishly, or even imagine them naked! Another technique is to imagine that you're performing alone in your room, and that the audience isn't really there. I find that for larger audiences, looking past them and towards the back of the room often helps, and it looks like I'm playing to the back of the audience, when in fact I'm avoiding eye-contact. Remember to compensate for this technique by actually occasionally and consciously making eye contact with every single person in the front row, even scanning/glancing them from right to left or left to right during your performance, but not making a big thing of it ie)-wondering what they're thinking of you: just do it automatically and it will create the illusion of connecting with your audience, despite your nerves!

I have also found a different kind of "anxiety factor" with time and/or age. After doing thousands of shows for hundreds of thousands of audiences, I have no doubt that I can stand in front of any age of audience, young or old, make them like me, and entertain them with my magic and/or music. I can even "plug in" a brand-new trick or two into a show, and also rely on some of my time-proven magic-tricks in the show. No problem. But lately, (in the last 10 years, I'm 60 as of this writing) I experience a feeling of dread and anxiety between shows, for no logical reason! Maybe it's biological; it certainly can't be psychological; maybe over time I've conditioned myself this way because in my younger years with several agents, I had to "produce", or do the shows so that we all made great amounts of money. Some weekends I performed 12 shows, (six on Saturday, another six the next day) no sooner packing up my tricks from one location and driving like a fiend halfway across town to the next location, unpacking and "psyching" myself up for the next several hundred people comprising my audience! Thank goodness for meditation, which still quiets my nerves and brings me back down to earth ("grounds me") helping me to pace myself! Perhaps the years of this pressure has frayed my nerves somewhat, resulting in great bouts of anxiety between shows, but then once I'm performing and immediately after, the rewards and joy I feel from performing for the amazing children and adult audiences more than compensates for this feeling. But it's still is worth mentioning nonetheless. It's not all fun and games between shows, what with practicing new sleights and routines, keeping up-to-date through trade magazines and videos, writing articles and books, producing DVD's and CD's, editing others' books, and seeing clients for my Theocentric Psychology and Clinical Hypnotherapy practice! The thing that still brings me the most joy is to see the look of wonder and laughter in the faces of my audiences!

When I'm on stage or performing for my audiences in general, I suddenly feel more comfortable and "at home" than if I'm trying to conduct idle "chit-chat" with friends or family. This all happened since that point in Winnipeg, after a year of shows back in 1982! I believe with many performances, you'll suddenly have that moment of being "present" and in the moment, rather than worrying in the back of your mind about which trick comes next, how the audience will respond, etc., and just focus on entertaining your audience with your magic and your personality.

Just enjoy performing, perform well, and if you can't, then don't.

10 TROUPING-PART 1: THE ILLUSIONS

"Trouping" among professional magicians generally means touring, and/or doing many shows, one after the other, either at a regular venue/location, or multiple ones.

This definition doesn't seem to include performing on cruise ships, which is a completely different category, and of which I have very little knowledge, nor experience; this is pretty much the only thing in the magic world that I've not at the time of this writing done. Performing, say, regular close-up/table-to-table magic at a regular venue is also not included in this category, however, I suppose that if you had a dozen or so close-up magic shows lined up, technically that would be touring or trouping, but strictly speaking, this term is reserved more for stage shows involving larger box illusions.

I purchased my very first illusion (larger, "box-trick") from a local Winnipeg magician/collector of magic, in the very early 1980's. He was a very famous corporate clown for many years in Manitoba and Saskatchewan, a fine magician in his own right specializing in what we refer to as manipulation magic involving complex sleight-of-hand miracles.

It was from he that I purchased my first "Zig-Zag Lady". This illusion was invented by magician Robert Harbin in the 1960's, who also invented a nifty bow-saw sawing a lady in half, folding table, and many other original larger illusions, and I pretty much had to own this if I was to "move up" in the eyes of local agents, enabling us to start to charge higher fees. I had also seen, a couple of years previously at Toronto's recreational park, (where I drew caricatures) a magician/comedian do a very entertaining act involving what we call a "Sucker Die-Box", what eventually became my sponge-ball routine culminating with a sponge number "4", and ending his show with his Zig-Zag Lady! I LOVED seeing this illusion live, as previously I had seen it numerous times on television, thinking it involved mirrors, but to my surprise and chagrin, it did not!

Essentially, your assistant (older magicians used to call them "box-jumpers"!!) steps into an upright, vertical cabinet, placing her face and left-hand through an opening in the upper third, her right-hand through an opening in the middle part, and her left-foot through a hole in the lower third. All body parts are real, I might add at this point, as some other illusions involve using dummy parts, or extra assistants in other cases, but this is a one-person illusion. The magician slides two completely solid blades through openings under the top third and above the lower third. He swings the illusion around (which is on casters) to show that the blades penetrated right through and out the back! Again, the girl's face, hand, and foot are visible the whole time, and in her hand she's waving a silk red scarf! Then, the piece de resistance: he slides completely off to one side the middle part, leaving a large gap in the middle; where IS her middle? With some Zig-Zag models, there's what we call a "tickle-box", or a small door in the middle section which is opened, revealing the girl's tummy and costume, which he tickles, all the while her hand containing the handkerchief waiving to and fro! It's a perfect, angle-proof illusion, suitable for stage, and even allowing for people from the audience to closely inspect everything before, during, and after, because there IS no funny business, nor anything to discover; the cabinet is exactly as it appears, and is not gimmicked in any way! I owned two versions of this illusion, the initial one purchased from my friend, and years later I had one custom-built for me from illusion plans. If you're a seasoned magician, you know who the illusion-builder is. I also had several other illusions built from his plans, including a "Mis-Made Lady", (which I also used to produce myself as a "Stack of Boxes", a guillotine, and a fabulous "Doll's House" pictured, (not from the Osborne plans) used to mysteriously produce my assistants.

Other illusions I owned while trouping also included two different "Metamorphosis" trunks, (where the magician is handcuffed, tied in a sack, locked in a trunk, and then switches places with his female assistant in the blink of an eye, who also ends up having a costume-change!) several suspensions, (which give the illusion that the girl is suspended in mid-air with no visible means of support, several bow-saws sawing-a-lady-in-half, a "Thin-Model Sawing a Lady in Half", (also by this famous illusion designer) not my favorite illusion, I prefer the simple bow-saw version, or better yet, two ropes which visibly and instantly penetrate through the centre of my body! I also owned several "Dagger-Chest" illusions, the quality of them varying greatly from maker to maker! My favorite? The one made by Mak Magic. I enjoyed using an acupuncture theme thanks to magician David Ginn. I found, after trouping for several years at county fairs, malls, and corporate events, that a beautiful (and easy) illusion involving producing a large, colorful bouquet of flowers (I use Abbott's "Botania") elicited (and still does) bigger "ooh's and ahh's" than the large, cumbersome illusions! As my fees started to go up, I slowly fazed out the larger cabinets and boxes, (which were also a pain to put together, especially in some cases where there were no back-stages before shows!) in favor of the "Acupuncture Cabinet", "Chair Suspension", and "Bow-Saw Illusion" which played huge, were easier to set up and transport; combined with my "Botania", I started trouping with a great new show that looked super, while garnering the same $350. fee for 45 minutes!

One set of shows at the scenic "Nickel Days" in Thompson, Manitoba, we were flown up from Winnipeg by prop-plane. As I was also producing doves and rabbits in my shows, in addition to performing "Metamorphosis", the "Zig-Zag" and "Broom Suspension", we smuggled my dwarf rabbit onto the plane under a very pregnant-looking wife's shirt! Another time, I was performing the "Zig-Zag" at St. Pierre-Joli's "Frog Follies"; I realized after returning home, that I had left part of the illusion at the venue! I had to drive a few hours back to retrieve the important part! Ah, the pleasures of trooping!

11 TROUPING-PART 2

Nothing was more exciting than trouping with my Magic Circus, the summer of 1988 and 1989.

I was originally asked by a famous local kids' festival in the winter of 1988 to submit a proposal to the provincial government, who would fund a province-wide tour, potentially, for myself and several other performance artists from Manitoba. Right around that time I was already assembling an entourage, or troupe if you will, of variety entertainers not unlike my original Kiddie Cabaret troupe. (which was the basis of my original television program) At the very least, I intended to put on several performances that summer at a kids' fest, which were also one of my agents. Because I no longer had the same performance artists and musicians that were in my original show, I decided to rename this potential touring troupe "Merlin's Magic Circus" and give it some kind of circus theme. Note: At the time, I called myself "Merlin", eventually Michael Merlin, Magic Mike Merlin, and finally just "Magic Mike". I had seen, several years earlier in Miami, Florida, a show put on at a famous clown circus establishment, which inspired me to upgrade the make-up and costuming for my own clowns in my show, and also "inspired" several clown skits, (which eventually made it to my TV-show and live performances) including "Clown College"! One of the skits involved a clown "ringmaster" getting his clowns to growl like lions and jump through a hoop he held; another segment included a silly-looking ballerina-type female clown pretending to walk a tightrope, (actually just a rope laid out on the ground) holding a little pink, French-looking parasol. This would become the nucleus of my Magic Circus touring troupe: I would invite kids up from the audience to perform these "skills", (including a "strongman" lifting light-weight plastic barbells) while dressed up in costumes I would slip over them; a magic-show segment performed by myself, the "ringmaster" with musical accompaniment by musical geniuses Arthur and the late Elijah (of a musical Klezmer group) on electric piano and guitar, respectively.

The proposal (which I presented before a large committee using video-tape and live presentation, included notes and promo-material as handouts) was accepted, and my little troupe was well on its way to a successful 15-town tour. The next year would include another 15 towns, some towns switched for others. A provincial government van was provided for us to drive to and from the shows, and a government-issued credit card was also supplied to pay for gas and any potential repairs to the older-model van, which fortunately we didn't have to use.

All members of my group (except for two) were professional, seasoned entertainers, and there was five of us. I dressed in formal magician's attire which doubled as the ringmaster's attire, and the rest dressed as clowns. All the "circus" props fit into a colorful, yellow wastebasket which I decorated with red vinyl trim. My magic-segment (which started off the show) consisted of my standard live show: a colorful silk handkerchief production, sponge-balls, (with an assistant, usually a child aged 8-10) and the "Miser's Dream". (I produced coins from everywhere, running out into the audience and plucking coins from the air, children's ears, etc., and dropping said coins, with a huge clunk, into a metal bucket, all the while to musical accompaniment!) I did the "Mutilated Parasol" as well, to musical accompaniment, with one of our clowns assisting: essentially a bunch of colorful silk hankies switch places with the colorful parasol cover, and then go back to their original state; an easy-to-perform illusion, but very colorful! My "Botania" (large and unexpected) flower production capped off the magic segment of the show. This segment ran approximately 15 minutes. Next up, was the previously-described audience-participation "circus" segment, and then I ended this 45-minute show with one more magic-trick, to resounding applause. Because we toured in the summertime, our costumes were hot and uncomfortable in the sometimes 110-degree Manitoba weather!

I recall in one town where our stage was on top of a flat-bed truck, that right in the middle of my magic segment there was an announcement over the loud-speaker that the tractor-pull was about to start, and most of my audience excitedly rushed off! "I was upstaged by the tractor-pull", I joke years later. Regardless of this, or if we were rained out, as long as we showed up, we got paid; a handsome $600. per show, most of which went to the other performers in my show, I might add, but they were all worth it!

Livestock

I used to produce doves and rabbits in my shows, but I eventually stopped doing this, because it was all too much to schlep!

I had all of the fancy and colorful boxes which would always keep the creatures cool and comfortable; (while giving the appearance that they weren't there) and on stage they would either appear or disappear from these boxes, but one day I decided to stop using "livestock" (old-school magicians' term for doves, rabbits, sometimes ducks, geese, elephants and horses!) as I wanted them just as pets. At one time, I inadvertently "raised" rabbits, as its hard not to...they magically multiply and then multiply again! I would use one rabbit in a group of 3 or 4 shows on a Saturday, then the other look-a-like rabbit in the next day's group of shows. I called the little white male with black-tipped nose "Hocus" and the female "Pocus". My two doves "Fluffy" and "Puffy", had a baby, "Baby Bird", and I raised him to troupe in my shows as well. Sometimes I would produce two doves in a show, or sometimes I would give the appearance of producing and then vanishing one dove, and then have it re-appear elsewhere. My doves were ring-neck doves, not the pure white ones one often sees magicians work with. It was thanks to a local amateur magician/dove-breeder who referred me to a dove-breeder in rural Manitoba that I got my first and only doves, as they live a long time. I always made sure that my animals were comfortable, and that I produced and vanished them in humane ways, as opposed to the questionable methods other magicians use. For example, in order to produce doves supposedly from nowhere, they have to lay in a tight-fitting pocket, restrained in a strait-jacket-like devise, and then quickly yanked out into view, or yanked out into an upside-down position, camouflaged behind a silk scarf until the magician releases them into view! My tricks with doves and rabbits looked less flashy because I used comfortable boxes for them to rest in prior to producing or vanishing them; kids were amazed regardless, (as were most of the adults) so who cares, as long as the creatures were comfortable?

One show, the birthday-boy was particularly rambunctious and talkative; I "magically" produced one of my doves, and while it was perched on my finger, I asked the child to take it on his finger; the dove was subsequently perched on the birthday-boy's finger as the boy continued to yell and act out. The bird then proceeded to defecate on the boy's good dressy pants, and surprisingly, nobody objected, not even his mother, who quickly cleaned the boy up after handing me my bird. Another successful show! I remember after one show (where I produced my doves) for the Jewish New Year at a North-End Winnipeg synagogue, as I was sitting with some of the people after my show, an older, European man turned to me, declaring proudly: "I think I ate a pigeon once in Europe."

Ah, the wonders of working with livestock!

12 COMMERCIAL OR FOR MAGICIANS?

In the world of magic, there are basically two types of audiences: a) lay-people/regular folk b) magicians (experienced, and inexperienced)

There are therefore tricks/illusions for lay-people, and tricks/illusions aimed at magicians.(I mean those who are more experienced and have seen it all and know all of the methods) In some instances, some tricks will overlap, and actually fool magicians; often times, these tricks can be tedious and boring, filled with complex and time-consuming sleight-of-hand, when a trick deck or gimmicked coin might have made the trick more visual, snappy, and interesting for the spectator, also allowing the magician leeway to relax, improvise his presentation and most importantly, ENTERTAIN, which as far as I'm concerned is the main reason for doing magic! I would much rather have my audience first be entertained, (laugh, for example) and secondly be fooled while I'm at it.

When I moved to Winnipeg in 1981 from Toronto, I inadvertently (due to my own lack of experience in the magic world) upset the experienced magicians. First, I charged an outrageously low fee for my shows, (which I felt justified at doing due to my lack of confidence and experience) and secondly because I by-passed a lot of difficult sleight-of-hand in favor of entertaining my audience; this wasn't because I couldn't do intricate sleight-of-hand, (I was very adept at coins and cards) but because I would much rather have, say, showed a deck of cards as appearing normal, then all blank, then all normal again, focusing on presentation. A sleight-of-hand-artist would have done all sorts of less-convincing and intricate moves to accomplish this, so focused on the sleights, that perhaps the presentation or patter might have suffered. Believe me, I saw plenty of this at the magic-clubs, and it just plain hurt to see all the knuckle-busting moves performed by the well-intentioned locals to accomplish the simplest of magical effects. I make no excuses for my methodologies, which made me the busiest and most commercial magician at the time, working at many bars and restaurants, and eventually corporate, private, and public events, malls, and fairs, not to forget birthday parties. I was having the greatest time, focusing on my personality and entertaining my audience first, and the tricks secondly, which apparently made for a successful formula. My audiences would laugh, and scream with delight AND amazement, which is exactly what I wanted, and still, hopefully, accomplish. I'm not bashing the "finger-flingers" here, merely pointing out my personal opinions and experience. There are amazing magicians out there who mainly use sleight-of-hand in their act, (usually to musical accompaniment) of which I still have the pleasure and honor of enjoying, but the methods are just not for me. I guess you can categorize me as a "Comedy Magician", if I must be stereotyped.

Nonetheless, there is a reason why I've shared this with you, and it's because in a couple of weeks I have what's known professionally as a "close-up gig", that is, I'll be "table-hopping", going table-to-table for a major corporate family restaurant doing my thing. It brought me back to my first regular restaurant gig doing magic at "September's" and also "Gabby's" in Winnipeg. How excited I was, pockets loaded up with sponge-balls, carting around a cutlery box filled with my close-up miracles, soft red velveteen working surface on top of it, and I intrusively placing this gaudily-painted box on top of the customers' tables; my enthusiasm obviously made them forget that they never asked that I come to their table, nor that the amount of room left for their meal was greatly diminished, but again, my enthusiasm must have blinded them; either that, or they were really nice, patient people!

Thirty-five years later, it will be myself, pockets and case (on the floor, out of their way) loaded up with the same tricks! This amazes me, because I've gone through hundreds of thousands of newer, more amazing close-up magic tricks, learned so many more sleights, and studied and practiced so many more tricks, many of which have made it into my stage show; but why not my close-up magic-show? To be frank, some newer ones have made the cut, and will be included, possibly a plastic spoon that twists itself out of shape that I give them to keep at the end of the routine, a coloring-page the size of a five-dollar bill that changes from a black-and-white line drawing to full-color, (this will take the place of the "bill-switch", where one denomination of bill visibly transforms into another denomination) and a few other ones; but the disappearing and appearing red silk hanky will still be present 35 years later, along with the cards that all go blank and normal again; heck, my "Clones" will make their appearance, (and disappearance) as well my Lucite "Hot Rod" will be present and many other what we call "chestnuts" in the world of magic! Why? Because my audience will be lay-people, not magicians. Why? Because these tricks are easy, they amaze, and they still ENTERTAIN.

13 OUT WITH THE OLD

It's been twenty-five odd-years since I moved from a vibrant, arts-and-entertainment-based city in the middle of Canada, where I enjoyed a vibrant career (actually several) involving doing stage and close-up magic for every conceivable special event imaginable; fairs, malls, wind-ups, you name it, Magic Mike was there! If there was a celebration in Winnipeg proper, or some other town or city within a six-hour driving radius, there I was, either the featured performer, or certainly one of the top three featured. I performed approximately 250 shows a year, PLUS my weekly television program, (which ran for 9 years) plus weekly appearances on a local kids' show. I guess you can say I was pretty busy. When I moved to this prairie city in 1981, there was a lull in the professional magic community, and there was not the same magic-fervor that had hit the rest of North America, what with magicians performing in restaurants and bars, and certainly at children's birthday parties. Everywhere in North America, wherever you would go, magicians had gainful employment and were in the public eye; high visibility for sure! World-famous magicians had regular television specials, and magic fever was everywhere. Little did I realize that this was only a temporary lull in the local magic community. Winnipeg was, and subsequently claimed again the crown for magic events and activities next to Toronto, Montreal, and New York. Winnipeg was the home of the International Brotherhood of Magicians, a world-wide organization that also originally published their magazine there. The Young Magicians Society had its birthplace there as well, started by Bill Brace. (deceased) A world famous escape-artist, the first ever gold-medal winner for magic, many other world-class performers all hail from Winnipeg. Last year's winner of

Britain's Got Talent, hails from Winnipeg. A "Magic Museum" exists in Manitoba as well, to name just a few magical accomplishments. Little did I realize that I would, in my youthful and naive enthusiasm for magic, be instrumental in the re-birth of the local magic community in Winnipeg, or so it was said upon my departure from this fine city by the then-treasurer of Winnipeg's Magic Circle. I simply moved to Winnipeg with a strong drive, nay, an obsession to perform magic anywhere and everywhere, and so I did! I also started the first real magic-shop in Winnipeg, until the magic counter at a large, local toy-store expanded it's selection and hired a magician, subsequently surpassing my sales. But enough of my love for magic rubbing off on Winnipeg.

This is about what I'm doing (or not doing) today. Any time, and every time there's a special event in Vancouver, (my home since 1994) I anticipate having been hired to do a show or two there, the reality being I have no local agent, (I have a great one in Winnipeg) nor have I even tried to acquire one here. I'm perfectly content at this point in my life (almost 62!) to do the odd show, here-and-there.

Long-gone are the 250 shows a year, but would I really want that for myself? That life was exhausting for a 20 or 30-something year-old, let alone for a 62-year-old! Besides, perhaps I'm coming to the realization that it's been long the time to step aside to make way for the younger generation of magicians, and to me that means the 30-something year olds, and younger. I'm told by workers at a local community center (who are 20 and 30-something-year-olds) that they never even noticed my age, but I certainly feel a difference from when I was 30-something, even though I'm in great shape and relatively healthy. My energy-output is just about the same as it always was, I know that. My local peers in magic (and I have a few who are working professionals my age and older) profess to work as much as they always did, although to really make a buck they have to perform elsewhere, that is Japan, the states, or points east, whereas my peers, say in Winnipeg, Toronto, and Montreal are still making a living and are busier than ever in their home cities.

It's a choice, I suppose, at this point in my life: winters, 30 or 40 below zero and paralyzing snow, but superior arts and culture and more than a living as an entertainer) or a relatively temperate paradise where outdoor activities year round exist, with a lesser arts and culture situation. At almost 62, I'm grateful for this easier life I have, for the clients I see evolve as Dr. Michael Likey, Doctor of Theocentric Psychology and Clinical Hypnotherapist, and the self-help books I write and sell globally on the Internet; magic, like it originally was for me at 14, before the joy got a little lost in touring and agents, is a joy again. I'm genuinely excited about this amazing art, as an inventor and marketer of tricks, a practitioner of new sleights, in seeing the joy, amazement and laughter in kids and parents' eyes, and much more. This renewed excitement for me about the art of magic surpasses "making a living" from it. Perhaps I can finally accept the fact that I am no longer in every special event, and can move over (if even a little bit) for other generations to share their craft. I know for sure (and am comforted by the fact) that I have left a legacy in Winnipeg that the younger generations will not be aware of.

Out with the old? Hardly; perhaps in with the new, but never out with the old!

14 SHAKING THINGS UP!

I recently did a special event show at a local Coquitlam/Vancouver Canada-area French community center; although I'm English, I was raised in Montreal, so technically I'm what we call out there an Anglophone (English-speaking) and a Francophone. (French-speaking) I feel really fortunate to have 3 languages, Yiddish being the third one.

I use these relatively smaller special events (average 30 kids per show) as a live "dress-rehearsal" if you will, for my larger shows, for example I'm having a show this month-end and next month-end where there will easily be at least 200 people in attendance each show, along with press coverage, mayor attending, etc. I love all sizes of show, whether there are 10 kids, or 10,000.

Nonetheless, I decided to shake things up this particular show, as many of the kids have seen my shows over and over again, even with my inserting tricks from my "B" or "C" shows into the main one. For the non-performers out there, most magicians have several cases of shows; their main show which they "troop" with, (tour with) and those secondary and third cases of tricks/shows just in case they have more than one show at a venue in a day, where potentially it may be the same people showing up to watch...it's always nice to "shake things up", or insert a batch of other tricks or combinations there of. Remember that I've been doing magic professionally since 1981...there is absolutely no venue, or special kind of event that I haven't performed in; from close-up magic in restaurants, corporate events and bars, to malls, fairs, auditoriums, and even glamorous fashion-shows! Then there was my TV-show of 9 years, which forced me to re-invent a lot of tricks especially for that! Thank God I owned a magic-shop and I was able to buy a lot of tricks wholesale; magic is one of the most expensive hobbies in the world! Then there were the scores of doves and rabbits I had as pets and featured characters in my show, and the props necessary to produce and vanish the creatures. So I've owned millions of dollars of magic equipment including huge stage illusions, (at almost 60 years of age, I've long gotten rid of those larger props) which I've used over and over again. I even moved to Vancouver with the show I toured with and kept as my stand-by for 7 years before that. Prior to that I had a whole other show that I trooped with for another 8 years; so I knew the ins and outs of all of those tricks, the audience's reactions, the jokes and bits of business that either I or children had improvised which became permanent lines in my show's scripts...seeming to be improvised to the audience but in reality having been said hundreds of times; I know the timing of every word, every nuance, so that the "sneaky stuff" (misdirection and sleight-of-hand) would not be noticed, all the while trying to be entertaining and affable! This time however, I wanted to completely challenge myself and do a brand-new, untested (at least not by myself) show. The kids in most audiences already seem to love me, I guess they sense that I love them, so that's half the battle: there's a saying in magic, that if the audience likes you, they'll also like your tricks, and I have found this to be 100% true. So, with only a month's rehearsal, for the first time since 1981, I did a completely new show!

Recently I've been enjoying the magic of a seasoned Canadian/Toronto veteran of magic. He was a "star" in the '80's around the same time that I was, and we have a very similar background: he's from Montreal and immigrated to Toronto as I did. He did a lot of T.V. like myself, and he's of a smaller physical stature like myself; what is it with us Easterners? Eccentric short people we are! Where we differ is that he's a creative magical genius who has come up with hundreds of thousands of original (and brilliant) tricks which he's selling on DVD, and promoting on social media along with his online learning annex for professional, intermediate, and beginner magicians; what an amazing teacher of magic he is, with his "organic" approach to magic, which works for close-up as well as stage magicians. Unbelievable. Perfect for me at this stage of my career! I believe we all need mentors, regardless of what stage of life that we're at, and he is certainly it for me right now. At various stages throughout my life, I had numerous role-models for magic, like many other magicians do, regardless of their age or level of professionalism!. At this stage of my life and career, I wasn't expecting to have another magician that I liked and admired; I couldn't relate to those "wondering" "street"-style magicians or horror-"goth" television illusionists. Too bad...because although their material is exceptional, their appearance and presentations are simply not for me! Discovering this Toronto magician, at this point, was obviously meant to be, especially because although as a pro I was aware of him in the '80's and '90's, I never bought his books; I didn't even know that many of the tricks performed on TV then and now were invented by him, including a pull-a-selected-card-out-of-an-inflated-balloon performed by David Copperfield on one of his specials was his! He even appeared last year on "Fool Me with Penn and Teller"! Needless to say, my new show was "heavy" with this Toronto magician's tricks!

The New Show

I'll spare you what my most recent "touring" show was like, but suffice it to say that I had already worked in two of that magician's tricks, including his card-out-of-balloon, a card trick involving a party sparkler, where the magician succeeds in spearing a selected card with a lit sparkler. Very visual and showy, deceptive, and yet easy-to-do!

Yes, the audiences LOVED those illusions, but they also loved the "B" tricks from my old shows like "ropes through my body", which plays big and folds small into my doctor's bag; and then there's the oversized beautiful sponge rabbits that multiply in a spectator's hands! It pained me to eliminate these two tricks! Honestly, the opening effect is also crucial, and I literally "have a million of 'em", but the one that works 100% of the time with great audience reaction is "rope to silk", so I decided that that would be the only effect from my old show that I would include. It got the strong reaction that I am used to! The new Toronto magician's effects included a magic plastic Coke loyalty card that transforms, a chopstick-impaled-through-a-coin, (with a "hypno"-swirl sticker placed on both sides) the very strong card-from-balloon, and sparkler tricks as the finale.

That magician recently released a fantastic DVD about routines involving a finger-ring mysteriously appearing on and off a piece of black, silky rope, and even includes the ring and beautiful rope! Since I had been performing a very similar illusion since 1993, I decided to integrate several of the moves from his routines, (which included a nice rope-routine) and despite the difficulty of the newly-learned routine, received one of the best reactions that I've ever received from one trick! I LOVE this trick/routine which is from his rope-and-ring DVD. I resurrected two more illusions that I've not performed since 1994, a very standard kids' show trick which is funny but baffling involving two large bamboo sticks and their "tissle and tassle", and another illusion where I freely count 6 jumbo cards, (and ONLY 6 cards!) removing three of them, but still having six cards over and over again! It usually evokes laughter and amazement, but this time (25 years later) it only seemed to encourage mild curiosity; this is one I'll do one more time in my next show to see if I need to change my routine (which I've done over hundreds of shows!!) or if that was just a freak reaction.

Nerves? No way! Maybe a little anxiety, but because I rehearsed the individual tricks over and over for a month and then strung them together in a logical order, I felt really liberated during the performance and successfully (I'm told) ad-libbed a lot of new lines that will go into my future shows. Don't be afraid to "shake things up"...it just might be what your show needs!

15 CHILDREN'S SHOWS

One of the things I love to do now after almost forty years of magic-shows, (3 or 4,000 of them!) are shows for kids! That includes special events/"family" shows as well as birthday parties!

I didn't start off as a kids' magician after relocating to Winnipeg, Canada from Toronto in 1981, although I had some birthday-party shows under my belt by then. My goal was to perform mainly for adult audiences in bars and lounges, with close-up magic, as well as a "platform" or "cabaret" show consisting mainly of "pseudo-psychic", a.k.a. "Mentalism" effects. I had doves in my stage-show, appearing and color-changing canes and candles, but I especially loved doing card-tricks on stage in which I was apparently "reading" spectators' minds. I must admit, I borrowed some effects from a well-known 1970's television "Mentalist"!

I must admit, I didn't enjoy kids at first, nor did I ever choose to have my own children, (I love my almost 40-year-old step-kids, however, from my second marriage!) but performing primarily for thousands of kids' events made me grow to love them, and vice-versa! I enjoyed their enthusiasm, honesty, and humor, and they enjoyed my silliness and magic-tricks! I made them laugh, I made them sing, and I believe I brought a sense of wonder into their lives, which I still hear today about from them, themselves now parents!

Earlier tonight, I performed at a birthday party at our local community center; I'm their "go-to" magician, when I'm available! At age 62, (I started at 25) I choose to no longer do as many shows: four or less a month is more than enough! I've recently "re-cycled" one of my four kids' shows since I'm starting to get some of the same kids attend these parties and special events at the community center. So the same, time-tested show ("A") that I've been mainly doing for many years goes into the magic-trunk, and out from my oversized leather doctor's bag (or sometimes a carpet-bag) comes show "B", also pretty strong, but less familiar to me, since it was my 1980's "go-to" act, and the other one "A" was my 1990's "go-to" show. The two other shows I mix and match with "A" and "B" sometimes. This current incarnation includes a "double-rope-through-my body" and the "Egg Can" effect, which I've re-worked to suit my style; I must admit, the advise given in professional kids'-show-magician David Ginn has heavily influenced the construction and routines of my kids' shows; I was thrilled to meet David in the 1980's at a magic get-together in Winnipeg; he even autographed one of his books that I owned, just one of many which he's written!

Regardless, something went very wrong with the "Egg-Can" effect tonight, unbenounced to the audience. Suffice it to say that an egg that I had supposedly pre-blown empty wasn't completely hollow, making for a sticky and stinky mess! The kids didn't notice anything unusual, thankfully, so the outcome was as it should be, but that's not the first time I had bad luck with an egg: in the 1990's, at the medieval feast at a hotel in Winnipeg, a whole egg that I had hidden in the front pocket of my white pants had broken just before my segment! The effect involved a silk handkerchief transforming into an egg, so the egg was a crucial part of the trick! I quickly drove home (which was minutes away, thankfully) and changed my pants, securing a brand-new egg. After that, I always performed that effect with a fake egg.

The point of this is, that we as magicians have an advantage over, say singers and musicians; the audience knows what the particular song is supposed to sound like, but they don't necessarily know what to expect with a magic illusion! In other words, we can change our routine, or even the outcome of the trick, without them even knowing that something might have gone wrong! Believe me, I've had to do this on several occasions, without batting an eye. One friend of mine, a famous television "escape artist", early in his magic career in Winnipeg, apparently produced a deceased dove from a fire-pan, while another gold-medal-winning Winnipeg magician, while attempting to secretly vanish into his coat-tails a dove, missed, sending the bird careening quickly in reverse to its early demise, smashing against a nearby wall! No doubt everyone was horrified; our mutual agent related these stories to me, in an effort to make light of me forgetting my bunny at home, which in the "spectacular" climax of my show, I was to produce; you win some, you lose some! After that, a former talent agent of mine (now deceased) always teased me before a show, asking, "Did you feed your rabbit? He looks kind of skinny"

16 THE HISTORY OF THE MAGIC MIKE WANDS

From Plastic To Wood And Back To Plastic Again

There was never just one first wand, there were several!

I purchased my first magic wands from a Toronto magic-shop in 1980, when a cigar-smoking, Groucho Marx lookalike with a New York accent was still the owner, and they were situated in the Yorkville-area of Toronto, Canada, back in the summer of 1981. I had just turned twenty-five, and I was also feeding my magic obsession, performing, practicing and purchasing as many magic tricks as I could as I had no idea if there was a magic shop in Winnipeg;, where I was shortly re-locating to.

The First Ones

The first wands I ever purchased included a standard black plastic one with white tips, and a plastic "gag" black and white one which when held by anyone else but myself went flaccid. I purchased that summer, as well, two "coin wands", as they are known in the business. One was a narrow metal one, covered with red glitter-tape, with a built-in rubber-band attached to a copper British coin. When the elastic and coin were secretly pulled down the length of the wand, with the coin held in place at the other end by my palm, it looked only as if I was holding that wand in my hand. With a slight release of pressure by that hand, the coin would jump up, and suddenly appear (as if by magic!) at the other end/tip of the wand. It actually looked good, but after some practice, the band broke, which I never replaced, nor did I end up using that wand for that purpose in my shows. It did however match the red motif of my close-up magic show, what with the red crushed velour close-up mat which was attached via Velcro to the makeshift close-up case. (a cutlery box I painted gloss black with white stars!) I did use the wand in all of my shows in Winnipeg from 1981 to approximately 1992 to misdirect audiences away from any sleight-of-hand I was doing in my shows.

The other wand was a longer, broader plastic-wand mainly black with white tips; this wand housed a secret plunger feature, which would secretly deliver into my hand, one-at-a-time, folding 50-cent pieces. It gave the illusion that I was producing coins out of thin air! I love that wand, and still have it, along with the red one.

The "Camirand" Wand

In Winnipeg from 1989 to 1993, I was also running a successful mail-order magicians supplies business. One of my suppliers by 1992 was a magnificent business from a suburb of Montreal. It was named for it's founder. Their raison d'être initially was to produce and teach splendid, elegant, and original magic material; their initial instructor/creator of new magic went on to produce many magic specials for television, and he also became one of David Copperfield's principle designers/inventors! One of their products was the "Camirand Wand", which I still own to this day. It's solid-wood with silver tips and perfect balance makes it still one of the more superior wands of it's kind in the world. I used to always use it with my brass cups and balls (from a Spanish manufacturer) and miniature baseballs from the late inventor Mike Rogers. I used a standard routine from the late Dai Vernon. Again I digress.

I used the Camirand Wand for years, even after relocating to Vancouver, Canada in 1994.

A few years after that, I remembered magic-legend Harry Blackstone Sr.'s gorgeous redwood wand with brass tips, with his name engraved on it, reposing under glass, which I had seen in a magic museum located in the basement of "Twin Cities Magic" in Minneapolis, MN. circa 1991. I never forgot the history and energy resonating from it, and to this day I still associate classy, classic magicians with this style of wand.

By 2002, a local Vancouver magic-illusion builder and friend, "Reg", (by far, responsible for the highest-quality "Multiplying Bottles" magic illusion in magic history, by-the-way) was creating magnificent redwood-and-brass wands! I knew I had to own a "Donnelly Wand", and I still do!

The Donnelly Wand

I asked Reg to engrave on one tip in fancy script "Magic", and on the other tip, also in script-type, "Mike", thus insuring and carrying on some sort of

"Magic Mike Likey heritage" once I'm gone. This, like the Blackstone wand, would be my official (generic) magician's wand.

But what of the "period", Celtic/medieval/"witchy" Magic Mike Likey of "Magic Mike's Castle" (TV-show) fame? What of his wand?

The Magic Mike's Castle Wand

In Winnipeg, circa 1990-1992, during my "Castle" (Celtic/"witchy") phase, I made my own wooden wand from a tree-branch.

Approximately three-quarters-of-an-inch in diameter, and ten-inches long, this sanded-smooth-and clear-lacquered wand also had a small crystal which I attached to one end, and some Viking Runes cut into the body of the wand, to give it a mystical "feel". Original in look and design, I always felt comfortable with this wand, counting on it's originality to match the originality of my medieval costume. Unfortunately, somewhere between Winnipeg and Vancouver, it "magically disappeared"! This is why I used the Camirand Wand for many years in all of my shows, "witchy" and otherwise. This is why I used the Donnelly Wand for other shows.

Today

Since 2013, I've been using an "updated" version of the "witchy" wand: a twenty-inch long branch, sanded, finished, and painted dark brown by myself, with a crystal at one end attached with glue and gold tape. The effect of this three-quarter-inch-thick beauty is that of "mystical majesty"; the end of which I hold even seems to have a natural, ergonomic shape which cups my hand as I hold it! This is the true, "re-born" and updated Magic Mike Likey of today, having come full-circle, so-to-speak!

In 2014, a plastic, tan-colored (to simulate wood) "Wizard's Wand" from China came to my attention through "Magie Parfait/Perfect Magic" in Montreal. This twelve-inch long wand is one-inch-wide at it's base, and tapers to one-quarter inch at the other end. Here's the thing: it has a small button, which when pressed, causes a small blue light at the tip to flash, while a "twinkling" sound is emitted. What a great kids-show wand! I've included it in every single birthday-party/children's/family show that I've performed at! Perfect! To hear the audience go "ahhh" while I use the wand is worth way more than the original twenty-dollar price of the wand!

I've also integrated into my children's shows a short, (four inched) clear-colored plastic, Chinese-made wand purchased at a Dollar Store, which pulsates various patterns of multi-colored lights from inside of it, enhanced via the semi-transparent colored plastic. It is the perfect wand for when I ask the audience to "throw their colors" at a black-and-white sad clown on a handkerchief, magically changing him to a happy, multi-colored clown!

The Real Magic

I love magic. Of course, the "real magic" is not in the wands, but in the smiles, laughs, joy, and wonderment I see and hear from my audiences. What a privilege it is to perform, and work my own magic!

17 A HISTORY OF THE MAGIC MIKE LIKEY CARPET BAGS

The Beginning

There is a world-famous Orlando, Florida, magician who also appeared as a clown in a 1960's U.S. television-show about magic. He is known as an inventor of tricks, and is also a successful entertainer. For these reasons I was excited to watch his show in 1989 at the "Red River Exhibition" in Winnipeg, an agricultural fair, whose equivalents include Toronto's "Canadian National Exhibition", and Vancouver's "Pacific National Exhibition". What struck me immediately, was that he walked out on stage with an oversized carpet-bag, also known as a "Mary Poppins Bag". He worked his complete act out of this large, attractive, tapestry bag, wearing a sort of "huckster/pin-stripe suit" . I've always had a fascination with carpet-bags, perhaps because they look so old and magical; how many times have we seen on television and movies magicians, witches, and other interesting characters carrying one, pulling from it potions and other magical artifacts? There is a sort of mystique about carpetbags, and I made up my mind right then and there that I would acquire one for my period-themed magic shows; up until that point, I'd been shlepping around a cumbersome trunk on wheels; how convenient and magical-looking would a carpet-bag look in my shows, what with colorful props and silk handkerchiefs coming out from it? I was once again obsessed.

My First Carpet-Bag

As luck (or fate?) would have it, modern carpet-bags, and carpet-bag luggage was all the rage in 1989! All I had to do was walk through any luggage department of almost any department store, and strike gold! A major department store in Winnipeg was my first stop, and 'lo and behold, there it was: the bag that would house, transport, and be instrumental in the look and execution of my live magic-shows! It was beautiful: a brown, paisley tapestry material, with brown leather handles! It even matched my medieval costume, with it's white and brown suede "feel".

This bag went through hundreds and hundreds of shows, and one of the handles was beginning to wear; I decided it was time to go back to that store and buy a spare one. This was easier said than done, as this style of luggage was beginning to wane in popularity; I had no choice but to buy a grey-paisley tapestry bag, but this one had longer handles, (a more feminine/hand-bag-look to it) but I didn't care, this would be the next bag once the current one wore out and would be retired to that great magic museum in the sky. The wonderful thing about this bag was that it housed all of my children's show props with ease; it even had a couple of interior pockets for carrying spare balloons and smaller props! Furthermore, I made my show even more self-contained by carrying a folding side-table (known in the trade as a "Harbin" table) in the bag as well! The bag and my Cittern in it's case completed my set up, both of which I'd throw into my hatchback and drive to a half-dozen shows in a day, back in the day. I must admit I started to get a bit carried away with the "self-contained" theme (ie- not needing any additional tables or chairs once I arrived at a show, by screwing folding TV-dinner tray legs to the bottom of my guitar case, so that the case would rest on its own legs so-to-speak, while my carpet-bag rested on it's own tripod-stand, which was screwed/attached to a flange at the bottom of the bag; the whole idea of spontaneity (ie-the bag sitting on a chair) seemed lost, so when I switched to the newer grey bag, I dropped the use of a tripod-stand for it to sit on.

I debuted the set-up during the week of Halloween 1989 at a mall show in Winnipeg; it was also the first time I sang an original warm-up song, "You Can Do Anything You Want", which later became one of the theme-songs of one of my TV-shows, "Magic Mike & Company". Depending on the size of the venue, I alternated using my carpet-bag with my trunk for housing and transporting my props in Winnipeg from 1989 to 1994, then into Vancouver shows from 1994 to 2004. I loved hearing the kids commenting that I "had a Mary Poppins bag", especially when I pulled an umbrella out of the bag to do a particular illusion...what a perfect tie-in! The illusion, by-the-way, is Abbott's "Mutilated Parasol".

I'd like to share at this point, a brief history of carpet bags in general.

A Brief History of Carpet Bags

A carpet bag is a traveling bag made of carpet, commonly from an oriental rug, ranging in size from a small purse to a large duffel bag.

The "carpet bag" was not invented as a pocketbook or handbag for women. Rather, it was the day's version of our modern "suitcase" that operated as a reliable traveling companion and carrier of a person's possessions.

Such bags were popular in the United States and Europe during the 19th century. They are still made to this day, but now typically as women's decorative small luggage and purses, although typically no longer out of old carpets. Carpet was the chosen material because, during the time, carpet in homes was a popular accent piece and the "remainder" pieces were easily bought to use for the construction of carpet bags. In a sense, the carpetbag was a sustainable invention because it used remnants of materials which otherwise would have gone unused.

The carpetbaggers of the Reconstruction era following the American Civil War were given their name from this type of luggage which they carried from the Scientific American Supplement, No. 561, October 2, 1886 "The old-fashioned carpet bag" is still unsurpassed by any, where rough wear is the principal thing to be studied. Such a bag, if constructed of good Brussels carpeting and unquestionable workmanship, will last a lifetime, provided always that a substantial frame is used.

Carpet bags sometimes also served as a "railway rug", a common item in the 19th century for warmth in drafty, unheated rail-cars. The rug could either be opened as a blanket, or latched up on the sides as a traveling bag. From Robert Louis Stevenson's *Travels with a Donkey in the Cévennes* (1879): "... my railway-rug, which, being also in the form of a bag, made me a double castle for cold nights."

One of the most popular carpet bag brands of the mid 1960s (known as "the California Carpetbagger" is Jerry Terrence Original Carpet Bag, aka: JT Carpet Bag. The company encouraged the use of brand new carpet material.

The Leather Doctor's Bag (Gladstone Bag)

After my hiatus from magic to earn a masters degree, then three doctorates in metaphysics, (I am Rev. Dr. Michael Likey, by-the-way...a clinical hypnotherapist, and Doctor of Theocentric Psychology among other things), I caught the "magic bug" again almost two year ago! To become obsessed with leather doctor's bags as an extension of my love for carpet-bags wasn't much of a stretch, thus, I own several standard black-leather doctor's bags, a beautiful brown leather one, and a vintage, (1920's, in almost perfect condition!) oversized leather doctor's bag imported from England, purchased through an Internet retailer. My intension was to replace the feminine-looking grey-paisley, long-handled tapestry bag with a larger, more masculine-looking, brown-leather doctor's bag, which suits me more nowadays. You'll almost always, when attending one of my live magic concerts these days, see me with either the large doctor's bag, or my steamer/upright trunk on wheels, and my Cittern or Dulcimer case, unless it's a non-period show, in which case, I'll have either my Ovation or Epiphone guitar, and props in the trunk or the bag. Recently I purchased from an online retailer an oversized, colorful brand-new carpet-bag, replete with leather trim, leather straps, and southwestern pattern on it! I expect you'll be seeing me do a lot of shows in the future with this bag and using my brand-new metallic, folding-table!

I should mention a brief history at this point of the Gladstone bag.

History of the Gladstone Bag

A Gladstone bag is a small portmanteau suitcase built over a rigid frame which could separate into two equal sections. Unlike a suitcase, a Gladstone bag is deeper in proportion to its length. They are typically made of stiff leather and often belted with lanyards. The bags are named after William Ewart Gladstone (1809–1898), the four-time Prime Minister of the United Kingdom.

Hinged luggage was first developed in the late 19th century. The first Gladstone bag was designed and manufactured by J G Beard at his leather shop in the City of Westminster.Beard was an avid admirer of Gladstone, and named it to memorialise his name.

Though the Gladstone bag developed into the typical flat-sided suitcase of today, modern leather versions are marketed which in fact are not Gladstone bags. Often these modern bags are made with soft, rounded sides, only opening at the top. This incorrectly named Gladstone bag is actually a kit bag, or a square-mouthed bag. The Gladstone bag has been mentioned numerous times in literature by Arthur Conan Doyle, J.D. Salinger, Tennessee Williams, Oscar Wilde, and many more.

There you have it! I guess you can say that magic is truly my "bag".

18 A HISTORY OF MAGIC MIKE LIKEY'S GUITARS

From Aria To Dulcimer

A beautiful 6-string acoustic "Aria" guitar was my first guitar, purchased at a downtown music-shop in Montreal by my dad (a professional Montreal show-drummer) for one of my birthdays. If they even make that particular model today, the closest is the Aria, Prodigy Series, AFN-15. It was a special experience, as a teen, to go with my dad to his favorite music store, and the great care he took in making sure they included a strap, pitch-pipes, and books of instruction. I learned many Cat Stevens songs on it, as well as my own original tunes. In those days, I also played Supertramp, Jim Croce, Meat Loaf, and many more. One day I went to the closet to play it, and to my horror, the entire bridge had lifted up, cracking (permanently) the fine wood finish and top of this guitar, which was ultimately ruined; I was heart-broken! I moved to Winnipeg from Toronto in 1981, bringing my nylon-string classical guitar with me; I forget who made it...my dad bought it for me from a Montreal hardware store in the Cote-des-Neiges area when I was in my late teens! I was a big Cat Stevens fan, and his style had been a major influence in my burgeoning music career both onstage as well as in my song-writing style. I was obsessed with Cat's "Ovation" acoustic guitars, which I had seen him play in one of his Montreal concert tours. One day I walked into a music shop in a Winnipeg Mall, and 'lo and behold, there hung a very affordable (and previously owned) "Ovation"! Feverishly I snapped down my credit card to purchase one of the greatest loves and investments in my professional career: I still own and occasionally play this 6-string wonder, which along with my "Yamaha" keyboards were..."instrumental" in my song-writing career!

The Ovation

I played my Ovation guitar for every one of my live concert and television appearances in Winnipeg and environs where I wasn't dressed up in my period costume from 1981 to 1994, for a total of well over 2,000 shows. I continued this tradition in my Vancouver appearances, (from 1994 until the present) alternating with my blond 6-string acoustic "Epiphone" as well, again, without my period garb. For the shows where I was in full period garb, I played my 12-string Cittern.

The Fisher Cittern

"Larry" is a gifted folk musician and instrument builder that I was fortunate to perform with in Winnipeg at hundreds of medieval feasts. Larry exclusively builds custom harps nowadays, (including one that a 1980's Celtic musician/singer used in a tour) though in my time in Winnipeg he built a wide assortment of instruments. I loved the 7-string flat-back lute-like instrument that he constantly used in his shows; it looked so "folky", "celticy" and "period"...perfect for my medieval-themed TV-show and live appearances! Since I only played 6 and 12-stringed guitars, in 1989 I asked Larry if he would build me a 12-string "Cittern", (which is the proper word for that lute-like wonder) or "English Guitar". Larry agreed. I was over the moon with excitement and anticipation; I knew that this treasured instrument would be with me always and everywhere "period" Magic Mike Likey would appear. The year before (1988) I had built a 6-string flat-backed lute from a kit I purchased from a Renaissance instrument-builder, but I felt that the finished product wasn't professional enough for me, hence I asked Larry about a Cittern. Darren, the voice-talent on my television show, suggested that we bring a mobile camera-crew out to video-record the making of the instrument at Larry's home workshop; both Larry and CVW agreed. It made for an educational and entertaining insert on my television show. By the time the instrument was finished, the public would have been exposed to, and expecting to see, this instrument in my live shows. It still to this days elicits "oooh's" when I lift it out of it's case.

The Epiphone

Another guitar besides the Ovation that I love which Cat Stevens (a.k.a. "Yusuf") plays, is a beautiful blond "Gibson" 6-string guitar. I was excited when my wife bought me for my birthday it's nearest relative, a 6-string acoustic "Epiphone", manufactured by Gibson. I love the look and deep sound of this guitar, since previously I was used to the sounds of the cittern and the Ovation, one shallower sounding, the other more "tinny". In non-period concerts, I alternate playing the Epiphone with my Ovation. I've had the Epiphone since 2012.

The Dulcimer

Around 2009, I saw two videos: one of Joni Mitchell and the other of Cyndi Lauper each playing their songs using a folk-instrument known as a Dulcimer. Although this instrument has 3, sometimes 4 strings, a full-range of notes and chords can be produced from it. This elongated, narrow-violin-shaped beauty has a Celtic/Maritimes sound/feel to it, and is traditionally played while you're seated with it sitting on your lap; for my concerts, I wear it like a guitar using a guitar-strap. This makes fingering the notes more difficult, but well worth it. It is also traditionally strummed using a pick (plectrum), while holding down the notes using a popsicle-stick-like flat piece of wood. I prefer using a pick, and using my fingers for the notes. I purchased this instrument online, along with a separate case for it, since local music-shops (at least in Vancouver) didn't even know what a Dulcimer is, let alone carrying a case for it! Sometimes I really miss Montreal or Toronto; I'm positive the Winnipeg Folk Festival store would also carry one. However, I digress. After receiving the instrument in the mail, I was anxious to learn how to play it, and as I did with guitar and electric keyboard, I taught myself. Note: my father sat me down at age three at his drum-kit, showing me the proper way to hold drumsticks, and even doing "rolls". He then had me play on the snare, tom-tom and cymbals; what a thrill that was! Regardless, in a short time I became relatively proficient with the Dulcimer, but I've only started playing it very recently in my live shows. Every time I remove it from it's case, it's exotic look elicits an "oooh" (as does the Cittern) from the audience. So far, I've only used it to play my still-trending song "The Bat", but I intend to play more songs with it in the future.

I intend to alternate between the Cittern and the Dulcimer for my period-shows, and the Ovation with the Epiphone for non-period concerts. After all, isn't variety "instrumental" for enjoying life?

Lately I've been seriously thinking about learning the banjo, just to shake things up in my new stage shows, after all, it goes with my "new" 1800's style costume...we'll see.

19 A HISTORY OF THE MAGIC MIKE LIKEY COSTUMES

From Tuxedos To Knee-Highs And Hoods

If you've been following my television show and live concerts since the mid-eighties, or my current web-series and live appearances, you'll notice a very similar look, or style, in my knee-high boots, shirts and vests (or waistcoats) with small variations very consciously planned as "Easter Eggs", for we nerds and trivia buffs out there! Who really cares? The answer, friends, fans, and nostalgia aficionados, is surprisingly more than we could imagine!

The Look Comes Together

From 1981-1987, sporting an afro and aviator glasses, I was performing in traditional, formal-wear magicians' garb, ie)-tuxedo with/without tails, tuxedo-shirt and tie, (either red or black tie with matching cummerbund) silver-tinsel waistcoat with tuxedo-pants, tuxedo-shirt and tie, or even tuxedo-pants, tuxedo-shirt and tie with gold-tinsel tuxedo-jacket!

I was completely ignoring the trend towards the more colorful "hippie-garb" popularized by magician Doug Henning, or the more relaxed (yet semi-formal) '80's-style of David Copperfield.

I had to be me, and if I couldn't me myself, then I'd at least be the more broadly accepted, cliché-magician in formal-wear. I even added silver-trim around the collar of my black tux and swapped out black buttons for silver buttons, after seeing many magicians with that style performing at "Magic Montreal", a major magic convention. It was all a "good-enough" fit for me, but it was still not entirely "me". I tried wearing Kaftans, (I was deep into Eastern spirituality and meditation) sometimes even a silk red Chinese shirt, not quite me, but getting there.

This is why, when doing magic-teaching seminars, I emphasize "finding your on-stage character/persona"; once you do that, everything else will come together: your dress, style/theme and music of your show, (if you use recorded music) even style and choice of props. You'll still maintain commercial-value without sacrificing art, and it will all become more original-looking than the next guy; agents will seek you out more; you may even have to alter your existing props (or even have custom-made ones) to suit your style, but you'll feel more comfortable, even more powerful on stage, but I digress.

Kiddie Cabaret

My original television show, "Kiddie Cabaret" (circa 1985-1988) featuring myself as a circus "ring leader" surrounded by clowns (literally) and puppets, and featuring blackout-skits a la "Laugh-In" was coming to an end; I was growing into another person, and as such, my first marriage was wrapping up too.

By 1988, my obsession with a combination of a little television-show from England, and an Irish musical group, (who also did the mystical-sounding soundtrack for the series) combined with the airing of a Simon and Garfunkel special on PBS, was (pardon the pun) instrumental in my transformation to the real me!

During the PBS special, Art Garfunkel was wearing a vest, unbuttoned, over his poet-shirt. (a poet-shirt looks Shakespearean, with puffy-sleeves, like in the "Seinfeld" pirate/puffy-shirt episode, but more understated; you know the style!) I still love that "Minstrel" style! Around that same time, I was enjoying the mystical interpretation of the Robin Hood tale which was airing on TV, what with the Irish band's moody, atmospheric soundtrack in the background; I knew I had to buy every single one of their albums available, and I did! You also may have heard of the Celtic Irish songstress who used to sing with this same group which was also her family, before she went solo.

Again, I digress.

Merlin's Magic Castle

When my first marriage broke up, all of the clowns departed my TV-show, leaving me with Darren (a clown and puppeteer from that show) who decided to stick with me during the transition.

As I was already evolving into some sort of "wizard"/medieval character any way, (my professional name was already "Merlin", later changed to "Michael Merlin", "Magic Mike Merlin", then finally "Magic Mike") I decided that the "show must go on", and one week in July of 1988, "Kiddie Cabaret" went off the air, and the following week "Merlin's Magic Castle" debuted! It was too soon for me to paint the now-famous castle set and props, so we used "Chroma Key", a technique that turns a drawing/sketch/image into a background image; I used a cut-and-paste (old school, I might add) of a children's book castle interior, making it different enough to avoid copyright issues, and voila, the illusion of me sitting in a castle was complete! I was wearing a wizard's costume that I had recently commissioned, replete with shoulder pads! (after all, it was the eighties)

I decided that this "minstrel" image was "me", after all, I was also playing guitar and singing semi-professionally for many years! I also decided that I would add some live music into my shows which I'd play on my 6-string Ovation guitar! I started writing songs that both kids would like, and adults could relate to; Cat Stevens' "If You Want To Sing Out" (from the movie "Harold and Maude") and the "Reading Rainbow" television theme-song heavily influenced my style; I began singing these songs on my own T.V.-show, as well as wearing the minstrel-style poet-shirt (custom sewn by a private Winnipeg seamstress) and paisley-vest. By 1989 my "medieval" boots were actually brown cowboy boots; I shortly thereafter found a great pair of brown, suede knee-high boots (on sale at a Winnipeg mall!) which I still occasionally include in my costume, although I've added extra flaps and straps since those days. I started off wearing a moustache and "Geraldo" glasses with the costume, but shaved and began wearing contacts for the first time, thus eliminating any visual "barriers" to my audience they might have created. I also grew my hair out, a bit.

The home-made pouch hanging from my belt was replaced with a more authentic one, as well as a brand-new poet-shirt, both of which I purchased at a Renaissance fair in St. Paul/Minneapolis; in those days, the fair was held every weekend in July and August.

Inspired by the "Robin Hood" 1980's series, I sewed a brown suede hood which I added to the ensemble.

For some reason (perhaps "inspiration" from David Copperfield) by 1992 I dropped the period-style in favor of wearing the poet-shirt tucked into tuxedo-pants; I began wearing white dress-shirts tucked into either tuxedo-pants or tight black jeans and black biker-boots.

Magic Mike & Company

Another reason for dropping the medieval/period-look, was because I felt that a more contemporary style suited my regular weekly appearances on a broadcast television children's show, whose host was a Juno-award-winner, and whose set was a contemporary attic; I decided to adapt a more contemporary look to my castle and also my garb there: rather than medieval days, the time was my castle "now"...not as much fun, as I eliminated the swords, cauldrons etc., but nonetheless an "evolution" of sorts at the time. I renamed the TV-show "Magic Mike & Company".

By 1994, both my own TV-show (which lasted 9 years total) and my friend, the Juno-award-winner's show, were both cancelled.

Vancouver

I decided that after having grown up for years in a cold, wintery climate (Montreal, then Toronto) and in the case of Winnipeg, for 6 months of the year for 13 years, that I would seek gainful employment in the more temperate climate of Vancouver, on the west coast of Canada. (notorious for it's 9 months of rain, but milder temperatures) In my move to Vancouver, I kept only the shirt, pouch, and boots, which are still in mint condition after 23 years, and I still wear them to this day in my current shows, alternating them with three other shirts/costumes...not a bad investment!

For some of my early Vancouver shows, (1994- 2005) I added a gold paisley vest and formal trousers, sometimes tucking my pants into my knee-high brown boots.

For other early Vancouver shows, (which included some malls, corporate, as well as kids shows) I also wore everything from a collarless white formal shirt tucked into either formal black pants, or black jeans, to suits and ties, to black tux, white shirt and white bow-tie. On other occasions, bolo-tie with short, black formal jacket combined with a white or black tuxedo shirt.

These variations in dress reflected my lack of personal direction; I no longer felt like the "Magic Mike" of old, so to speak; I was no longer a practicing graphic designer, (except for my own personal projects) nor caricature artist; (though still writing and illustrating my own self-published childrens' books) I had morphed into an alternative wellness practitioner and clinical hypnotherapist; as I earned my bachelors and masters degrees, I became qualified to be a metaphysical minister and author of self-help books. I started to phase out the magic shows in favor of eventually doing spiritual counseling. I forgot to just have fun!

Dr. Magic Mike

After an eight-year hiatus from magic to earn a bachelors and masters degree, and three doctorates, (2005-2013) I resumed my magic career with a vengeance, resurrecting my magicians' supplies business, this time completely on the Internet. Simultaneously I began to have a clearer picture of myself by the time I authored my third self-help book: I could see my "new-old" onstage persona and costumes again! This also coincided with the brand-new, updated versions of my original TV-show, in the form of a web-series and podcast! Full circle, but even better than before!

My generic costume (except at corporate events) today includes the poet-shirt (I alternate between the original Minneapolis Renaissance Fair one, a "witchy", pointy-sleeved, high-collar "vampire"-style shirt locally made, another one (sort of a combination of the poet's and vampire one) also locally made, as well as the white, collarless formal one, combined with a red-velour waistcoat with gold buttons worn over formal black pants or tight black jeans, with black cowboy boots, or pants tucked into my original brown suede knee-highs, or my newly-acquired black suede, or black leather knee-highs. The overall look and feel being visually consistent from show-to-show. I will sometimes appear at family shows wearing what I call "Magic Mike 1990": poet-shirt over pants with belt and pouch over that, my newly-sewn brown suede hood, and knee-high brown-suede boots. I've added a "dragon's tooth" on a leather string that I wear around my neck. In lieu of the tooth, I wear a replica of "Lily Munster's" oversized bat on a chain pendant. I usually wear either a goth-style ring on my right index finger, or a replica of Dracula's ring, styled from the old movie Dracula. I add a bat-stud earring in my left ear lobe to complete the "bat theme", as I also have written and perform an audience-participation, "trending" song called "The Bat"! As a lifelong fan of magic and old-school spooky horror movies, my "Magic Mike Likey" onstage identity is now whole and complete!

Ironic that my original "Magic Mike's Castle" persona existed long before other magicians started calling themselves "Magic Mike ____", long before other wizards such as Harry Potter, or even the male stripper, "Magic Mike". I'm sure that as a result of all of this, there are numerous advantageous marketing opportunities that I've not yet explored!

As stated earlier, I've recently put together an 1800's style costume; I've always loved the "Steampunk" movement, reminiscent of great changes during that period! Thanks to H.G. Wells and Jules Verne's writings during that period, our imaginations, dreams, and hopes are all the more lifted!

20 A HISTORY OF THE MAGIC MIKE LIKEY TRUNK

I was "inspired" to switch from a red suitcase and decorated folding TV-dinner trays to a trunk one day in the early eighties, when I was booked to perform at the Brandon Fair, two hours west of Winnipeg, Manitoba, Canada.

It was one of those situations where I was one of several stage acts, introduced by emcee Len Andree (deceased): almost immediately after one act finished, Len would kill some time on stage with a game or contest, to allow the next act to clamber up and set up their show.

Famed Vancouver television celebrity and ventriloquist Peter Rolston (deceased) was on before myself, so I was able to enjoy this seasoned professional's show.

One thing I noticed was the ease with which he switched from one vent dummy to another: he was using a steamer-trunk, or a trunk which stood upright, which housed his ventriloquist figures! As soon as he was done, he merely closed the trunk and exited the stage to resounding laughter and applause, wheeling off the trunk with ease, as opposed to fumbling, zipping, stuffing, and folding!

After my show, I gave it some thought, and remembered there was an old army footlocker (metal trunk) resting unused upstairs in the unfinished attic of my Lanark home in Winnipeg.

Feverishly I brought it down, insulation falling on me as I gingerly stepped off the wooden retractable ladder which led up to the space, discreetly hidden by a small trap-door in the ceiling.

At that time, my first T.V.-show, "Kiddie Cabaret" was in it's second or third season, and one of the writers/clowns on the show, Darren, arrived at my home, offering to help me to transform the old army relic into a thing of beauty, worthy of my audience's adoration.

We attached four wheels to the underside, I lined the trunk with a furry blue fabric, and he installed a shelf in one half of it. I later installed pockets made of the same black, faux-leather chesterfield-style material that I covered the entire thing with. To finish it, I glued a gold bunny-in-the-hat on the front, just in case people couldn't identify this as a magician's prop. In those days, I was relatively fresh from a larger city, so the compulsory glitz-and-glamour "tinsley" backdrop and yes, even waistcoat, had to dominate the look of my typical eighties show. The trunk was relatively understated in comparison to the rest of my gaudy show, which consisted of glittery, brightly-painted props and boxes and silk handkerchiefs; after all, I believed that more was, well...more.

Several years later on one of my vacations to Miami, Florida, (a hub-bub of magic action!) I came across a brand new trunk at a local department store. This trunk subsequently went through hundreds and hundreds of shows, reincarnating and re-inventing itself (as I did) with a red-furry covering, even a grey, black-and-mylar motif which (pardon the pun) reflected the then-popular "Industrial"-look/feel that a certain famous American television magician made popular in the nineties.

Recently, after using an oversized leather doctor's bag, sometimes alternating it with a stand-up fabric suitcase on wheels (depending on the venue/size of the show) for my shows, I've gone back to the "magic" trunk: I was given for Christmas a brand-new black trunk purchased from a major U.S. department store, and delivered in more than enough time for me to install pockets, etc. in time for this years Christmas show! It's identical to the one I used for years but which was long gone...full-circle, baby! I've added my "Magic Mike's Castle" logo, laminated, and hung from the handle to update/customize my current "incarnation".

I'll continue to alternate (again depending on the size/location of the show) between my beautiful new trunk and my leather doctor's bag, and sometimes the carpet-bag, hopefully honoring the "Magic Mike Likey" tradition of trunks and carpet-bags, hoods, knee-high boots, poet's shirts, and all things medieval/period-themed.

21 CONCLUSION

I'm very grateful to those of you who have bought this book, and have chosen to read it as far as you have, wherever you have. It is my humble life, such as I perceive it, up to this date of June, 2018. I will be turning sixty-two in a month, and for the first time in many years, I'm feeling great about it, I'm even planning on actually acknowledging it to others! For the first time in twenty-five years, I can truly say that I am completely and optimistically looking forward to the future, while truly being in the "present", which I wasn't doing for many years. I chose, instead, to run positive, past-experiences through my mind, as I carried on my day-to-day existence, never feeling completely "satisfied" and fulfilled. I even initially wrote this book with my Winnipeg market in mind, but since doing a very positive and optimistic "closure" recently about my "Magic Mike" character/persona/"life" in Winnipeg, even going through the emotions of grieving, I have come out the other end of an illusionary tunnel of sorts, and I am now feeling more present and fulfilled, grateful for the ups and the downs not only in the last twenty-one years, but throughout my entire life! This book is not only for my Winnipeg audience, but for everybody! I see, now, how throughout my life, a "Higher Intelligence" was in the background, always with me, throughout those supposed "ups and downs". I refer you at this point to a famous bit of writing, given to me by my good friend Darren in 1993, while I was still in Winnipeg; it was written, unbenounced to me, by an author from out this way, in White Rock, B.C.! It's called "Footprints", and the end goes like this: "My son, my precious child, I love you and I would never leave you. During your times of trial and suffering, when you saw only one set of footprints, it was then that I carried you."

I realize now, partially thanks to my wife Sue, that everyone is doing the best that they can do, and I truly forgive, and see mostly only the "God" in others, like the term "Namaste" means: "God in me sees God in you!"

I have mostly worked through the low self-esteem that I allowed myself after the ups and downs of settling into the west-coast initially, thanks to Higher Intelligence, and to own personal-growth, metaphysical tools, again inspired by, and my having been led to it, by Source; I can almost regularly again feel unconditional love for everyone, feeling love and compassion and seeing the Light within them more easily again, as in the past. I am feeling a lighter and lighter heart like a child, that feeling of relief and freedom just about there, as before. I believe that my real growth and healing is also as a result of my letting my inner-child loose, (again, thanks to the love, strength and compassion of Source) and performing once again, my magic.

This morning, as I was sitting having a coffee at a local retail establishment, before returning home to write this, I was reading one of my favorite book, Ernest Holmes "The Science Of The Mind", and this came to me: "Performing Is My Medicine." When I'm performing, I'm totally not "about myself", I'm free and selfless, channeling pure joy and love, and in turn, receiving it; this is the basis of all good, honest spirituality, which supports "oneness" with God/"Christ-Conscious Awareness", (which is what it's called in New Thought terminology) essentially conscious awareness of ones soul's onement/merging with the Mind and Spirit of God. When this occurs, there is healing, there is compassion and love, there is growth and understanding and experiencing of a "Peace that passeth all understanding".

I have come full-circle with this knowing, with this living a complete life of sharing and experiencing that which I always knew to begin with! It gets better, and deeper, and I wish all of you a knowing, a living of this complete and utter peace, love, and joy! May God's light, compassion, love, and peace within you, see that same light within others; may you touch others with your love, just with your presence, no matter where your journey takes you.

Dr. Michael Likey,
June 2018,
Coquitlam, B.C., Canada.

AFTERWORD

I'm so pleased and excited to have written this book, sharing major milestones of my life with you. I'm also very grateful that you purchased this and read it! Who would have thought?

Indeed, it was also difficult including everything related to my life in magic, as much of it is forgotten already!

As they say, things only get better with time!

MEMORIES: PHOTOS

Myself and mum-circa 1957

My father circa 1957

My mum, circa 1950's

Mum and dad circa 1950's

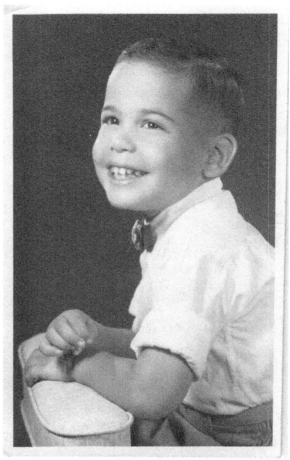

Myself, age 4, circa 1960

Myself, age 7, circa 1963 Goyer Street apartment

Myself, age 12, circa 1968

Myself, age 16, circa 1973

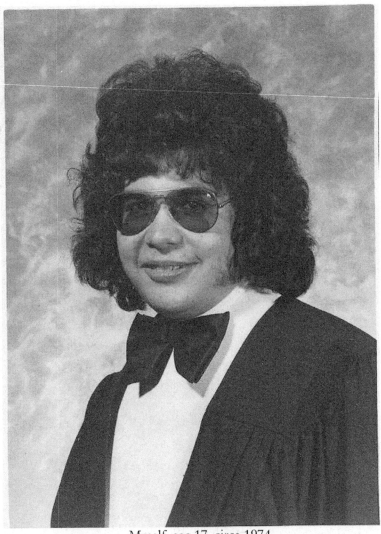

Myself, age 17, circa 1974

Myself, age 19, circa 1976

Above: 1981

Left: 1983

Left: 1981

Bottom: 1993

Bottom: 2015   Right: 2015

Left: Desmond and Forgetful, Animated-version, 2014

Left: Magic Mike's Castle (circa 1990)

Right:
2016

Right: 1987

Bottom: 1987   Right: 1989

Left: 1994

Bottom: 1988

Top Left: 2015

Top Right: 2014

Bottom: 1991

Left:
1983

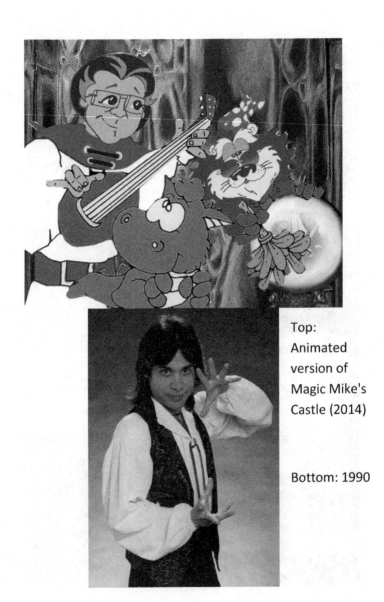

Top:
Animated
version of
Magic Mike's
Castle (2014)

Bottom: 1990

Left: Kiddie Cabaret, 1987

Bottom: 1993

Top:
1986

Left:
1983

Bottom:
2000

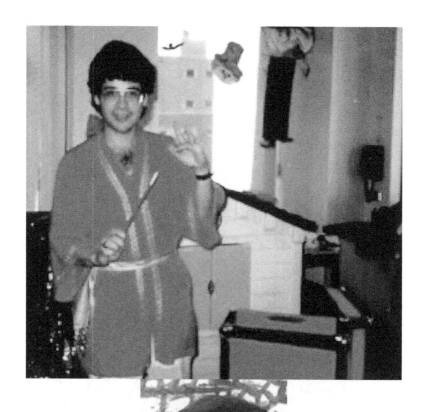

Top: 1989

Bottom: 1992

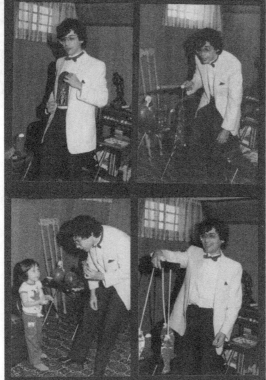

Top:
1987

Bottom:
1983

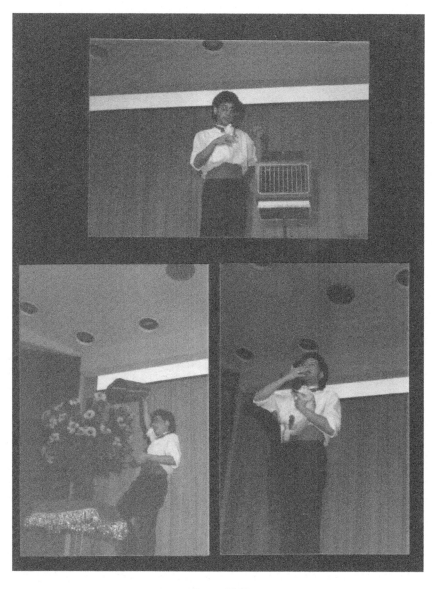

Top: 1987

Top: 1982

Above: 1992

Below: 1993

Variety Club contributions on television for raising money
doing caricatures: 1989, 1990, 1992, 1991

(Top) Animated version of Magic Mike's Castle, circa 2014

Bottom: 2015

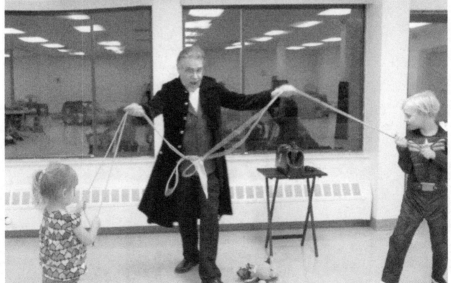

Bottom: Halloween, 2015

Today: 2018-plus, no glasses, the miracle of eye-procedures!

ABOUT THE AUTHOR

Dr. Michael Likey

MAGIC MIKE LIKEY

Because Michael Likey has distinct careers, one as Magic Mike Likey, and the other as Dr. Michael Likey, we will present both separately, starting with...

Magic Mike Likey

In the 1980's and '90's, Magic Mike Likey, professional magician, musician, and published creator and designer of magic illusions and proprietor of his magic-shop "Merry Minstrel Majick", hosted the longest-running television show about magic in Winnipeg, Canada,
"Magic Mike's Castle"! He performed grand stage illusions as well as close-up magic. His "Magic Circus" and "Kiddie Cabaret" shows toured extensively.
Today, Dr. Michael H. Likey, Ph.D., carries on the "Magic Mike Likey Universe" with the
"Magic Mike Likey's Castle Mysteries" podcasts on BlogTalk Radio and Spreaker Radio, and the all-new
"Magic Mike's Castle" webcasts on YouTube! He also teaches magic and performs close-up as well as stage-magic for old and young alike.

Contact: magic.mike.likey@gmail.com

Facebook: https://www.facebook.com/magic.mike.likey

Twitter: https://twitter.com/drmichaellikey

Website: http://magicmikelikeymagician.weebly.com

Linkedin: https://www.linkedin.com/in/magic-mike-likey-710b7286

YouTube:
https://www.youtube.com/channel/UCSZjpb5N_D1ljAsd46YResQ

Now we present Michael Likey's other career as...

Dr. Michael Likey

Dr. Michael Likey is an International Author, Clinical Hypnotherapist, Doctor of Theocentric Psychology, Producer/Host of his BlogTalk Radio show, Live-Streamed Video-Broadcasts, and creator of his Transcendence System. He has an H.Dip. (*Diploma of Clinical Hypnotherapy*) from The Robert Shields College of Hypnotherapy, England. Michael is also certified through Robert Shields as a *Fear Elimination Therapist*, (2004) and is also a triple-Doctoral graduate: a D.D., *Doctor of Divinity Specializing in Spiritual Healing*, from the University of Metaphysics, a Ph.D. *Specializing in Mystical Research* from the University of Sedona, and a PsyTh.D., *Doctor of Theocentric Psychology*, from the University of Sedona, Dr. Masters, CEO. Both the University of Metaphysics, and the University of Sedona, as well as it's parent organization, The International Metaphysical Ministry, were founded by Dr. Masters, CEO. Dr. Michael is the author of the popular and globally-available books "Spiritual Mind-Science And Your Soul", "The Science of the Soul", "Magic Happens!", "Journey of the Mind, Journey of the Soul", "The Spiritual Laws Of The Universe", "Scientific Prayer", and "Dr. Likey's Transcendence System" in addition to a dozen e-books (available on the Amazon Kindle Store), and is also Founder/CEO/Spiritual-Director of his own spiritual gatherings/programs.

He is a Member of the International Metaphysical Ministry and the Association of Ethical and Professional Hypnotherapists.

Contact: dr.likey@gmail.com
Facebook: https://www.facebook.com/Dr.MichaelLikey
Twitter: https://twitter.com/drmichaellikey
YouTube: https://www.youtube.com/user/SoulScienceTV
Website: http://www.drmichaellikey.com

Magic Mike Likey Products

DVD's

Magic Mike Likey's Top Ten Favorite Magic-Tricks (Instructional DVD)-ASIN: B00XM2FLNO

Magic Mike's Castle: Season 4-The Webseries (Based On The Popular TV-Show)-ASIN: B00WL6LGAY

The Adventures Of Young Magic Mike-DVD/Animated Cartoons-ASIN: B00WL6LKNW

Magic Mike Likey's Open/Closed Prediction (Original Magic-Trick)-ASIN: B00YZ84V0I

CD

The Ballad Of Young Magic Mike (Kids' Music CD)-ASIN: B00WAKMI7G

BOOKS

The Adventures Of Young Magic Mike (Large Format, Full-Color Comic-Book)-ISBN-10: 1511741821

Magic Still Happens! (Official Autobiography)-ISBN-10: 1515079414

Magic Mike Likey also has a number of DVD's of original magic-tricks. Go here to see them all:
https://magicmikelikey.wordpress.com/magic-mike-likey-store/

Works by Dr. Michael Likey

Books

- **Touched by the Wind**-ISBN-10: 171900062X

- **Higher Thought: Glimpses, Insights, and Snippets**-ISBN-10: 198752070X

- **Reiki: A Legitimate Healing Modality-The Dissertation**-ISBN-10: 1985025515

- **Mystical Meditation**-ISBN-10: 1983952753

- **Affirmative Prayer-Treatments**-ISBN-10: 1983810851

- **Western Psychology Vs. Eastern Psychology**-ISBN-10: 198161091X

- **Spiritual Mind-Science**-ISBN-10: 1973780690

- **How to Pray, Meditate & In-Vision Properly**-ISBN-10: 1973771926

- **Practical Tarot**-ISBN-10: 154840313X

- **Developing Your Psychic Awareness**-ISBN-10: 154839968X

- **Everything is Energy**-ISBN-10: 1548434027

- **Meditation, Metaphysics & Self-Hypnosis**-ISBN-10: 154845138X

- **Hypnosis or Meditation?**-ISBN-10: 1548438987

- **Happiness IS Possible!**-ISBN-10: 1548428736

- **Meditation, Scientific-Prayer & Psychosomatics**-ISBN-10: 1548453129

- **In-Visioning/Imaging**-ISBN-10: 1548007420

- **The Christ Mind**-ISBN-10: 1546539395

- **The Mind of the Universe**-ISBN-10: 1545463816

- **Mystical Wisdom Complete**-ISBN-10: 1543020305

- **Mystical Self-Hypnosis**-ISBN-10: 1542755301

- **Real Problems, Real Solutions**-ISBN-10: 1540447588

- **Mystical Wisdom**-ISBN-10: 1535347775

- **Working Through Trauma Spiritually**-ISBN-10: 1537443100

- **The Mind-The Key to Spiritual Healing**-ISBN-10: 1537319566

- **Dr. Michael's The Key to the Soul**-ISBN-10: 1532946929

- **Dr. Michael's Complete Soul Oracle Cards Manual**-ISBN-10: 1530829623

- **The Complete Spiritual Laws of the Universe**-ISBN-10: 1530735173

- **Speaking Thoughts Into Existence**-ISBN-10: 1517327148

- **Master Reiki**-ISBN-10: 1515026248

- **Dr. Likey's Transcendence System**-ISBN-10: 1514755289

- **Spiritual Mind-Science and Your Soul**-ISBN-10: 1514275104

- **Scientific Prayer**-ISBN-10: 1512183717

- **Journey of the Mind, Journey of the Soul**-ISBN-10: 1440131074

- **The Science of the Soul**-ISBN-10: 1462061885

- **Magic Happens!**-ISBN-10: 059569473X

CD's

- **Affirmative Prayer-Treatments**-ISBN-10: 1983810851

NOTES